A Continental Guide to Philosophy

To my students, past, present, and future.

A Continental Guide to Philosophy

John Douglas Macready

EDINBURGH
University Press

Edinburgh University Press is one of the leading university presses in the UK. We publish academic books and journals in our selected subject areas across the humanities and social sciences, combining cutting-edge scholarship with high editorial and production values to produce academic works of lasting importance. For more information visit our website: edinburghuniversitypress.com

© John Douglas Macready, 2022

Edinburgh University Press Ltd
The Tun – Holyrood Road, 12(2f) Jackson's Entry, Edinburgh EH8 8PJ

Typeset in 10/13 Gill Sans Nova by
IDSUK (DataConnection) Ltd

A CIP record for this book is available from the British Library

ISBN 978 1 4744 8677 4 (hardback)
ISBN 978 1 4744 8680 4 (webready PDF)
ISBN 978 1 4744 8678 1 (paperback)
ISBN 978 1 4744 8679 8 (epub)

The right of John Douglas Macready to be identified as the author of this work has been asserted in accordance with the Copyright, Designs and Patents Act 1988, and the Copyright and Related Rights Regulations 2003 (SI No. 2498).

Contents

Acknowledgments	ix
Glossary	x
Timeline	xiii
Introduction	1
Three basic questions	3
A continental tour of philosophy	4
How to use this book	7
How to read philosophical texts	7

PART I METAPHYSICS
WHAT IS REAL?
PLATO AND DESCARTES

1. Plato: The Hunt for the Real	13
The aim of philosophy	13
Being and appearance and the problem of difference	15
The Vermeer forgeries	16
The problem of identity and difference	18
How to give an account of the real	19
Only forms are real	22
The hunt for a slippery beast	23
2. Plato: The Net of Language	26
The problem of being	27
The problem of language	31

	Imitation and knowledge	32
	The hunt for being: four views	33
	The five kinds	35
3.	Descartes: Mind and Reality	38
	The *Meditations* are spiritual exercises	39
	The substance of reality	39
	Meditation 1: doubting reality	42
	Meditation 2: the reality of me	46
	Meditation 3: the reality of God	47
4.	Descartes: Truth and World	53
	Meditation 4: judgment and truth	54
	Meditation 5: God, things, and ideas	57
	Meditation 6: the reality of the world	59

PART II EPISTEMOLOGY
HOW CAN WE KNOW WHAT IS REAL?
HUME AND KANT

5.	Hume: The Mind is an Assemblage of Ideas	67
	A conceptual revolution	67
	Hume's clash with rationalism	68
	A new kind of philosophy	69
	Hume's atomism and associationism	71
	The Cartesian ego vs the assemblage of the self	72
	Innate ideas vs copies of impressions	73
	Knowledge vs belief	74
	The fragile connection between cause and effect	76
6.	Hume: Skepticism and Truth	79
	Probability and belief	80
	The illusion of connection	81
	Are we free or determined?	83
	Should we believe in God or miracles?	85
	Skepticism as philosophical therapy	87
	Hume and the idea of race	87
7.	Kant: The Architecture of the Mind	92
	Hume's problem and Kant's awakening	93
	Critical philosophy	95
	Knowledge and judgments	96

	Mathematical judgments are synthetic *a priori* judgments	98
	Natural Science judgments are synthetic *a priori* judgments	100
8.	Kant: Virtual Reality and the Limits of Reason	105
	The problem of reality and appearances	106
	The threefold synthesis	108
	Reason and the three dialectical illusions	110
	Metaphysical judgments are synthetic *a priori*	116

PART III ETHICS
HOW MIGHT WE LIVE AUTHENTICALLY?
NIETZSCHE AND ARENDT

9.	Nietzsche: Become Who You Are!	123
	How to know yourself	124
	Three exemplary qualities of an authentic life	132
	The dangers of an authentic life	134
10.	Nietzsche: The Creative Life	137
	Modern culture is dehumanizing	138
	How to become a child	140
	Modern culture is egoistic and tyrannical	141
	Three images of creative spirits	142
	The meaning of life is to contribute to culture	143
	The two sacraments of culture	145
	Beware of the four enemies of culture	146
11.	Arendt: Think What We Are Doing!	149
	The prejudice of philosophy and worldlessness	150
	The recovery of the public world	151
	The two ways of life	153
	The pre-philosophic view of the active life	154
	The philosophical view: political action as work	155
	The modern view: political action as labor	158
12.	Arendt: The Political Life	161
	Labor is natural and necessary	162
	Labor is not work	163
	Work makes the world	165

Action reveals who we are	167
Behavior vs. action	170
Conclusion: Philosophy for Life	173
Suggestions for Further Reading	176
Bibliography	181
Index	188

Acknowledgments

Philosophical thinking is collaborative, and this book is the product of numerous collaborations. It was inspired by Brent Adkins' superb book, *A Guide to Ethics and Moral Philosophy*, and I have tried to emulate its pedagogical structure and style in this present work. It was also inspired by conversations with my students and colleagues at Collin College, where I have the great privilege to teach and explore the three questions around which this book is organized. I am grateful to my colleagues Levi Bryant and Jeff Courtright, who have inspired and challenged me while at Collin College, and who graciously read early drafts of this book. I am also grateful to several colleagues outside my college, who generously agreed to read specific chapters and provide substantive feedback: Nancy McHugh, Tom Sparrow, Kurt Brandhorst, Jeffrey Bell, Andrew Cutrofello, Jeffrey Church, and Samantha Hill. I owe any clarity, insight, or precision in this book to their helpful comments. I am also thankful for Carol Macdonald at Edinburgh University Press, who first prompted me to consider writing this book. Her keen insight and confidence in this project made the review and publication process a pleasure. Finally, I am grateful for the love and support of my wife Kelly and our son Jack, who put up with early morning writing sessions and stacks of books.

Glossary

a posteriori (*Kant*) – a type of knowledge after experience
a priori (*Kant*) – a type of knowledge before experience
Action (*Arendt*) – the unpredictable and irreversible activity of beginning something new
Analytic (*Kant*) – a judgment in which the predicate is contained in the subject
Antinomies of Reason (*Kant*) – paradoxes of rational inquiry
Apollonian (*Nietzsche*) – the drive toward order
Becoming (*Plato*) – what is in process
Being (*Plato*) – what is
Being and Appearance (*Plato*) – the distinction between what is and what seems to be
Body (*Descartes*) – a material substance that takes up space
Clear and Distinct (*Descartes*) – quality of a perception that is immediately known and beyond doubt
Communicative Action (*Arendt*) – the public disclosure of who we are to others through words and deeds
Compatibilism (*Hume*) – freedom and determinism are not mutually exclusive
Creative Spirits (*Nietzsche*) – free individuals who create their own values
Culture (*Nietzsche*) – the archive of human excellence and creativity
Cultural Duty (*Nietzsche*) – the duty to perfect nature in ourselves and contribute to culture

Dionysian (*Nietzsche*) – the drive toward disorder

Egoism (*Nietzsche*) – an ethical position that seeks to maximize one's self-interests

Empiricism (*Hume*) – the view that we know reality through experience

Fallibilism (*Kant*) – the view that absolute certainty about reality is impossible

Forms (*Plato*) – perfect, immaterial models of imperfect, material things

Idea (*Descartes*) – mental representations of objects

Idea (*Hume*) – a mental copy of an impression

Ideals of Reason (*Kant*) – unconditioned aims of rational inquiry

Identity and Difference (*Plato*) – the relationship between sameness and otherness

Imagination (*Descartes*) – the embodied capacity for representing objects

Impression (*Hume*) – a sensory perception of reality

Intellect (*Descartes*) – the passive capacity for understanding objects

Judgment (*Descartes*) – the decision to affirm or deny the truth of an idea

Labor (*Arendt*) – the cyclical and necessary activity for maintaining biological life

Logos (*Plato*) – an account of something in language

Method of Division (*Plato*) – technique for dividing things into formal categories

Mind (*Descartes*) – an immaterial substance that thinks

Natality (*Arendt*) – human birth that initiates a new expression of humanity

Necessary Connection (*Hume*) – the belief that every effect *must* have a cause

Non-being (*Plato*) – what is not

Plurality (*Arendt*) – the paradoxical condition of equality and distinction that makes action possible

Probability (*Hume*) – principle for justifying beliefs by a superiority of evidence

Rationalism (*Hume*) – the view that we know reality through reason

Skepticism (*Hume*) – methodological doubt about the certainty of beliefs

Substance (*Descartes*) – an independently existing thing with qualities

Synthetic (*Kant*) – a judgment in which the predicate expands the knowledge of the subject

Transcendent (*Kant*) – knowledge beyond possible experience

Transcendental (*Kant*) – knowledge restricted to *a priori* conditions of possible experience

True Educator (*Nietzsche*) – one who liberates you to become your authentic self

Unfashionable (*Nietzsche*) – out of sync with the common order of things

vita activa (*Arendt*) – the active (political) life

vita contemplativa (*Arendt*) – the contemplative (philosophical) life

Will (*Descartes*) – the active capacity to decide

World (*Arendt*) – the shared network of objects and orientations between human beings

Worldlessness (*Arendt*) – the modern loss of trust in the shared world

Work (*Arendt*) – the productive activity of making an artificial and durable world

Timeline

- Plato (c. 428–347 BCE) *Sophist* (c. 365)
- René Descartes (1596–1650) *Meditations on First Philosophy* (1641)
- David Hume (1711–1776) *An Enquiry Concerning Human Understanding* (1748)
- Immanuel Kant (1724–1804) *Prolegomena to Any Future Metaphysics* (1783)
- Friedrich Nietzsche (1844–1900) *Schopenhauer as Educator* (1874)
- Hannah Arendt (1906–1975) "Labor, Work, Action" (1964)

Introduction

My own reality is determined by the *way* I know and *what* I know reality to be.

Karl Jaspers, *Philosophy of Existence*[1]

In the spring of 1945, three weeks after the Allied victory over the Nazis, a middle-aged painter of modest skill but immense wealth was arrested in Amsterdam for perpetrating one of the most lucrative hoaxes in art history. Han van Meegeren had been a struggling Dutch painter in the early twentieth century, never managing to cultivate his talents sufficiently to achieve the fame of other Dutch artists like Rembrandt or Mondrian. He was by all accounts an average painter. His most successful work was a sentimental painting of a doe that was mass-produced and marketed as a representation of a deer owned by Princess Juliana of Holland. Art critics had deemed his work clichéd, cold, shallow, and best suited for the market rather than the gallery. Incensed by the rejection of the critics, van Meegeren hatched a plan to dupe them and earn a sizeable profit.[2]

In 1923 he began developing techniques to create perfect forgeries of the seventeenth-century Dutch painter Johannes Vermeer. These were not forgeries of existing Vermeer paintings but new paintings in the style of Vermeer, which van Meegeren sold as authentic, newly discovered works by the artist. Van Meegeren knew that art historians had speculated about the influence of Michelangelo Merisi da Caravaggio on Vermeer's painting style, and he decided to capitalize on this speculative assumption. If he could create a painting with explicit references to Caravaggio but executed in the style of Vermeer and using

---

[1] Karl Jaspers, *Philosophy of Existence*, trans. Richard F. Grabau (Philadelphia: University of Pennsylvania Press, 1995), 78.
[2] My recounting of the story of Han van Meegeren relies upon Edward Dolnick's book *The Forger's Spell: A True Story of Vermeer, Nazis, and the Greatest Art Hoax of the Twentieth Century* (San Francisco: Harper Collins, 2009).

materials and techniques employed in the seventeenth century, then the experts just might think his forgery was an authentic Vermeer. So, that's what he did. His most successful forgery was titled *Christ at Emmaus*, which was painted on a seventeenth-century canvas with paints mixed according to formulas of the same period. Modeled on Caravaggio's *The Supper at Emmaus*, the forgery was clumsily executed and did not exhibit the depth and quality of authentic paintings by Vermeer. But because the painting was clearly modeled on Caravaggio's, and art historians and critics were aware of the possible connection between Caravaggio and Vermeer, the poor quality of the work was overlooked. It was thoroughly examined by experts in 1937 and determined to be an authentic work by Vermeer. The Rembrandt Society immediately purchased van Meegeren's forgery for the equivalent of what would be $3.9 million today.

However, the most significant event in van Meegeren's career as an art forger occurred in 1942, when he sold a Vermeer forgery titled *Christ with the Woman Taken in Adultery* to a Nazi-sympathizing banker and art dealer named Alois Miedl, who then traded the painting to the Nazi Reichmarschall Hermann Goering in exchange for other paintings. Toward the end of the war, Goering had hidden the painting in a salt mine to avoid its theft, but in 1945 Allied forces discovered it and traced its origin to van Meegeren. He was arrested and charged with collaborating with the Nazis and selling Dutch cultural artifacts to them. Seeking to avoid the shame and punishment of being a Nazi collaborator and Dutch traitor, which could have entailed a death sentence, van Meegeren confessed to forging several paintings and selling them for immense profits, and was sentenced to a year in prison. In spite of his career as an art forger, van Meegeren's fake Vermeers have drawn the attention of art critics. Today, his work hangs in the Rijksmuseum and the Groninger Museum in the Netherlands, as well as in private collections.

The story of van Meegeren is a cautionary tale about how forgers of reality can fool us. Van Meegeren's paintings were *like* the paintings of Vermeer, but they were not *real* Vermeers. Van Meegeren, like all forgers, was a master of imitation, creating persuasive appearances that even fooled the experts. So, how can we inoculate ourselves against forgers of reality like van Meegeren who traffic in persuasive delusions? In this book, I hope to persuade you that the practice of philosophy might just hold the answer.

Three basic questions

If there is an activity common to all philosophers, it is asking questions. Philosophers are insatiable inquirers, and this activity is what makes philosophy possible. In fact, it is no exaggeration to say that questioning is the engine of philosophical thinking. Questions disrupt our certainties, illuminate new paths for thinking, and provoke us to wonder, which, as Plato and Aristotle knew, is the beginning of wisdom. Thus, the search for wisdom begins with questioning and the realization that we are not wise—that we lack precisely what we seek. When philosophers ask questions, they are attempting to outline the contours of what they lack, so they can pursue it. It is precisely this pursuit of what is missing that can dispel illusions and make our lives worth living.

What is real?
How can we know what is real?
How might we live authentically?

These three questions represent the fundamental questions of philosophy and mark its three main divisions of *metaphysics, epistemology,* and *ethics. Metaphysics* is the branch of philosophy concerned with identifying ultimate reality. For ancient philosophers like Plato, metaphysical questions had to be answered before epistemological or ethical questions could be answered. *Epistemology* is the branch of philosophy that tries to determine the scope and limits of our ability to know reality. As we will see, epistemological questions became the focus of modern philosophers like Descartes, Hume, and Kant. *Ethics* is the branch of philosophy that attempts to actualize the insights from metaphysics and epistemology in human existence. Ethics examines the various ways we might live in accordance with what we know to be real. What is important to notice is that these branches are interrelated. Our answers to the first two questions will have a direct impact on how we choose to live our lives. All of us live out answers to these questions, but most of us never take the time to critically examine them. This book provides you with an opportunity to examine your answers through a critical study of how some of the most significant philosophers have answered these questions. Your goal should not be to find a philosopher you agree with and adopt his or her answers, but to learn how to develop your own answers to these questions by thinking more clearly and consistently about them.

A continental tour of philosophy

The history of philosophy can be thought of as an art gallery filled with paintings by various artists. Each painting is a representation of reality from a particular perspective and makes use of distinct methods and styles to express what each artist conceives. The paintings, you might say, are answers to the three basic questions of philosophy. Although painting and philosophy might seem very different, both disciplines share a creative impulse. Painters create images and philosophers create concepts. If questions are the engine of philosophy, concepts are its product. Philosophy is, therefore, a creative activity—it creates concepts in order to understand the various phenomena it investigates. Concepts are the way we get a grip on reality; they are intellectual paintings of reality. Philosophy, then, is the ongoing inquiry into reality and the perpetual creation of concepts that allow us to come to terms with that reality in order to live more authentically.

Our gallery tour will be curated from the perspective of *continental philosophy*. Continental philosophy is a broad tradition of inquiry within philosophy that originated on the continent of Europe and encompasses a wide variety of theoretical orientations (e.g. phenomenology, existentialism, critical theory, psychoanalysis) and methodologies (e.g. structuralism, post-structuralism, hermeneutics, deconstructionism). It has its origins in the critical philosophy of Immanuel Kant and the subsequent reactions to his thought in the nineteenth and twentieth centuries by philosophers such as G. W. F. Hegel, Friedrich Nietzsche, Henri Bergson, Edmund Husserl, Martin Heidegger, Jean-Paul Sartre, Maurice Merleau-Ponty, Frantz Fanon, Gilles Deleuze, Emmanuel Levinas, Hannah Arendt, and others. Although continental philosophy is theoretically diverse, it has four main conceptual orientations that will inform the interpretations of the six philosophers we will consider.[3]

---

[3] The conception of continental philosophy as expressive of four features is drawn from Leonard Lawlor's *Early Twentieth-Century Continental Philosophy* (Bloomington: Indiana University Press, 2012), viii.

First, continental philosophy is oriented toward the *immanence* of our lived experience instead of the transcendence of abstract ideas. "Immanence" is derived from the Latin word *immanere*, which means to "dwell in," and stands in contrast to "transcendence," which comes from the Latin word *transcendere*, which means to "climb above." Continental philosophy takes our embodied existence in time as its starting point for inquiry. *Second*, continental philosophy emphasizes the priority of *difference* and multiplicity in our immanent experience instead of sameness and unity. In emphasizing difference, continental philosophy seeks to challenge the idea that everything and everyone can be understood or explained through a single idea or unifying principle. Instead, continental philosophy attends to how difference is a fundamental and inescapable feature of reality. Consequently, continental philosophy is suspicious of grand narratives and totalizing concepts like race, gender, or class that obscure or eclipse human differences. *Third*, continental philosophy seeks to turn language, which is governed by logic, into an activity of *thinking* that is beyond logic, and therefore open to difference and variation within our immanent experience. *Fourth*, continental philosophy seeks to challenge the idea that the whole of reality (essence) can be given or exhausted in our fixed categories and concepts, and it seeks to foster the *perpetual creation of new concepts* that account for the differences we encounter in our immanent experience (existence). So, our gallery tour will attend to these continental themes, emphasizing the transitions from transcendence to immanence, from unity to plurality, from language to thinking, and from essence to existence.

We will begin our tour of philosophy by considering Plato's answer to the metaphysical question, "What is real?" Plato was searching for an unchanging, transcendent reality that could serve as an objective measure for the changing reality he encountered through his senses. He thought he had located this reality in an intelligible realm of forms that our minds have access to through the medium of language, but as we will see, difference haunts the reality Plato discovers. After Plato, we will leap from the ancient world into the modern world and examine René Descartes' answer to this same question. Descartes' historical situation led him to answer the question in a very different way. In the wake of the scientific revolutions initiated by Kepler, Copernicus, and Galileo, and the declining intellectual authority of Christianity,

Descartes conceived reality as substance and developed a scientific method for knowing this reality with certainty. As we will see, the inquiries of Plato and Descartes into the nature of reality assume a fundamental distinction between reality and illusion, and both of them create new concepts that allow them to articulate the features of reality in language and avoid being duped by false appearances.

While Plato and Descartes thought we could know reality, other philosophers were not so sure. David Hume thought we should first clarify the scope and limits of our knowledge before determining what is real. He thought the rationalists were trafficking in illusions when it came to reality, and that if we understood how the mind worked, we could avoid falling into these illusions. Hume's answer to the question "How can we know what is real?" is an empiricist answer: we know reality primarily through the senses, and only secondarily through reason. As we will see, Hume reorients us back to the plurality of our bodily and sensory experience of the world. After Hume, we will turn to Immanuel Kant, who attempted to reconcile the competing views of the rationalists and empiricists. Kant showed us how our knowledge of reality is the product of both concepts and experience, but he also showed us how limited our knowledge of reality actually is.

We will end by exploring Friedrich Nietzsche's and Hannah Arendt's answers to the ethical question, "How might we live authentically?" The use of "might" rather than "should" in this question is intentional and important. "Might" suggests that there are many possibilities for living an authentic life, while "should" suggests there is only one standard for authenticity. Nietzsche and Arendt wrote during historical periods when absolute standards and values had lost their authority, and humanity faced the task of creating new values and concepts to live by. Nietzsche saw the creative life of the artist as an authentic way of living, because the artist created his or her own life like a work of art, and this creation contributed to culture. In contrast, Arendt argued that the political life was the most authentically human way of life. She emphasized the need for human beings to act together to build and sustain a common world through their words and deeds. Both of these ways of life are possibilities for living one's life, but they are not the only possibilities. It is my sincerest hope that by the end of this book, you will have started thinking about how *you* might live authentically.

How to use this book

The purpose of this book is to provoke you to ask the metaphysical, epistemological, and ethical questions for yourself and to formulate your own answers to them. The authors and texts we will consider are presented as models for *how* to think about these questions, not as final answers to be adopted. This book is a *guide* to philosophical practice—to the practice of philosophical questioning and thinking. One of its guiding assumptions is that philosophy is a human activity that everyone engages in—everyone wonders about what is real and fake, what is true and false, and how they might live their lives. However, it takes practice to learn how to think carefully and critically about these important questions, and we can learn how to think by reading exemplary authors.

This book should be used as companion to the texts being considered in the following chapters. Readers will want to first read the philosophical texts for themselves, followed by this *Guide*, and then some of the supplementary texts suggested in the "Suggestions for Further Reading" section at the end of this book. Reading philosophical texts will seem challenging at first, but with consistent practice, you will begin reading with greater efficiency and insight.

How to read philosophical texts

Reading philosophical texts takes patience and careful attention. Philosophers are notorious for writing in opaque or difficult prose replete with neologisms and obscure technical language. It is natural to feel disoriented when you first begin to read a philosophical text. However, it is important to keep in mind that philosophers use language as a tool to communicate their thinking, often creating new concepts and pushing language to its limits. Their aim in using language in this way is to disrupt our common ways of thinking about things, so that we can see things we have been missing or overlooking. The language they use is intentional and precise, and to understand a philosopher, you must learn how to analyze this language.

Every philosophical text is the attempt to answer a question through the creation of concepts and the development of an argument. The question identifies the phenomena to be investigated, and the concepts provide the lenses through which to see and interpret the phenomena. This allows the philosopher to develop an argument that answers the question through a series of claims based upon evidence that can be evaluated and its implications explored. To understand a philosophical text, you have to understand these five elements: the *question* being asked, the *concepts* being used, the *claims* being made, the *evidence* offered in support of the claims, and the *implications* of the argument.

When you first begin to read a philosophical text, whether it is an essay or a book, be attentive to the *question* the author is trying to answer. The answer the author argues for in the text will be meaningless unless you know the question he or she is asking. This question may be implicit or explicit and will usually be indicated in the opening paragraphs or in an introduction to the work. It will be helpful to write this question in the margins of the essay or book to serve as a reminder as you follow the argument to its conclusion. In this book, I have provided general questions for each text, but you will want to pay attention to the particular questions that each author asks.

Once you know the question an author is asking, you can begin reading the text and attending to the *claims* that the author makes along the way. A claim is statement in which the author takes a position on a topic. There will be a main claim that serves as the answer to the author's question, and there will be a series of subordinate claims that serve as reasons in support of that answer. It will be worthwhile to mark these claims in the text as you read, so that you can retrace the argument when you finish reading and evaluate it.

Each of the claims made by an author will be supported by *evidence*. Evidence is the collection of facts or reasons that show that a claim is true. You may find yourself agreeing with a claim by an author, but its truth will rest on the quality of the evidence. To philosophize well, it will be important to get into the habit of evaluating claims based on the evidence presented. This evidence might be a series of reasons, or a logical principle, or a historical or scientific fact, but it could also be common human experience. Whatever it is, it needs to be critically evaluated to determine whether the claim being made is true.

Along the way, an author of a philosophical text will be creating and developing a series of *concepts* that function as lenses to view a given set of phenomena. Concepts are the way philosophers create new ways of seeing things. As concepts—which may be ideas, principles, or theories—are introduced, it will be helpful to circle them, and list them in one of the empty pages in the back of the book along with a succinct definition and page number where the concept occurs. Understanding the concepts that a philosopher uses is essential to learning how to *see with* the philosopher, but this understanding will not come from learning a series of definitions. To understand the conceptual architecture of a philosophical text, you will need to read closely and carefully in order to pick up the style and nuance of the philosopher. Understanding philosophical concepts is akin to learning how to speak a language fluently versus merely memorizing vocabulary.

One of the most important lessons we can learn from philosophy is that thinking has consequences. Every concept a philosopher develops has implications for how we see the world, others, and ourselves. The arguments that we take to be true have implications for how we think, speak, and act. As you read philosophical texts, it will be helpful to keep asking yourself, "So what?"—"If I accept this way of seeing, or assent to this claim, how will this change my life?" Thinking through the implications of a philosophical position allows you to begin philosophizing for yourself so that philosophy can be in the service of your life. Make a habit of always bringing philosophical ideas back into your own experience—try them on, walk around in them, and see how they fit or don't fit.

My hope is that this little book will function as a guide as you walk through the gallery of the history of philosophy. It will introduce you to each philosopher, discussing each of their paintings of reality, and explaining their unique styles, techniques, vocabulary, and methods. In the end, I hope it will inspire you to begin philosophizing for yourself by making the three questions pursued in this book your own and formulating your own answers.

PART I METAPHYSICS

WHAT IS REAL?
PLATO AND DESCARTES

Metaphysics

The two philosophers you will read about in this section are Plato (427–347 BCE) and René Descartes (1596–1650). Plato is one of the most significant thinkers in the history of philosophy. He was a student of Socrates and related to Solon, the lawmaker whose constitutional reforms made Athenian democracy possible. Plato's works deal with the most fundamental philosophical questions, and he used human dialogue to dramatize philosophical thinking. He wrote works on metaphysics, epistemology, ethics, politics, religion, law, rhetoric, education, and mathematics.

Plato and Descartes are separated by two millennia in which immense intellectual, social, religious, and political changes occurred that dramatically altered how we understand reality and the way philosophy is practiced. Religious authority was being challenged by emerging scientific knowledge about the physical universe, and Europe was embroiled in the Thirty Years' War. Amidst these uncertainties, Descartes turned inward to seek a firmer foundation upon which to reestablish our most deeply held beliefs about reality, God, and ourselves on scientific grounds. He wrote works on optics, mathematics, logic, physics, meteorology, theology, the emotions, and the scientific method.

Although Plato and Descartes occupy different historical periods, they are both ultimately concerned with the same, metaphysical, question: What is real? This question seeks to distinguish what *is* from what merely *appears* to be, in order to avoid epistemological illusions. For this reason, both Plato and Descartes will offer an account of reality and how it can be known.

Both Plato and Descartes think reality is stable and unchanging, and that it is accessible to human reason. The point of these chapters is to identify what Plato and Descartes understood this reality to be, but also to understand how and why they came to their conclusions. Once we have analyzed their arguments for reality, we can begin to evaluate for ourselves whether their accounts are accurate and compelling.

1

Plato: The Hunt for the Real
(*Sophist*, 216a–231e)

Key terms

Being and Appearance – the distinction between what is and what seems to be
Identity and Difference – the relationship between sameness and otherness
Method of Division – technique for dividing things into formal categories
Forms – perfect, immaterial models of imperfect, material things
Logos – an account of something in language

The aim of philosophy

For Plato, the practice of philosophy involves distinguishing what is real from what is fake. Philosophers want to ensure they are not duped or misled by what appears to be real but is not. It is not surprising that when Plato described philosophical education in his *Republic*, he described it as an escape from a dark cave where shadows are confused with reality (Plato, *Rep.*, 514–520a).[1] In distinguishing the real

---

[1] I will be using citations like this throughout the book to make it easy to find these references in Plato's dialogues. The citation has three parts. The first part indicates the author's name ("Plato"). The second part indicates the particular dialogue being cited. The third part indicates the Stephanus number—a numbering system for Plato's complete works developed by Henri Estienne (1528–98) during the Renaissance—located in the margins of the dialogue. For references to Plato's *Sophist*, I will be using Plato, *Sophist*, trans. Nicholas P. White (Indianapolis: Hackett Publishing, 1993). For references to Plato's *Republic*, I will be using Plato, *Republic*, in *Plato: Complete Works*, ed. John M. Cooper, trans. C. D. C. Reeve (Indianapolis: Hackett Publishing, 1997).

from the fake, philosophers seek to determine what something *is* and not simply what it *appears* to be—philosophers want to liberate themselves from delusion and know the true nature of things.

Plato's dialogue the *Sophist* has exerted an immense influence in continental philosophy. Martin Heidegger devoted an entire course to it in 1924–25 and opened his magisterial *Being and Time* with a quote from the dialogue. Hannah Arendt, who attended Heidegger's lecture course on the *Sophist*, claimed that her book *The Human Condition* was indebted to insights from those lectures. The *Sophist* was also an inspiration for Emmanuel Levinas's philosophy of otherness in *Totality and Infinity* and Gilles Deleuze's philosophy of difference in *Difference and Repetition*. To understand why the dialogue has had such a significant impact we have to understand how it describes the relationship between being and appearance.

The dialogue opens with Socrates emphasizing this central philosophical concern. In response to Theodorus' introduction of the Visitor from Elea (sometimes translated as "Stranger") as a "philosopher," Socrates asks whether Theodorus might be mistaken about the nature of the Visitor and might have brought along "a god without realizing it" (Plato, *Soph.*, 216a). Even when Theodorus responds that he calls all philosophers "divine," Socrates presses his point even more, "But probably it's no easier, I imagine, to distinguish that kind of person than it is to distinguish gods. Certainly the genuine philosophers who 'haunt our cities'—by contrast to the fake ones—take on all sorts of different appearances just because of other people's ignorance" (Plato, *Soph.*, 216c). Socrates's distinction between real and fake philosophers raises an important question: "What is a philosopher?" or, more precisely, "What is the nature of a philosopher?" Once this question is answered, it becomes possible to distinguish *real* philosophers from *fake* philosophers. Thus, the aim of philosophy, for Plato, is to determine what is real.

Plato uses language as the instrument for discovering reality. One of the first things to notice about Plato's *Sophist* is that it is a *dialogue*. A dialogue is a conversation between two or more people about a particular topic structured by a question and answer format. For Plato, language has its own logic, so if one follows it, one will eventually arrive at an account of what is true or real. Socrates recommends this dialogical method to the Visitor when he tells him that one of the first great philosophers, Parmenides, "used questions to generate a very fine discussion" (Plato, *Soph.*, 217c). However, most of Plato's dialogues raise questions that are not answered at the end of the dialogue. Most of them end in confusion or paradoxes. So, what is Plato up to?

Plato's dialogues can be understood as invitations *into* the practice of philosophy; they do not tell readers *what* to think; they teach readers *how* to think. They are like Jackson Pollock's splatter paintings, which express the activity of the painter rather than being a depiction of reality. Similarly, Plato's dialogues express the activity of philosophical thinking rather than declaring what is true. They invite the reader into the activity of thinking in language. In this way, they should be read as training manuals for thinking.

Being and appearance and the problem of difference

The *Sophist* is part of a trilogy of dialogues—the *Theaetetus*, *Sophist*, and *Statesman*—that recount an ongoing conversation between Socrates, Theaetetus, Theodorus, and the Visitor from Elea. The *Sophist* continues the conversation of the *Theaetetus*, which centered on the question, "What is knowledge?" However, when Theodorus comments on the philosophical nature of the Visitor, the central question shifts from "What is knowledge?" to "What is a philosopher?" Socrates points out that there are many answers to this question on offer because sometimes the philosopher appears to be worthwhile, and at other times worthless, sometimes a statesman, at other times a sophist, and even sometimes a madman (Plato, *Soph.*, 216d). Socrates is raising one of the central problems of philosophy here—the problem of *being and appearance*. How are we to distinguish what *is* (philosopher) from what simply *appears* to be (fake philosopher), and how might being and appearance be related?

The distinction between being and appearance shows up in the dialogue as a distinction between what Plato called *forms* (being) and *copies* (appearance). For Plato, the forms are the immaterial models of everything that exists; they are the objects of our knowledge, and we can represent (copy) them in language through the words we use. For example, the verb "is" is a representation of the form *being*. Notice, the word "is" is not being itself, it is a copy of the form in language. The truthfulness of our statements about reality hinges on the close resemblance of our language to the forms, and so being (forms) and appearance (copies) are related through imitation (resemblance). When we speak truthfully about reality, we create accurate copies of the forms in language (likeness), but when we speak falsely, we create inaccurate copies of the forms in language (appearances). What is important to notice in this distinction between copies that resemble the forms (likenesses) and copies that do not (appearances) is that what sets them apart is their *difference* from the forms. For Plato, the greater the difference, the greater the falsity. Things are true only to the extent that they correspond to the original model of the form; to the degree that something does not correspond to the original model of the form, it is false. In the *Sophist*, the Visitor and Theaetetus will attempt to banish difference from language in order to grasp reality. But, as we will see, difference persists in the dialogue.

The Vermeer forgeries

Let's think through the problem of being and appearance in a more concrete way by returning to the story of Han van Meegeren and considering whether his paintings were real or fake, or whether he was a genuine artist or just appeared to be one. It is clear that the paintings were real, insofar as van Meegeren actually painted them, although not with the artistic skill of Vermeer. But it is also clear that in attributing the paintings to Vermeer, he was attempting to deceive others about their value, so the paintings are certainly fake Vermeers. In order to determine whether van Meegeren was a genuine artist, we would first need to determine what an artist *is*—identify the essential feature or characteristic that makes an artist an artist—and then determine whether or not van Meegeren possesses this characteristic. It is not enough to declare oneself an artist or to have others declare you an artist, any more than it is enough to declare a painting an authentic Vermeer. What is at stake in the problem of being and appearance is whether or not we are being duped by fakes and forgeries or whether we have encountered something that is authentically real. Being deceived about reality can have undesirable implications.

For example, Plato argues that a real philosopher is someone "whose thoughts are truly directed towards the things that are"—to the unchanging forms of beauty, truth, and goodness—but fake philosophers turn their thoughts only to the things that appear to be—to "the ever-changing sights and sounds of experience" (Plato, *Rep.*, 500b, 476b). What is interesting to note about this description of real philosophers is that their point of reference is the unchanging reality of the forms—the immaterial models for everything that exist. Philosophers look to the forms as a measure for reality. So, philosophers love the form of beauty itself, which never changes; while fake philosophers only love beautiful things, which constantly change. Consequently, fake philosophers are unable to explain why beautiful things are beautiful.

It is now well established that Vermeer used a camera obscura to create some of his most famous paintings. The camera obscura was a box-like device with a single pin-hole through which an image of what was outside the box could be projected onto a screen or canvas through the use of light and mirrors. It is believed that Vermeer constructed darkened cubicles equipped with a lens and mirrors in the back of the rooms where he painted some of his masterpieces like *The Music Lesson*. Inside this darkened cubicle, an image of the room outside would be projected onto a canvas at precise geometric scale, so that Vermeer could reconstruct the room and his subjects outside on the canvas, preserving the depth, scale, lighting, and perspective of the scene.[2] Like the real philosophers who look to the forms as the measure of reality, Vermeer looked to the geometry of the room as the measure for his paintings. He tried to copy the reality of the room on his canvas so that the painting resembled the reality of the room. There is no evidence that van Meegeren used a camera obscura to construct his fake Vermeers; instead he imitated the themes, gestures, and techniques of other paintings. Reality was not important to van Meegeren, only appearances. Real philosophers, as we will learn, try to copy reality in their language, so their verbal images resemble reality; fake philosophers only try to speak persuasively without any reference to reality, so their verbal images do not resemble reality. The consequences of mistaking a real philosopher for a fake one are obvious: you will be misled about the truth of things.

---

[2] I have relied on Philip Steadman's *Vermeer's Camera: Uncovering the Truth Behind the Masterpieces* (New York: Oxford University Press, 2001) for this account of Vermeer's use of the camera obscura.

The consequences are similar regarding the true and false statesman. An authentic statesman takes as his primary goal the common good of the people he serves and the state he governs, and all of his actions are directed to those ends. However, an inauthentic statesman is someone who deceives the people into believing his goal is the common good when it is actually satisfying his own interests. This can lead to tyranny and oppression. The same can be said of true and false friends. A true friend is loyal and trustworthy, but a false friend is not. Imagine sharing your deepest secrets with someone you thought was your friend but who turned out to not be. Because they have no loyalty to you, it is unlikely they could be trusted not to share your secrets. So, failing to distinguish what is real from what is fake can have terrible implications for us intellectually, politically, and personally. This is what is at stake in the question: "What is a philosopher?"

The problem of identity and difference

In order to answer the question "What is a philosopher?," Socrates asks the Visitor from Elea to distinguish between a sophist, a statesman, and a philosopher.

> SOC. But if it's all right with our visitor I'd be glad to have him tell us what the people where he comes from used to apply the following names to, and what they thought about these things?
> THD. What things?
> SOC. *Sophist, statesman,* and *philosopher.*
> THD. What, or what kind of thing, especially makes you consider asking that question? What special problem about them do you have in mind?
> SOC. This: did they think that sophists, statesmen, and philosophers make up one kind of thing or two? Or did they divide them up into three kinds corresponding to the three names and attach one name to each of them? (Plato, *Soph.*, 216d–217a)

There are three important things to note about how Socrates sets up the problem that the Visitor and Theaetetus are to resolve. The first thing to notice is that Socrates isn't asking them to describe what sophists, statesmen, and philosophers *do*; he's asking them to identify what they *are*. It is not sufficient to say that philosophers love wisdom or statesmen care for the state. In order to know you have encountered an authentic philosopher or statesman, and to avoid being deceived by a fake, you have to know what each of them are—you have to know what their nature is.

The second thing to notice is that Socrates indicates that *names* correspond to what a thing *is*. This means that language is the medium through which that nature of things is expressed. The Visitor calls this use of language *logos*, which is a Greek word that means "to give an account of something." To give an account of something could take the form of a single word, a definition, a more lengthy speech, or piece of writing. It is a way of gathering together all of the essential features of something in an explanation of what that something is.

The third and final thing to notice is that Socrates indicates a method for pursuing the answer to the question he poses, a method for dividing things into *kinds* or *categories*. In order to group things together by kinds, you must identify the features common to each thing. For example, all artists make things. Some artists make sculptures, some make paintings, some make music, and some make furniture. So, we could group sculptors, painters, musicians, and carpenters into the category of makers because they all share the common function of making. But there's a problem. Sculptors and musicians are not the same thing; sculptors make statues and musicians make music. They are both makers but they do not make the same things. They are simultaneously the same and different. How can this be? This is called the problem of *identity and difference*, and it is a central problem in the *Sophist*.

How to give an account of the real

In order to give an account of the nature of the philosopher and distinguish him from the sophist and the statesman, the Visitor from Elea proposes to first give an account of the sophist, then the statesman, and finally the philosopher. The account of the sophist is given in Plato's *Sophist* and the account of the statesman in his *Statesman*; however, the account of the philosopher is curiously missing. It is not clear whether Plato intended to write a dialogue called *Philosopher* and never did, or whether the account of the philosopher emerges in the conversations of the other three dialogues. Whatever the determination is, it is clear that a method is introduced in the *Sophist* for giving an account of what is real; it is called the *method of division*. As the Visitor explains, the method of division is a way of giving an account of what something *is* by beginning with a particular name or kind of thing, and then dividing it into two types, determining which type the object being pursued fits into, and discarding the other type (Plato, *Soph.*, 218c). This type is then divided again, and the object is again located in one of the types. This process continues until the essential nature or reality of the thing being pursued is discovered. The Visitor suggests they test the method first on something "easy to understand" before attempting to give an account of the sophist, so they settle on the figure of the *angler*.

The hunt for the angler begins by determining whether he is an expert or a non-expert (Plato, *Soph.*, 219a). It is worth asking why the Visitor chooses to begin with the category of *expertise* rather than another category (see Figure 1.1). Why, for example, didn't he begin by asking whether the angler was human or inhuman, living or non-living? The answer has to do with the aim of the inquiry, namely, the nature of the angler. Presumably, the angler is what he is because of what he does, namely, angling. The Visitor chooses to begin with the angler's skill or function rather than his nature because he seems to think that the function of the angler will reveal his nature. Once it is determined that he is an expert, the first category is established, and the process of dividing each category into two types or forms begins and continues until the angler is discovered in a form that can no longer be divided. Once the angler has been discovered, a tally of all the categories that the angler was found to be in is given in a clear account (*logos*) of the angler. Figure 1.1 gives an outline of the hunt for the angler.

There are two important points to notice about this method of division. The first is that the method proceeds from a general category to a specific instance of that category. These two categories are usually referred to as *genera* (general categories) and *species* (specifications of a general category). By moving from what is general to what is specific, it becomes possible to isolate what is particularly unique about the angler that distinguishes him from everything else. This unique feature is the angler's nature. Therefore, at the end of the process of division,

The Hunt for the Angler (219a-221c)

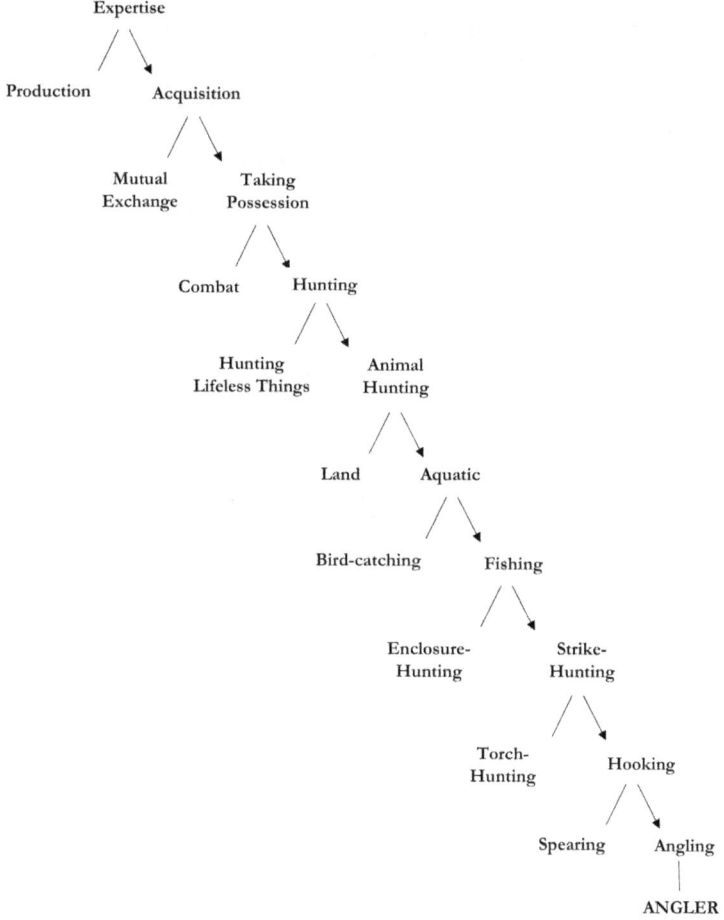

Figure 1.1

the Visitor is able to gather up all of the forms of the angler identified in the process and provide a clear and full account of him.

> So now we're in agreement about the angler's expertise, not just as to its name; in addition, we've also sufficiently grasped an account concerning the thing itself. Within expertise as a whole

one half was acquisitive; half of the acquisitive was taking possession; half of possession-taking was hunting; half of hunting was animal hunting; half of animal hunting was aquatic hunting; all of the lower portion of aquatic hunting was fishing; half of fishing was hunting by striking; and half of striking was hooking. And the part of hooking that involves a blow drawing a thing upward from underneath is called by a name that's derived by its similarity to the action itself, that is, it's called draw-fishing or angling—which is what we're searching for. (Plato, *Soph.*, 221b–c).

The second important point to note about this method is that it isolates the "thing itself"—the angler's nature—within a *form*. This means that the nature of the angler is a form—angling—that interacts with the other forms from which it descends. By implication, this means that what is really real are the forms. But what are forms?

Only forms are real

In order to understand the importance of the forms and what Plato meant by this concept, it is necessary to consider one of the most famous images in all of philosophy—Plato's Allegory of the Cave, which occurs in book seven of Plato's *Republic*. It recounts the mythical journey of a prisoner, who has been confined by chains in the depths of a cave since birth, to the brilliant light of the outside world (Plato, *Rep.*, 514a–520a). It is a journey from ignorance to wisdom. In a related mathematical image called the Divided Line, given just prior to the Allegory of the Cave (Plato, *Rep.*, 509d–513e), Plato describes the steps of this intellectual journey as a movement from opinion (appearance) to knowledge (being). According to Plato, we only have knowledge of something when we see or understand its *form*. The Greek word translated as "form" is *eidos*, derived from the Greek verb *idein*, "to see," which was also a metaphor for knowledge for Plato. To *know* is to *see* what something is—to understand how something presents itself to the mind. In fact, we get our English word "idea" from this Greek word, although, as we will see, Plato distinguished forms from ideas. A form is an immaterial and perfect model of the thing it stands for; it is what we know when we understand something. For example, the form of Beauty is the perfect model of anything that is beautiful, and, Plato would add, things are only beautiful because they participate or share in the form of Beauty. This means that only the forms are really real; everything else is a copy or a diminished reflection of the form. Therefore, when the Visitor gives an account of the angler, he is identifying (seeing) the form in which the angler participates and that makes him what he is, namely angling.

Let's recall that the central question of the *Sophist* is "What is a philosopher?," and that the Visitor and Theaetetus are pursuing this question by distinguishing the philosopher from the sophist and the statesman. Now that they have determined the appropriate method of inquiry and tested it out on the angler, they can investigate the nature of the sophist. The one pitfall they must avoid in their hunt is mistaking the sophist for a philosopher or a philosopher for a sophist. As we will see, this is no easy task.

The hunt for a slippery beast

Just as the search for the essential nature of the angler aimed at identifying the singular expertise of the angler, the Visitor and Theaetetus now seek to discover the singular expertise of the sophist. One would expect that by applying the same method of division to the sophist, one would arrive at a single expertise that makes the sophist what he is; however, the method proves incapable of capturing the "slippery" sophist (Plato, *Soph.*, 231a). The Visitor describes the search for the nature of the sophist as a "hunt" for a complex "beast" who is capable of escaping into the underbrush of each side of the divisions they make. For example, in the first hunt for the sophist it is determined that his expertise, like that of the angler, is an expertise of acquisition that involves taking possession through hunting (Plato, *Soph.*, 221d). However, in the second hunt it is determined that the expertise of the sophist is an expertise of acquisition, as in the first hunt, but when the form of acquisition is divided into hunting and exchanging, the sophist is placed in the form of exchanging instead of hunting (Plato, *Soph.*, 223c). This means that the sophist can be located in multiple forms—that of a hunter and of an exchanger—and if he can take many forms, he will have multiple natures instead of one. This is precisely what the Visitor and Theaetetus conclude. After six attempts at capturing the sophist beast with the net of language, they are left with six different *appearances* of the sophist but not his *being*.

> **First Hunt**
> The sophist is "a hired hunter of rich young men" (Plato, *Soph.*, 221c–223b).
>
> **Second Hunt**
> The sophist is "a wholesaler of learning about the soul" (Plato, *Soph.*, 223c–224d).
>
> **Third Hunt**
> The sophist is "a retailer of learning about the soul" (Plato, *Soph.*, 224d–e).
>
> **Fourth Hunt**
> The sophist is "a seller of his own learning" (Plato, *Soph.*, 224d–e).
>
> **Fifth Hunt**
> The sophist is "an athlete in verbal combat, distinguished by his expertise in debating" (Plato, *Soph.*, 224e–226a).
>
> **Sixth Hunt**
> The sophist purifies souls from "beliefs that interfere with learning" (Plato, *Soph.*, 226a–231b).

However, the Visitor and Theaetetus encounter an additional problem at the conclusion of the sixth hunt. In describing the expertise of the sophist as that of cleansing souls from false beliefs and discriminating between being and appearances, they have come dangerously close to confusing a philosopher with a sophist or a sophist with a philosopher. Unwittingly, the method of division has led them to describe the expertise of Socrates, but misapply it to the sophist. The philosopher has appeared in the disguise of the sophist, just as Socrates mentioned at the beginning of the dialogue (Plato, *Soph.*, 216b). It is not lost on

Socrates, who has listened silently to this entire conversation, that he has been indicted for being a sophist who corrupts young men by selling them his instruction on triumphing in debates. The similarities between the philosopher and the sophist were not carefully distinguished, and consequently the account of the sophist failed to capture his true nature.

This is an important lesson in learning to practice philosophy; the hallmark of authentic philosophical thinking is the ability to make clear and precise distinctions. This ability prevents the philosopher from being duped by appearances and sets her on the path to discovering what is real. However, there is another lesson that Plato would have us learn from the limitations of this method, and it is this: language cannot be the measure of reality; rather, reality is the measure of language. For Plato, the central aim for a philosopher in making careful and precise distinctions is to get the language about reality right—to allow reality to form itself in language instead of language forming reality. The former is philosophy; the latter is sophistry.

Summary

For Plato, immaterial, universal forms are real. We access the real through accurate and precise language. Philosophy is the practice of searching for reality through rational inquiry and expressing reality in language. Philosophers use the forms as models and try to copy them in language. The immaterial, universal forms are the rule and measure of whether we have given an accurate account of the real in language.

Questions

1. Do you think it is possible to distinguish reality from appearances?
2. What did Plato get right, or wrong, about the relationship between reality and language?
3. Are Plato's forms real?

2

Plato: The Net of Language
(*Sophist*, 232a–268d)

Key terms

Being – what is
Non-being – what is not
Becoming – what is in process

In the previous chapter, we saw that Plato claimed that only the forms were real. The forms, let us recall, are universal, unchanging, and immaterial models that exist independently of the mind and world and serve as paradigms for everything that exists. For example, the form of Tall applies to every particular instance of tallness—things are tall only to the degree that they correspond to the form of Tall. Moreover, the form of Tall does not change; it remains the same despite the changing of particular instances of tallness. For example, the form of Tall does not change when you are no longer as tall as your sister; it becomes the standard by which your sister is determined to be taller than you. Additionally, the forms are not material, so you cannot find them in the world as you might find willow trees, pomegranates, and armadillos; rather, the forms are the conditions that make things in the world intelligible. For example, when we understand the form of Tall, we can understand when one thing or person is taller than another. The forms, then, are the universal models for everything that is, and the most general form is Being. For Plato, the aim of philosophy is to grasp intellectually (or "see") the forms of things. We have knowledge of something when we can understand its form. This is precisely what Theaetetus and the Visitor want to accomplish in their pursuit of the sophist; they want to understand the form of the sophist.

The problem of being

After Theaetetus and the Visitor complete the sixth account of the sophist, they realize that the sophist has taken many forms. He appeared as a hunter of wealthy young men, a wholesaler and retailer of learning, an educational entrepreneur, a skilled debater, and a soul purifier. The problem is that the nature of the sophist seems to be many things rather than one thing. But how can this be? Does the name "sophist" refer to one thing or many? If it applies to one thing, then the many appearances of the sophist must be disguises that conceal his true nature. If the name applies to many things then each of the many things is not a sophist but something else. Theaetetus and the Visitor want to know the form of the sophist—what he is—not simply what he appears to be. This dilemma points to what philosophers refer to as *the problem of being*.

For Plato, being is the most general of all the forms, and therefore the most general form of reality. Everything that *is*—Venus fly traps, motorcycles, cicadas, concepts like large and small—shares in, or participates in, the form of Being because each thing has the feature of *isness*. But how can we apprehend the form of Being if it is immaterial and independent of the world? As we saw in the last chapter, Plato sees language as the appropriate medium for apprehending Being. To understand why Plato thinks language can function in this way, we need to return to an important concept in Plato's philosophical toolbox: *logos*.

The Greek noun *logos* is derived from the Greek verb *legein*, which means both "to speak" and "to gather." To speak, for the Greeks, was to collect or gather one's thoughts in a symbolic system of signs so that thinking could be operationalized to represent reality. To get a sense of how the Greeks understood the relationship between language and reality, consider the experience of watching a film with a friend and then discussing it. When your friend asks you what you thought of the film as you are walking out of the theater, you do not have an immediate response or a prepared review of the film, so you try to put your thoughts into words that communicate how the film made you feel or to indicate the insights you gained. Your mind tries to find the words and phrases that best represent your thoughts and feelings about the film. In this way, language functions like the clothing we wear on our bodies to present ourselves in the world. Language gives sensible form to our immaterial thoughts by gathering them together in a meaningful and sensible representation. This is what it means to give an account—a *logos*—of something: to represent reality in language. However, this raises an interesting question. If language is a medium for representing reality, how can we be sure the representation is accurate? After all, clothing conceals just as much as it reveals. Similarly, language freezes reality into a system of signs. It is, therefore, entirely possible that someone could *mis*represent reality by using language that conceals reality instead of revealing it. This happens when people lie, or make false statements because they are confused about reality or want to intentionally confuse others about reality. But how can we know if what is expressed in language is an accurate representation or misrepresentation? It seems that we would need some kind of measure or standard by which to judge what is expressed in language.

In a letter that is attributed to Plato called the "Seventh Letter," the author claims there are three necessary requirements to have knowledge of the nature or being of any object: the *name*, the *definition* (*logos*), and the *image*.[1] Contemporary philosophers of language refer to these elements as the *signifier* (name), *signified* (definition), and the *referent* (image). *Names* are the words or terms we use to signify things in statements. For example, in the statement, "Socrates is a philosopher," "Socrates" and "philosopher" are names that signify particular things. In order for this statement to be intelligible, the names—"Socrates" and "philosopher"—must be clearly defined; that is, an account must be given of what is meant by each name—a *definition* of the terms. *Images* are the physical and sensory referents or objects that are *signified* (definitions) by the *signifiers* (names). We have knowledge when we can recognize an image by way of a name and give an account of it. This connection between language and knowledge can be represented in the following "semiotic triangle," which is, well . . . an image (Figure 2.1).

The six accounts of the sophist that emerge in the discussion between Theaetetus and the Visitor are definitions broadly construed. The problem is that there are multiple definitions of a single name, making it difficult to know which one to apply to the sophist. Consequently,

---

[1] Plato, *Letter VII*, in *Plato: Complete Works*, 342b.

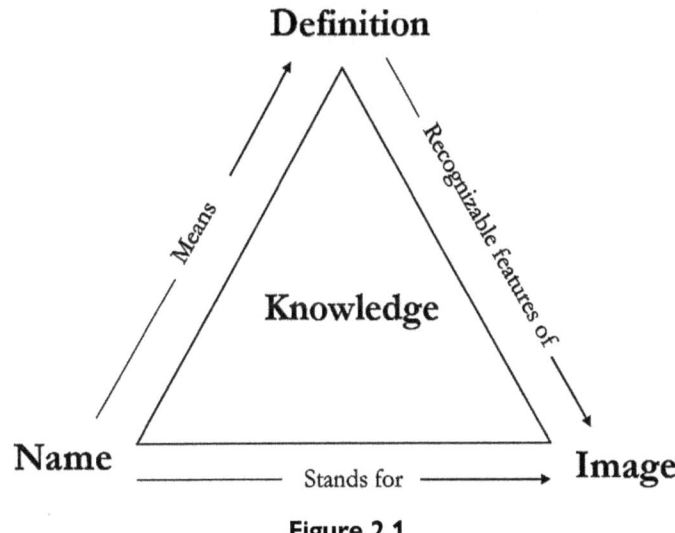

Figure 2.1

Theaetetus and the Visitor are unable to arrive at any knowledge of the sophist's nature. The sophist, as the Visitor points out, "appears to have expert knowledge of lots of things," but "if somebody takes him to be an expert at many things, then that observer can't be seeking clearly what it is in his expertise that all of those many pieces of learning focus on ..." (Plato, *Soph*., 232a). This insight suggests that if names, definitions, and images are *necessary* to have knowledge of something, they do not seem to be *sufficient*. Something else is needed—a fifth element added to that of name, definition, image, and knowledge—the form of the thing itself.

If only the forms are real, then it is important to understand what the forms are. Plato makes clear that the forms are not concepts or thoughts in the mind; rather, they are the object of our thoughts—they are what our thoughts and the language we use to express our thoughts seek to capture. The forms exist independently of our minds and language. In fact, as we will see, they are the measure or standard by which we can judge our concepts and statements to be either true or false.

If we expand Plato's semiotic triangle, we can see how the forms function as the ultimate objects of our knowledge about reality (see Figure 2.2). We have *knowledge*, Plato argues, when can give account of

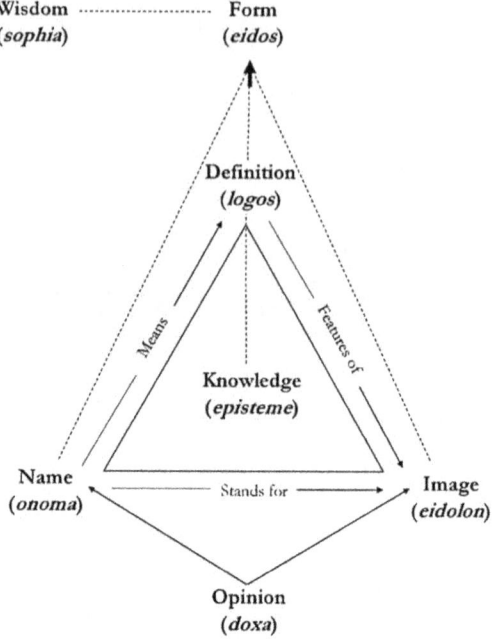

Figure 2.2

something in a definition and apply its corresponding name to a sensible representation of it, and we attain *wisdom* when we have knowledge of the forms. If we merely apply a name to an image without clearly defining the name we're applying, we only have an *opinion* about reality.

The definition uses terms that Plato argues are symbolic representations of immaterial forms. For example, the statement "Socrates is a man" is comprised of three terms: "Socrates," "man," and "is." "Socrates" is the *subject* of this statement, "man" is the *predicate*, and "is" is the *copula* that joins the other two terms together. The *subject* is who or what is spoken about in the statement. The *predicate* (from the Latin verb *praedicāre*, "to declare or say") is what is said about the subject. The *copula* is the verbal hinge in the statement that indicates how the subject and the predicate are related.

Socrates	**is**	**a man**
Subject	Copula	Predicate

To say that Socrates is a man is to define or give an account of his being—his nature or essence. The predicate explains what the nature of Socrates is. This is the kind of account that Theaetetus and the Visitor want to give of the sophist and of being itself. When the names "sophist" or "being" are defined, they refer, Plato argues, to immaterial, stable, and universal paradigms for everything that can be, and the highest of these paradigms is Being. The forms, then, are ultimate reality, and the ultimate referents of our language. For this reason, Plato unites thought and being in language. Because of this, reality can manifest itself in language when we discuss the meaning of the words we use and the way we use them—just as Theaetetus and the Visitor have been doing throughout the dialogue.

The problem of language

The Seventh Letter indicates that in order to grasp the fifth element (the form), the other four must be obtained, and this can only occur "when all of these things—names, definitions, and visual and other perceptions—have been rubbed against one another and tested, pupil and teacher asking and answering questions in good will and without envy—only then, when reason and knowledge are at the very extremity of human effort, can they illuminate the nature of any object" (Plato, *Letter VII*, 344b). Language is a limited medium; every statement reveals and conceals aspects of an object. This is why it is necessary to engage in lengthy dialogues with others about a topic: every twist and turn in the conversation between Theaetetus and the Visitor reveals a new glimpse of the sophist, but it also conceals some aspect of the sophist. As the Visitor points out, language is like a net (Plato, *Soph.*, 235b), but the problem with nets is that they have holes. This allows us to see an important insight about philosophy and language: the deepest insights about reality cannot be expressed in words but can only be experienced as flashes of insight made possible by the performance of language. We make use of, or perform, language, not to represent reality—it will always slip through the holes in our nets—but to create the conditions for reality to show itself in language. The more we name, define, and represent objects, the more their true nature—their form—is illuminated. Just as when lightning flashes in a dark sky and illuminates the contours of trees, houses, and other objects on the earth, so also the performance of language illuminates the forms.

Imitation and knowledge

The Visitor and Theaetetus reexamine the six accounts of the sophist, and determine that there is a single expertise the sophist exhibits: *imitation*. The sophist imitates real things through language—"spoken images" (Plato, *Soph.*, 234c). However, there are two types of imitation. One type of imitation is "likeness-making," which preserves the proportions and features of the original in the image that is created—recall Vermeer's use of the camera obscura to preserve geometrical scale in his paintings (Plato, *Soph.*, 235c). The other type is "appearance-making," which does not preserve the proportions or features of the original, but instead creates an image that appears to be something that it is not. Given that knowledge consists in the interrelationship between name, image, and definition, appearance-making can be distinguished from likeness-making by the absence of a definition—the lack of an account of the essential features of an object. To better understand this distinction, let's return to the case of Han van Meegeren. Remember that van Meegeren did not copy existing paintings by Vermeer—he did not try to create *likenesses* of existing Vermeer paintings; instead, he created paintings that *appeared* to have been painted by Vermeer. The expertise of the sophist is similar—he creates spoken images that appear to express knowledge of things but do not. The sophist is therefore a forger of wisdom.

This conclusion by the Visitor and Theaetetus opens up a new problem that will require them to reject a long-held philosophical belief. If a sophist is capable of appearance-making through language, then he is capable of speaking what is not—non-being. The philosopher Parmenides had argued that this was impossible. You cannot, he argued, think or speak what does not exist. Sure, you can conjure images of unicorns in your mind, and you can describe all of the features of a unicorn in language. But in doing so, Parmenides would argue, you have not thought or spoken what does not exist; you've thought and spoken what does exist—horses and horns—in a confused way. However, if Parmenides is right, false beliefs and false statements are impossible, because false beliefs are beliefs in what *is not* (non-being), and false statements are statements about what *is not* (non-being). The problem is: both beliefs and statements *are* (being). Theaetetus and the Visitor cannot accept the absurd implication of Parmenides' view that false beliefs and statements are impossible. This leads them to overturn that view and arrive at a paradoxical conclusion that will govern the rest of the dialogue: "*that which is not* somehow is, and ... *that which is* somehow is not" (Plato, *Soph.*, 241d). To resolve this dilemma, they decide to investigate what being is before turning the topic of non-being. If they can clarify these two important terms, they will be able to distinguish between the practice of philosophers and the practice of sophists. The investigation shifts from the sophist to being itself.

The hunt for being: four views

Theaetetus and the Visitor consider four ways that philosophers have conceived of reality: *monism*, *pluralism*, *materialism*, and *idealism*. Some, like Parmenides (515–450 BCE), argued that being is one thing and the many things that *are* are part of that one being. This view is called *monism*. The problem with this view is that in claiming that "'all things' are just one" (Plato, *Soph.*, 242d), the one being is understood to be the same as the totality of "all things." However, this means that the totality is distinct from the one being because the one being cannot be both the one itself and the totality itself. Moreover, this claim involves a plurality of terms (names) that all *are*: one, being, and totality (see Figure 2.3). If each one of these things *is*, then being must be something separate and independent of each of them, and therefore, being cannot be any one of them.

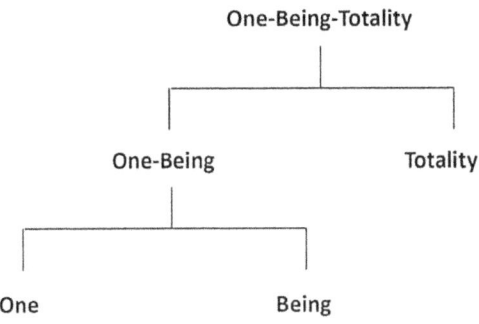

Figure 2.3

Others, like Democritus (460–370 BCE), Heraclitus (535–475 BCE), and Empedocles (494–434 BCE), claimed that reality is comprised of fundamental elements like earth, air, fire, and water, or qualities like hot and cold, or love and strife. This view is called *pluralism*. The problem with this view is that if there are two elements—hot and cold, for example—each of which must *be*, then this means that *being* is a third element that makes each one to be.

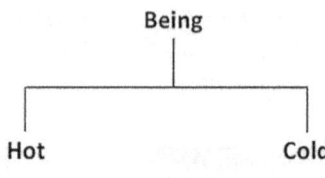

Figure 2.4

As the Visitor asks, "What shall we take this being to be? Is it a third thing alongside those two beings, so that according to you everything is no longer two but three?" (Plato, *Soph.*, 243d–e). This kind of questioning could go on forever because the being of each element of reality must be explained, which requires positing *being* as an additional thing.

Other philosophers, as the Visitor points out, "define being as the same as body" (Plato, *Soph.*, 246b). Like the Titans described in Hesiod's *Theogony*, these philosophers are at war with the *gods* of heaven, who view being as something separate and independent from the physical world of material objects. For the giants, only matter is real, and there is nothing beyond the material world. This view is called *materialism*. Materialism has a long and rich history in philosophy; instead of seeking a reality beyond the physical world, it seeks it within the world. For materialists, the forms are to be found within physical objects instead of independent of them. In this way, the materialist can be understood to be demystifying the world. The problem with this view is that if all there *is* is matter—being is simply physical—then how can immaterial virtues like courage, wisdom, generosity, love, or justice be accounted for? Surely, these virtues are exhibited in physical bodies, but their being is not material.

The final way of conceiving reality that the Visitor presents is the view of "the friends of the forms" (Plato, *Soph.*, 248a). These philosophers theorized that there are fundamental forms that exist independently of the physical world and are the basis for the reality of everything that is. This view is called *idealism*. The idealists separate being from becoming and non-being, so that reality is conceived of as universal and unchanging. If only the forms are real, *being* is the most fundamental form. But the idealist position has a troubling implication: if reality is universal and unchanging, then whatever is particular and undergoing change is not real. But this can't be true. For example, the minds of the Visitor and Theaetetus are changing throughout the dialogue as they pursue the question about the nature of the sophist, but their minds are certainly real. Moreover, the concepts of *being*, *becoming*, and *non-being* are names that can be defined and applied to certain phenomena, so they are real. So, the idealist view, just like the monist, pluralist, and materialist views, seems unable to account for the *being* of becoming and non-being, and does not seem to be able to explain how something can be undergoing change—moving from one state to another (e.g., from ignorance to knowledge)—and still be real.

The five kinds

Although each of these views describes some aspect of reality, they do not offer a complete account of it, and some of these aspects are in conflict with one another. For example, both the monists and the idealists emphasize the unity and stability of reality—being, they argue, is characterized by sameness and being-at-rest. However, the pluralists and materialists emphasize the variability and instability of reality—being, they argue, is characterized by difference and change. In their discussion of these four views, the Visitor and Theaetetus come to realize that each of these characteristics of reality *is*—change and rest *are* (Plato, *Soph.*, 250a), and sameness and difference *are* (Plato, *Soph.*, 255b–e). This leaves us with five forms: *being*, *change*, *rest*, *sameness*, and *difference*, and being seems to be the most

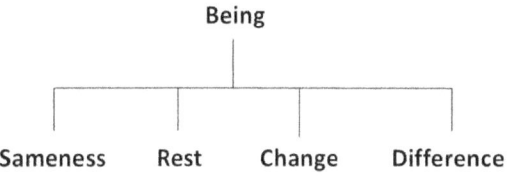

Figure 2.5

prominent among them because, while being is distinct from each of the other forms, each of them *is*.

Each of the five forms is a referent of the terms we use when we speak or write. For example, in the statement "Philosophers are not sophists," we are making use of being, sameness, and difference. However, not all forms can be linked together in statements and remain intelligible. For example, the statement "Philosophers are not philosophers" is incoherent because it links sameness ("philosophers" and "philosophers") and difference ("are not") together. Some forms "fit together with each and some don't," says the visitor (Plato, Soph., 253a). What this suggests, as the Visitor points out, is that the forms are like letters in the alphabet—some are consonants and some are vowels—that can be linked together to make intelligible statements (Plato, Soph., 253a). In any given word, the consonants are like the bricks and the vowels are like the mortar that holds the bricks together. Similarly, some forms are like bricks—they are categorical like being and non-being—while other forms are like mortar—they are structural like sameness, difference, rest, and change. This means that there is an inherent logic in language that provides the measure for language. Instead of language being the measure of reality, reality—understood as the forms—is the measure of language. Reality can therefore be expressed in language when someone has knowledge of the forms and expertise in "the weaving together of forms" (Plato, Soph., 259e). This is precisely the knowledge and expertise that the philosopher is purported to have and the sophist claims to have.

However, in the final account of the sophist, where the Visitor and Theaetetus attempt to finally distinguish the philosopher from the sophist by describing the sophist as an "appearance-maker" and the philosopher as a "likeness-maker," the sophist still bears an uncanny resemblance to the philosopher. The Visitor indicates that the sophist "uses short speeches in private conversation to force the person talking with him to contradict himself"—a method used by Socrates to help his conversation partners realize their errors (Plato, Soph., 268b). So, the philosopher (being) and the sophist (appearance) remain largely indistinguishable, which suggests that being and appearance are not ultimately separate but related. The dialogue ends not with a definitive answer about the nature of reality but with a demonstration of how to think about what is real.

Summary

For Plato, we have knowledge of reality when we can give an account of being in language. We do this by using names that are clearly defined to apply to images, and the definitions we provide indicate the form and essence of what we name. Language is thus a medium for expressing what is real. However, in order to have an accurate and precise account of reality, we must know how to weave the forms together in language. This is the expertise of philosophers. They are likeness-makers who try to express reality in language through knowledge of the forms. Sophists, on the other hand, are forgers of reality. They are appearance-makers, who express opinions about reality in language without knowledge of the forms.

Questions

1. Can reality be expressed in language?
2. Can getting our language right about reality prevent us from being duped by appearances?
3. What is the difference between a philosopher and a sophist?

3

Descartes: Mind and Reality
(*Meditations on First Philosophy*, I–III)

> **Key terms**
>
> Substance – an independently existing thing with qualities
> Mind – an immaterial substance that thinks
> Body – a material substance that takes up space
> Clear and Distinct – quality of a perception that is immediately known and beyond doubt

Almost 2000 years separate Plato and René Descartes, but both are ultimately concerned with the same question—What is real?—even though they answer this question in very different ways. Plato's answer was, as we have seen, that only the immaterial forms are real, and this reality is the measure for our knowledge and claims about the world of our experience. However, in conceptualizing reality as immaterial and independent of the world, Plato gave philosophy a *transcendent* orientation—philosophy, on his account, attempts to go beyond human experience to apprehend the unchanging realm of the forms. One consequence of this view is that some things turn out to have more reality than others; if the forms are ultimately real, the reality of the world is diminished. Descartes' answer will be very different. Instead of directing our attention to a reality outside of human experience, Descartes reorients philosophy so that we can discover reality within our *immanent* mental experience, and this is especially clear in the style of his *Meditations*. It turns out, for both Plato and Descartes, the answer to the metaphysical question—What is real?—is intrinsically related to the epistemological question—How can we know what is real? Recall that the epistemological question in Plato's *Theaetetus* prompts the metaphysical question of the *Sophist*. Similarly, in

Descartes' *Meditations*, the epistemological question leads to the metaphysical question. As we will see in Part II, the epistemological question becomes central in modern philosophy.

The *Meditations* are spiritual exercises

In order to begin reading Descartes' *Meditations*, it is important to understand what kind of book it is. The word *meditation* in the title suggests that Descartes intended the book to be read as a spiritual exercise (spiritual in terms of subjective experience, not necessarily religious) not as a philosophical *treatise*. Descartes had learned the value of meditative practice while enrolled at the Jesuit college of La Flèche in Anjou, France in the early seventeenth century, where students received both a theological and a philosophical education in addition to the other classical fields of study like Greek, Latin, logic, geometry, mathematics, rhetoric, astronomy, and music. It was at La Flèche that Descartes was exposed to the *Spiritual Exercises* of the Catholic saint Ignatius of Loyola. As part of his theological and spiritual formation, he went on weeklong spiritual retreats where he engaged in meditative practices created by Loyola. In these exercises, the meditator imagines himself to be involved in various events in the life of Jesus, in order to cultivate a devotion as well as the theological virtues of faith, hope, and love. Descartes invites the reader of his *Meditations* to engage in a similar kind of exercise, but whereas the *Spiritual Exercises* were intended to indoctrinate the meditator, Descartes' *Meditations* were intended to initiate the meditator into philosophical practice. Just as Plato's dialogues were training manuals in *how* to think rather than in *what* to think, so also Descartes' *Meditations* are exercises in philosophical thinking, with an emphasis on the priority of reason rather than imagination. Descartes' aim in the book is therefore to help the reader discover reality for himself or herself rather than simply telling them what reality is. This reality will be turn out to be *substance*.

The substance of reality

Descartes took up a critical stance toward the classical philosophies of both Plato and Aristotle. While Plato had argued that the forms were the immaterial paradigms of everything that exists, his student

Aristotle argued that the forms were a design feature of actual things, instead of entities that existed outside the world. This meant that the nature or essence of something was the result of how its matter was formed. For example, Plato would argue that we know the nature of a flute by having knowledge of the immaterial form of flute-ness. But Aristotle claimed that even if there was an immaterial form of fluteness independent of the world, it would be no use to us in explaining the nature of flutes in this world because it would be too general and abstract to account for all the particular kinds of flutes we encounter. Instead, Aristotle argued that everything we encounter in the world is a *substance*—an independent entity that we can point to in the world and describe in terms of its qualities or attributes.[1] Substances are literally what stand under (Latin, *sub* "under"+ *stare* "stand") the qualities and attributes of any given thing; a substance is what we identify when we make statements like, "*This* is a *flute*" (*This* indicates the substance of *this particular flute* and *flute* indicates the *universal form of all flutes*). A substance, for Aristotle, is composed of *matter* and *form*; the matter is the physical stuff out of which something is made, and the form is the shape or design of the matter. The formal design of a substance makes it what it is.[2] For example, Aristotle argues that human beings are "rational animals" because they are composed out of matter that has a rational form. Only substance is real for Aristotle, and substance is the object of philosophical inquiry—it's what we know when we say we have knowledge of something.

While Aristotle held that there are many types of substances in the world, Descartes claimed that there is only one *infinite* substance—God—that expresses itself in two *finite* substances—bodies and minds—that are wholly dependent on God for their nature and existence (see Figure 3.1). For Descartes, a substance is "a thing which exists in such a way as to depend on no other thing for its existence."[3] Given

---

[1] Aristotle, "Categories," in *The Complete Works of Aristotle*, vol. 1, ed. Jonathan Barnes (Princeton: Princeton University Press, 1984), 2a.11–12.
[2] Aristotle, "On the Soul," in *The Complete Works of Aristotle*, vol. 1, II.412a.9–26.
[3] René Descartes, "Principles of Philosophy," in *The Philosophical Writings of Descartes*, vol. 1, trans. John Cottingham, Robert Stoothoff, and Dugald Murdoch (New York: Cambridge University Press, 1985), AT VIIIA.24, 210. The English translations of Descartes' texts are keyed to the critical edition of his work, *Oeuvres de Descartes*, edited by Charles Adam and Paul Tannery. All citations for Descartes in these chapters

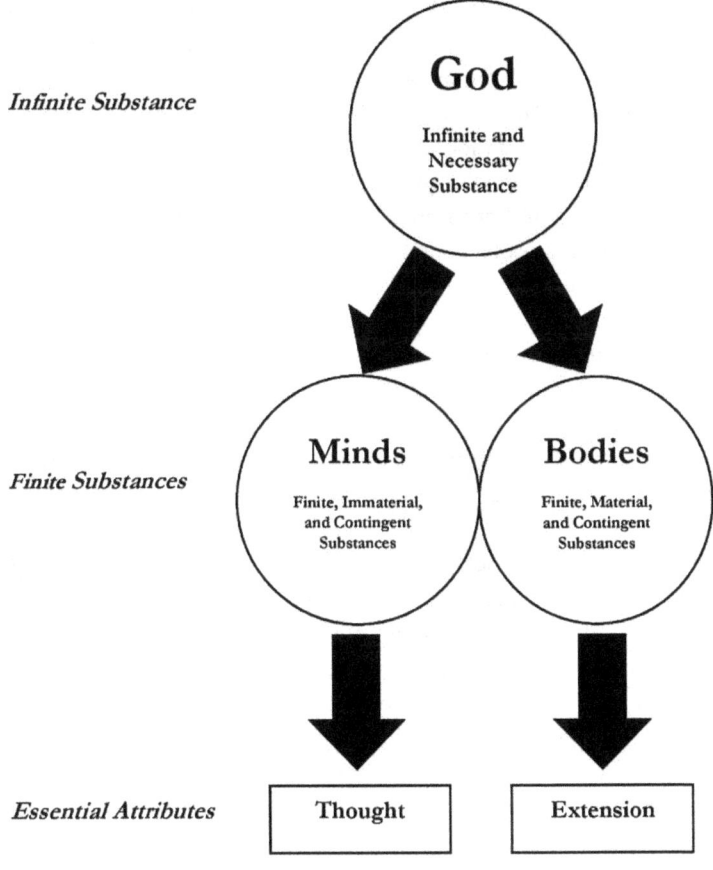

Figure 3.1

that a substance does not depend on anything else for its existence, only an independent and necessary being like God meets the strict criteria of a substance. God must therefore be an infinitely perfect and necessary substance and everything else is a finite, imperfect, and dependent substance. Every substance also has an essential attribute that makes it what

---

will indicate this by using "AT" to refer to the Adam and Tannery edition, followed by the volume and page number. The Adam and Tannery numbers are typically found in the margins of translations of Descartes' texts. All quotations from Descartes' *Meditations* will refer to Descartes, *Meditations on First Philosophy*, third edition, trans. Donald A. Cress (Indianapolis: Hackett, 1993). All other quotations will refer to the standard English translation cited above, *The Philosophical Writings of Descartes*.

it is. We have knowledge of a substance, Descartes argues, when we know its essential attribute. For example, the essential attribute of bodies (physical objects) is that all material objects are extended in space by their specific dimensions (extension), and the essential attribute of minds is the activity of thought in its various modes of sensing, imagining, reasoning, and judging (thought). In short, *bodies take up space* and *minds think*. If reality is substance, and the most immediate substances we are in contact with are our bodies and minds, then we have to begin our search for reality in the immanent experience of our bodies and minds. But, Descartes says, that's just where our problems begin.

Both Plato and Aristotle had claimed that the quest for knowing reality begins with what we can perceive with the senses and works backwards by abstracting from particular objects in the world to either a general, immaterial form, or a general substance. Descartes thought this way of philosophizing was on shaky ground because, as everyone is aware, the senses are not always reliable—sticks look bent when they are put in water, and food tastes different when we are sick. If we begin with the unreliable information from the senses, we will never attain a knowledge of reality that is free from error. Given that the history of philosophy was built on these shaky foundations, it is likely, Descartes thought, that much of what we have taken to be true is false. He realized that philosophy, for all its devotion to the pursuit of reality, might have led us astray. For him, there was only one option open to the philosopher seeking true reality: the entire house of philosophical knowledge would need to be torn down to its foundations and rebuilt.

Meditation 1: doubting reality

In the opening sentence of the first meditation, Descartes expresses a universal human experience—the experience of learning that one has been deceived. "Several years have now passed since I first realized how numerous were the false opinions that in my youth I had taken to be true, and thus how doubtful were all those that I had subsequently built upon them" (AT VII.17). Everyone has realized, at some point, to a greater or lesser degree, that what he or she once believed to be true is false. Santa Claus turns out to be a parental ruse; friends and lovers turn out to be less than loyal; words we thought we knew the meaning of for years turn out to mean something else; religious convictions are exposed as unsubstantiated myths. But there is an additional problem: each of these false opinions, because we believed them to be true, ended up serving as a foundation for other beliefs and opinions. Beliefs are formed within a larger network of other beliefs—each one depending on the other. The realization that our most fundamental beliefs about the world are false strikes a devastating blow to the foundations of our knowledge. The only way to resolve this problem is to disabuse ourselves of every opinion that admits of any doubt, so that we can discover what we know beyond any doubt, or as Descartes puts it, we have to "raze everything to the ground and begin again from the original foundations" (AT VII.17). The only way to avoid false beliefs or opinions is to discover what we can know for certain, and build everything we know on those certain foundations.

In order to accomplish this task, Descartes invites the meditator to set aside any belief or opinion that admits of any doubt or is not completely certain (AT VII.18). It's important to note that the beliefs or opinions that are set aside are not set aside because they are *false*—they may turn out to be true—but they are set aside because they are not *certain*. Something is certain if it cannot be doubted. It's also important to note that the doubt that Descartes employs is a method for arriving at the truth about reality rather than a descent into complete skepticism about reality. Doubt is a tool used to chip away uncertain beliefs in order to arrive at what is certain. We can think of this methodological doubt as akin to restoring a mural on the wall of an ancient temple that has faded under layers of paint and dust. In order to reveal the ancient artwork underneath, we have to remove the dust and other material accumulations in a careful and systematic way.

Descartes' methodological doubt takes place in three phases. In the first phase, he doubts any information received from the senses because our senses do not always provide reliable information about reality (AT VII.18–19). For example, a stick appears bent when it is placed in water, when it is actually straight. Note that this does not mean the senses are *always* unreliable, only that they are *sometimes* unreliable, and given that they are sometimes unreliable, the information they provide cannot be beyond doubt. This has a devastating implication. If we set aside all the information derived from the senses, this would include everything we see, hear, smell, taste, and touch; inevitably, this includes the external world of trees, cars, buildings, iPhones, lattes, our lovers, friends, pets, and our own bodies. If we cannot trust the senses, we cannot trust that there is an external world or that we have a body.

"But, wait!," you might say. If the senses are *sometimes* reliable, then some of the information they provide can be trusted, and if that is the case, why should we set aside everything we received from the senses? You would have to be completely crazy to dismiss *everything* the senses convey. Right? Descartes raises the same objection, but for a very specific reason. He points out that those who "insist that they are kings when they are utter paupers, or that they are arrayed in purple robes when they are naked" are under the sway of beliefs produced by the imagination that admit no contrary information from the senses (AT VII.19). What makes these beliefs compelling is that they have an internal consistency that leads the believer to accept them as true. What is more, these beliefs function as a framework for the acceptance or rejection of other beliefs—anything that fits into the belief structure ("I am a king robed in purple") is accepted, and anything that does not fit into this belief structure ("I am a naked pauper") is rejected. Note also that these beliefs are so convincing that we base our identities on them, and all our feelings and actions are derived from them. When Descartes asks the meditator to entertain the possibility that he might be insane, he is pointing out that our beliefs can be consistent—all of them fit together and explain each other—without being true.

In the second phase, having set aside all knowledge derived from the faculty of the senses, Descartes turns his wrecking ball of doubt on the faculty of the imagination. As he will point out in the sixth meditation, the imagination is a faculty that is "turned toward the body"—it makes use of the feelings and data delivered by the senses (AT VII.73)—this is why it can present complexes of coherent beliefs, because it makes use of the standards of sensory experience. But, if the information of the senses is unreliable, then the residual images that the imagination conjures from sensations like a magician, despite their apparent coherence, are even more likely to be unreliable because they derive their resources from sensory experiences that are doubtful. The imagination is, like Plato's sophist, an appearance-maker rather than a likeness-maker because it lacks a strong connection to reality. In fact, when we consider, for example, the musings of the insane, or the hallucinations of people on psychedelic drugs, or our own dreams, for that matter, we often describe these as being "out of touch with reality." We recognize, as Descartes did, that the imagination is even more unreliable than the senses. To return to our reading of the *Sophist*, the insane and dreamers mistake appearances for reality. Descartes asks the meditator to consider the implications of the unreliability of the senses and the imagination for the knowledge of his own body. He realizes that he has no grounds for believing that the fire he sees is real, or that the hands holding the newspaper in front of him are his, because the senses are sometimes unreliable; and if he is merely imagining these things, because he has gone insane or is dreaming, he is even less certain of their existence (AT VII.19). This means, of course, that he cannot know whether he has a body, whether he is sane or insane, or whether he is dreaming or awake. But this still leaves the possibility that all of these beliefs and opinions about the world and himself could be verified through a supernatural being like God, who exists independently of the meditator.

If there is a supremely good God who can be trusted to guide us to the truth about reality, then the meditator will be able to overcome the doubts about reality that have arisen and anchor his knowledge in God's revelation. But Descartes does not think the existence of such a being can be established so easily, at least not in the way traditional proofs for the existence of God have been offered. Traditional proofs attempt to derive the existence of an ultimate cause like God from the effects perceived by the senses—working back from sensory effects to a rationally deduced cause. Given that the senses are unreliable, this method of proving the existence of God cannot lead to certainty because the starting point is doubtful. Moreover, there is no way to establish the goodness of God. If there is a supernatural being that exists, he might have evil intentions and be bent on deceiving us. If this is the case, the meditator is left without any way of knowing what is real and what is not. Everything, it seems, can be doubted.

Descartes imagines an even more startling possibility: What if everything we think we know is a delusion perpetrated by an "evil genius" (AT VII.22)? This question has become the stuff of science-fiction films like *The Matrix*, where human beings live in a simulation and their bodies are used as fuel cells for the computer program that controls them. Descartes entertains the possibility that his perception of reality is a simulation because he wants to rid himself of any belief that is open to doubt. Given that the goodness of God cannot be readily established on certain grounds, it is possible that God could have evil intentions—this does not prove that he does, only that he *could*. This possibility requires Descartes to set aside the proposition of a good God who cannot deceive us until it can be established on more certain grounds.

Meditation 2: the reality of me

The doubt employed in the first meditation exercise was so destructive and disorienting that the meditator is left feeling as if he has "suddenly fallen into a deep whirlpool" and is unable to reach its bottom or emerge from its surface—the meditator is literally drowning in doubt (AT VII.24). Having doubted the external world, information received from the senses, and images produced by the imagination, as well as raising the possibility of an evil genius simulating everything he perceives, the meditator is left without any foundations for his knowledge.

But in the midst of swirling doubt, Descartes leads the meditator to realize that no matter how total his doubt, doubting is a mental activity that must necessarily occur in a thinking subject, and this thinking subject must exist (AT VII.25). This insight leads him to conclude that he is a "thinking thing" (AT VII.28); that is, he is a thinking *substance*. Descartes identifies his essential nature to be mental not physical, so that even if his bodily senses are deceived about the existence of the external world, his mind exists and operates independently of the body. This provides the meditator with his first indubitable foundation for knowledge: he exists.

The fruit of this insight comes out in Descartes' example of the wax. The meditator is asked to consider a piece of wax that is solid, tastes like honey because it has just been taken from a honeycomb, smells like flowers, has a distinct color and size, and is hard and cold. But when this same piece of wax is moved near a fire, all the sensory qualities change; the wax is no longer solid and hard, but gelatinous and flexible; it loses its floral scent and honey taste; its shape changes, and it is no longer cold but hot (AT VII.30). If our knowledge comes from our bodily senses, then we must conclude that the second piece of wax is distinct from the first piece of wax because its sensory qualities are completely different. But Descartes points out that in spite of the material changes in the wax, the mind still knows that it is wax—and the same wax—prior to the transformation. From this he concludes, just as he has done about his own existence, that the wax has material and immaterial aspects. With the senses, we perceive the material qualities of the wax, its shape, size, odor, taste, and color; but with the mind, we grasp the immaterial essence of the wax. The meditator, as a thinking substance, grasps the essence of the wax "through the mind alone" (AT VII.31). The important implication in this example is that the mind is capable of knowing reality independently of the senses and the imagination. But how is this possible?

Meditation 3: the reality of God

The discovery in the second mediation that one cannot doubt one's existence is a powerful insight. It appears to provide a solid foundation for knowledge, but it raises a problem: it leaves the meditator locked inside his own subjectivity (philosophers call this the *Cartesian ego*) with no way to verify his experience and ideas because he cannot escape his subjectivity, and the senses are unreliable. Descartes has essentially painted the meditator into a corner, so that he must verify his ideas within his mental experience alone. The meditator is like a person who has been locked in a room since birth with no knowledge of anything outside the room. Any knowledge he gains about the world outside the room must be deduced from clues he discovers from within the room itself. For the meditator, this means that any inquiry into the origin of his ideas must begin within his experience as a thinking substance—he will have to begin by examining his own thoughts. But to do this, he will need a criterion for determining whether a thought is true or false.

Descartes has concluded from the first two meditations that he exists as a thinking substance, and that this knowledge of himself is true because it is *clear and distinct*. A perception is *clear*, Descartes tells us in his *Principles of Philosophy*, if it is "present and accessible to the attentive mind"; and a perception is *distinct*, if it can be separated from all other perceptions and remains clear (AT VIIIA.22). So, a clear and distinct perception will be one that is beyond doubt and immediately known to the meditator. The meditator's discovery that he exists fits this description, and so Descartes lays down a "general rule" to guide the meditator in discovering what is true: all clear and distinct perceptions are true (AT VII.35). But there is a problem, the first meditation has already convinced the meditator to be wary of clear and distinct perceptions because we could be under the influence of a deceptive God or an evil genius. It might therefore be the case that what we clearly and distinctly perceive is false, and this means that even the meditator's idea of himself as a thinking substance still leaves room for some doubt. To remove this doubt, and to establish that one exists beyond any doubt, he must determine whether his ideas are self-caused or caused by another, and if caused by another, whether this other (God) is capable of being deceptive (AT VII.38).

Given that the meditator must begin with the contents of his own mind, Descartes asks the meditator to catalog the contents of his own mind, and what he finds are *ideas, affects, volitions,* and *judgments*. Affects, volitions, and judgments are all ways that we *respond* to objects of our thought, but ideas *are* the objects of our thinking. Ideas, for Descartes, are "images of things"—they are representations of the objects of thought, paintings of the mind, if you will, of things like "a man, or a chimera, or the sky, or an angel, or God" (AT VII.37). Descartes points out that all ideas are either innate within the mind (not produced by us), adventitious (originate outside of us like the idea of human being), or are fabrications (produced by us like the idea of a chimera) (AT VII.37). Consider each of the "ideas" Descartes has described. Each of these mental paintings are representations of some object of thought (note that the idea is not the object but the representation of the object—this is important to remember: an idea is a representation of something, not the thing itself), but they have been painted according to different standards. For example, the idea of a human being is painted according to the standards provided by sensation—human beings have bodies with two arms and legs, and are an intermingling of a mind with a body. However, a chimera (a Greek mythological being with a lion's head, a goat's body, and a serpent's tail) is a mosaic made up from other ideas according to standards of the imagination. Now consider the idea of the sky—the expansive blue or grey field I see when I look up—which always exceeds my perception of it, so that my idea of the sky is always *mine* and never the whole sky. This idea is painted according to the standards of my mind, but a part (*my* sky) is taken to be a representative of the whole (*the* sky). This is interesting, because the idea of God—an immaterial, supernatural being who is all-powerful, all-knowing, and everywhere-present—can never be totally grasped by the mind, and so, like the sky, God will always be greater than any representation of the mind. But the idea of God is distinct from the other ideas that are listed in that it cannot be based on the standards of the senses, because we have never seen, heard, smelled, tasted, or touched God; nor can it be based on standards of the imagination, because the imagination makes use of data from the senses, and we know God isn't an object of sensation. The idea of God, Descartes will argue, is innate in the mind (AT VII.51).

Let's return to Descartes' insight from the second meditation exercise, namely, that we are thinking substances distinct from the body. This is where Descartes thinks any proof for the existence of a God who could have given us our existence must begin—from reason alone. The senses are unreliable, so any proof that begins with material effects and works its way back to an immaterial cause is doomed to failure because it begins with uncertain information. If I am a thinking substance, I must begin with the idea of God I have in my mind. Descartes has already observed that there are degrees of reality—there are infinite and finite substances, necessary and contingent substances, minds and bodies—so some things have more reality than others. But what about ideas? According to Descartes, every idea can have either *formal* or *objective* reality, or both (AT VII.41). The formal reality of an idea is the actual reality of something in the world, and the objective reality of an idea is what the idea directs our mind to—its content. The metaphor of painting is helpful for understanding this distinction. Let us return to van Meegeren's painting of *Christ at Emmaus*, which depicts Jesus at the table with some of his disciples. There is a difference between the reality of the painted Jesus to which the painted image directs us (objective) and the actual reality of the historical Jesus (formal). The former is a representation of the latter. Now consider a painting of a Klingon (a fictional species from the television series *Star Trek*). Because Klingons do not actually exist (sorry to disappoint *Star Trek* fans), the painting of a Klingon has objective reality because it represents the *object* of our thought, namely, Klingons, but it lacks formal reality because it doesn't correspond to an actual reality in the world. Descartes claimed that our ideas can have objective reality even if they don't have formal reality. We can cause ideas in our minds that don't correspond to any formal reality in the world. What Descartes wants the meditator to consider is whether the idea of God in his mind has objective reality, formal reality, or both. He thinks it must have both.

Let us consider first the objective reality of the idea of God. What is the content of this idea? Descartes tells us that he "understand(s) by the name 'God' a certain substance that is infinite, independent, supremely intelligent and supremely powerful, and that created me along with everything else that exists" (AT VII.45). This is the content of this idea—the object of our thought when we think the idea of God. But does this idea have formal reality; that is, is there an actual being like the one we have represented in our minds? Isn't it possible that the idea of "God" has no more formal reality than the idea of a "Klingon"? Descartes did not think so, and his reasoning is based upon his understanding of cause and effect.

Descartes thinks the *principle of causality*—every effect must have a cause—is beyond doubt and is a trustworthy guide for determining the origins of our existence (AT VII.40). But there is a supplementary principle that Descartes contends must be employed in deducing the origins of his existence: the cause of any effect must have more reality than its effect (AT VII.40). This is called the *principle of causal adequacy*. Consider again the example of van Meegeren's *Christ at Emmaus*. It would be absurd to claim that the painting had as much reality as the painter, because the painting did not produce itself, and will not, in turn, produce a painter or other paintings. It seems clear that van Meegeren has more reality—more power and abilities—than the painting of *Christ at Emmaus*. If the principle of causal adequacy holds, and Descartes is certain it does, then the origin of our existence must have more reality than we do, and this he claims is God.

If the idea of God in the meditator's mind is an effect, it must have a cause, and given that the objective reality of this idea is of an infinite, perfect, omniscient, and omnipotent entity, the cause of this idea must have at least as much reality in it. But, if this is true, then the cause of the idea of God in the meditator's mind must be infinite, perfect, omniscient, and omnipotent, and these are not qualities the meditator possesses, so the idea of God could not have been created by the meditator, but must have come from an infinite, perfect, omniscient, and omnipotent cause independent of our minds. This, Descartes concludes, means that the idea of God has both formal and objective reality.

For Descartes, God is the one substance (reality) from which everything else is derived. All bodies and minds, including his, are attributes of this one God, and the essence of these bodies and minds—extension and thinking—are modifications (modes) of these attributes. This explains why we have innate ideas that are clear and distinct, because they are expressions of God. If it can be shown that God cannot deceive us, then these ideas can serve as a certain foundation for our knowledge of reality.

Let us conclude by examining the pressing question implicit in the third meditation, "How did I come to exist?" Did I create myself? Did some*one* or some*thing* create me? Did I come from nothing? Imagine for a moment, Descartes proposes, that you created yourself. Would you not have made yourself perfect rather than imperfect, so that you would not be a being saddled with doubts and desires, fearing your own death, but a being who knew everything, was content, and would live forever (AT VII.48)? This clearly is not the case, so we cannot have created ourselves. It is even more absurd to conclude that we came from nothing because every effect must have a cause, and to conclude that the cause of our existence was nothing violates the principle of cause and effect. But could it be that some*one* or some*thing* independent of us provided us with the reality of our existence and the clear and distinct ideas in our minds? Descartes thought this was the inevitable conclusion every meditator must draw.

Summary

Descartes offers an immanent account of reality from a rationalist perspective by using methodological doubt and a series of meditations designed to initiate the meditator into a philosophical discovery of reality. Reality, he argues, is a single, necessary substance (God) that expresses itself in the modes of bodies and minds whose natures are extension and thought, respectively. We access this reality through innate ideas in our mind, which allow us to deduce that we exist, and that our existence depends on another (God) who is the source of these ideas. Philosophy is, therefore, the practice of removing all ideas that admit doubt to discover what is certain.

Questions

1. Is doubt an effective method for discovering what is certain?
2. Can we trust any of the ideas in our minds to represent reality accurately?
3. Are Descartes' arguments for the existence of God convincing?

4

Descartes: Truth and World
(*Meditations on First Philosophy*, IV–VI)

Key terms

Judgment – a decision to affirm or deny the truth of an idea
Will – the active capacity to decide
Intellect– the passive capacity for understanding objects
Imagination – the embodied capacity for representing objects
Idea – a mental representation of an object

By the end of the third meditation, Descartes has achieved his stated goals for the *Meditations*, namely, to demonstrate the existence of God and the soul philosophically rather than theologically (AT VII.1). So, what is the purpose of the final three meditations? The short answer is that Descartes does not just want to know reality; he wants to make use of this knowledge. So, while the first three meditations are *theoretical*, the final three are *practical*. Let us recall that Descartes has guided the meditator in turning away from the material, finite substances of the world, like his body, to the immaterial, infinite substance of God. Any reader who has followed Descartes in these meditations will have gained a new understanding of him or herself as a finite substance whose existence is certain but contingent and which originates from an infinite substance that created and sustains him or her. Descartes now intends to turn the meditator back to the material world of finite substances from the perspective of the infinite substance of God. Recalling Plato's cave allegory, we can understand the first three meditations to be a journey out of the cave, and the final three meditations to be a return to the cave. For Descartes, philosophy cannot just aim at understanding reality; it has to make us capable of living more rational and tranquil lives—philosophy has to be useful for life. He wants to guide the meditator not simply in philosophizing about life, but also in living philosophically.

One of the lingering problems left over from the third meditation is whether God can deceive us. Descartes has certainly given the meditator sufficient grounds for affirming the existence of God, but he has not yet demonstrated that an infinite substance who is omnipotent (all-powerful) and omniscient (all-knowing) is incapable of deception. If Descartes can show that God cannot deceive us, then he can show that we can trust the faculty of judgment and the innate ideas in our minds to give us certain knowledge about the world. The task of philosophy will then be to learn how to use this knowledge for living a more rational life—a life that is consistent with reality.

Meditation 4: judgment and truth

In the fourth meditation, Descartes eliminates the possibility that God could deceive him with a simple argument: If God is perfect, and the will to deceive is an indication of imperfection, then it is impossible for God to deceive anyone. The meditator has already arrived at a clear and distinct idea of God as "independent and complete," which means that God depends on nothing and lacks nothing (AT VII.53). Any being that is complete, or perfect, does not seek anything outside of itself—it has everything. A perfect being, for example, would not doubt anything because it knows everything, and it would not desire anything because it has everything it needs to be satisfied. Deception is an attempt to gain something one does not have by persuading or causing someone to believe something is the case when it is not. Consider the case of a liar. The liar wants you to believe something is true when it is actually false, or wants you to believe something is false when it is actually true. The operative faculty in lying is the *will*. The will is an expression of human freedom that enables us to decide what to do or not do, or what to affirm or deny. Note that to will something is not simply to *desire* it, but to *decide* that it become the case. The liar freely decides to misrepresent reality, so that a falsehood is mistaken for the truth. Descartes contends that God, although he is all-powerful and can do anything he wills, would never deceive anyone, because to deceive someone, even for sadistic pleasure, would be to seek to obtain something one does not have—in the sadistic case, the pleasure of seeing someone mistake a falsehood for the truth. If God exists, and he is the source of our existence as thinking substances, and of the ideas we have, and if it is impossible for him to deceive us, then we now have a criterion for truth.

But, wait a minute. We make errors in judgment all the time. If God gave us the faculty of judgment, and he is not capable of deceiving us, why do we frequently fall into error? To answer this we need to understand how Descartes understood the mind—the thinking substance that we are. Let us recall that there is only one infinite substance, God, that expresses itself in two, distinct, finite substances—bodies and minds—which have the attributes of extension and thought, respectively. Our minds are modifications of the one infinite substance of God, and the functions of our minds (e.g., understanding, will, and judgment) are modifications of the immaterial, finite substance of our minds. Descartes explained this in his *Principles of Philosophy*, where he distinguished between two types of mental operations: *operations of the intellect* (perceptions like sensations, imagination, and pure understanding) and *operations of the will* (volitions like desire, aversion, assertion, and denial) (AT VIIIA.17). For Descartes, the two operations of the mind—intellect and will—are passive and active functions of the mind, respectively, that are intertwined (see Figure 4.1). The problem is that while the understanding is limited to finite objects like ideas, the

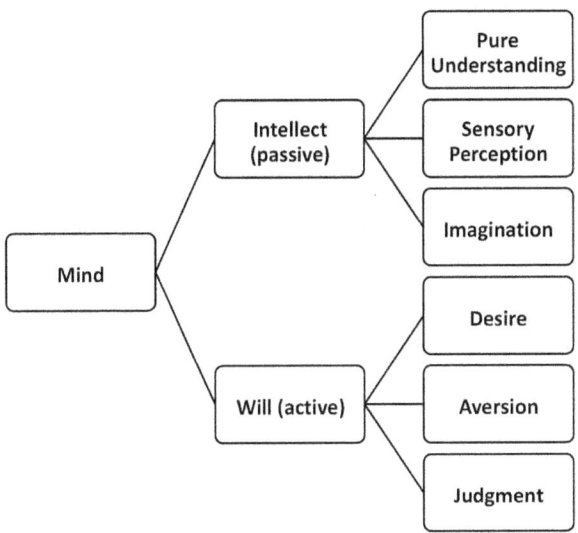

Figure 4.1

will—our power to freely choose or decide—is unlimited: it is infinite. We can will anything! We can choose to buy a new car or iPhone, we can decide to believe that alien life forms exist in our galaxy, or we can decide to believe we can fly by jumping off a cliff and flapping our arms rapidly. There seems to be no limit to what we can will. The will, it would seem, is capable of making decisions beyond the limits of our understanding, and this is why we make errors in our judgments, which Descartes understands as a mode of the will.

The faculty of judgment, according to Descartes, is given to us by God, and since it has already been established that God cannot deceive us, the meditator is forced to conclude that the faculty of judgment, *when it is used correctly*, will lead us to truth instead of error (AT VII.54, 58). So what does it mean to use the faculty of judgment correctly or incorrectly? Descartes places the human being in the middle of what medieval theologians called the Great Chain of Being, which extends from the absolute being of God to complete non-being (AT VII.54). God is the most complete reality, and everything that extends below him (e.g., angels, human beings, animals, plants, rocks) has less and less reality. Therefore, Descartes argues, as long as we focus our intellect on God, who cannot deceive us, we will use our judgment correctly and arrive at truth, but if we allow our will to extend beyond what we understand, we inevitably fall into errors of judgment (AT VII.54). We deceive ourselves when we make decisions about things we do not understand. The problem is not with our faculties but with how we use them. In fact, if we consider the will as the power "to do or not do the same thing, that is, of being able to affirm or deny, to pursue or to shun," and that this power is infinite, we will realize that "we bear a certain image and likeness of God" (AT VII.57). But we are not God, and when we allow our will to reach beyond the boundaries of the clear and distinct ideas provided by the intellect we make errors (AT VII.58).

Consider the errors in judgment that art critics made when they evaluated the forgeries of Han van Meegeren. They had hypothesized that there may have been a period in which Johannes Vermeer created religious paintings, and when they saw van Meegeren's *Christ at Emmaus*, and considered the seventeenth-century materials of the painting, it seemed to confirm their assumptions. However, hypotheses and assumptions are not certain; they are productions of the imagination guided by the will. Descartes would argue that the errors of the art critics stemmed from their misuse of the faculty of judgment. Had they confined their judgments to what they knew to be certain, instead of what might be true, the Rembrandt Society would have avoided paying almost $4 million for a forgery. The same is true for us: to avoid errors in judgment, we have to confine ourselves to what we know to be true—what is clearly and distinctly perceived to be true or good. When we allow ourselves to will what *might* be true or good, we fall into error.

Meditation 5: God, things, and ideas

Given that the meditator has now discovered how to avoid errors in judgment, she can now determine whether we can have knowledge of an immaterial God and material things, and whether either—which were subject to doubt in the first meditation—actually exist. The fifth meditation is not only a demonstration of the existence of God and things from reason alone, it is also an exercise of the newly discovered and verified capacities of the thinking substance. Descartes would have the meditator walk around the mind, flipping switches, and trying out operations, so to speak, to get a feel for how she ought to live as an embodied mind in the world who is capable of avoiding error and pursuing truth. The point of this exercise is to see whether the meditator, who as a thinking substance has been locked inside her own subjectivity since the second meditation exercise, can establish a connection with the material world again. To do this, Descartes recommends that she begin with the ideas in her mind.

If we examine the contents of our minds, we will find a collection of ideas—some are clear and distinct, and some are not. One clear and distinct idea is *extension*—the mental representation of quantities expressed in number or dimensions like height, width, and length. It is beyond doubt that if material objects exist, they are extended in space and have dimensions. However, we do not merely have an intellectual idea of extension, we can also produce images of extension with the imagination. We can imagine a triangle, for example, and even if this imagined figure does not exist in the world, it nevertheless has a certain nature—three equal sides—that we clearly and distinctly perceive with the mind (AT VII.64). Moreover, as Descartes points out, pure mathematics and geometry are the disciplines for demonstrating the truth of these ideas (AT VII.65). The important point in this exercise of the intellect and imagination is that the idea of extension is not something we *will* to be the case—triangles are not figments of our imagination; rather, it is innate in the mind and inescapably true. This leads to an important implication: we can clearly and distinctly know the nature of material things. For example, the idea of a triangle is a mental model for all triangular things we might encounter in the world. If our idea of the nature of a triangle is true, it must correspond to the nature of things in the world. This means that mathematics and geometry—as investigations of extension—can serve as means for understanding material things in the world. However, if we can establish the existence of material things from ideas in the mind, Descartes argues, then might we do the same with the existence of God? Yes (AT VII.65).

Descartes guides the meditator through a medieval argument for the existence of God called the *ontological argument*. The argument was first formulated by St. Anselm of Canterbury (1033–1109) in a little book called the *Proslogion* that attempts to convince an atheist of God's existence from reason alone. The simplified form of the argument is the following:

Premise 1: God is that than which no greater can be conceived.
Premise 2: Things can exist merely as ideas in our understanding or also in reality.
Premise 3: Things that exist in reality are greater than things that only exist as ideas in our understanding.
Premise 4: If God existed only as an idea in our understanding, then he would not be that than which no greater can be conceived, because God existing in reality would be greater.
Conclusion: Therefore, God must exist in reality.

By Descartes' time, this argument had been discredited by philosophers like Thomas Aquinas because it assumes from the beginning that human beings can have knowledge of the essence of God. However, Descartes does not want to reinvigorate the debate about the validity of this argument—he thinks he has already proven God's existence in the third meditation—he wants the meditator to test-drive his theory of innate ideas and the criteria for truth, the clear and distinct perceptions of the mind. He wants to demonstrate that when we use the powers of the mind correctly, we can have certainty and achieve a tranquility of mind known only to those who are not plagued by doubts and uncertainties.

Descartes thinks that if we think about God the same way as we think about triangles, we will conclude that just as triangles exist, so also does God exist (AT VII.65). His formulation of the argument is as follows:

Premise 1: God has all perfections.
Premise 2: Existence is one of these perfections.
Premise 3: Perfection entails existence.
Conclusion: Therefore, God exists.

For Descartes, the proposition "God exists" is just as certain and true as the proposition "a triangle has three equal sides." Moreover, the idea of God in our minds cannot be a product of the imagination or will because, as has already been established in the third meditation, an idea of an infinite God cannot be produced by a finite human mind since every cause must be greater than its effect. This puts the meditator in a strong position regarding the reality of the world. If we have innate ideas that are clear and distinct—and one of them is of God who cannot deceive us and has given us a faculty of judgment that can lead us to the truth about reality when used properly—then we now have a bridge from the inside of our minds to the reality of the external world.

Meditation 6: the reality of the world

In the final meditation exercise, Descartes finishes building the bridge from the inner subjectivity of the meditator to the vibrant external world, so that the meditator can understand herself not merely as a thinking substance separated from the body, but as an integrated whole—an embodied mind in the world. In the first meditation, Descartes had discovered a distinction between the immaterial mind and the material body because of the differences in their operations—the mind can grasp the unchanging nature of things while the body only grasps the changing qualities of things through sensation. However, in the sixth meditation, he finds that the body and mind are joined together as an integrated whole. He claims that our mind is not like a sailor in a ship. If we are simply a mind in a body the way a sailor is in a ship, he argues, then the pains and pleasures we experience in life would never be *our* pain or *our* pleasure—they would be simply be *a* pain or *a* pleasure (AT VII.81). But we get hungry, accidently shut our fingers in doors, drink sour milk, and feel the warmth of an embrace from a lover or friend. These experiences suggest to us that we are an embodied mind the world. But, how do we know the world exists?

The meditator, throughout these exercises, has been trapped inside her own subjectivity and the external world has only remained a possibility. While the meditator has become convinced of her existence and of the existence of God, as well as the reliability of the clear and distinct ideas that are innate in her mind, this only suggests that the external world is *possible*—it does not establish that that world *actually* exists. For Descartes, the key to establishing the existence of the external world is to distinguish between the operations of the imagination and sensation. While the imagination *actively* envisages objects as if they were present, the senses are merely *passive* to the objects they report on (AT VII.79). Consider, for example, the perception of a vanilla milkshake. You see it on the table in a large glass with condensation beading on the outside of the glass. Your mind knows what a vanilla milkshake is conceptually, and you can remember previous experiences of drinking a vanilla milkshake. This allows you to make the experience present again through the activity of the imagination, so that you can create an index of the sensory qualities to expect when you drink the vanilla milkshake in front of you—it will be cold, sweet, textured, and smooth. If we were only active minds, our bodily experience would never contradict our mental experience, but this is not the case. We often find that our sensory experience does not correspond to our mental expectations. For example, imagine that, after deciding to drink the vanilla milkshake in front of you, you discover much to your disgust that it was made with mashed potatoes and salt rather than milk and sugar. This suggests to Descartes that the senses are *passive* to something *active* external to us—something acts upon us against our will (AT VII.79). What the careful meditator discovers is that there must be a world external to the mind that acts upon our bodies in such a way as to produce sensations that we like (pleasure) or do not like (pain). Moreover, since we have established that God exists and cannot deceive us, we must conclude that the ideas produced in us by objects in the external world are not illusions but reality.

To make Descartes' argument clearer, let us conclude by imagining him responding to an argument against the reality of the external world popularized by Elon Musk, called the Simulation Argument,[1] which holds that the reality we experience is most likely a computer-generated simulation:

Elon Musk: I read your first meditation last night, René, and I think you are right that we can't know anything about the external world, and this is because I think there is strong evidence to suggest that we are living in a computer-generated simulation.
René Descartes: What makes you think that?
EM: Well, when I was a kid, we used to play a video game called Pong. It was simply rectangles on a screen that you could move from right to left or up and down with a hand-held device to bounce a square off so that another player could do the same. It was a lot like tennis but digital.
RD: Sounds riveting (sarcasm).
EM: It was for the time, but now we have fully immersive computer games that produce a virtual reality. I can, for example, battle cyborgs who have taken over the earth with futuristic weapons, and even feel the impact of explosions on my body.
RD: That is very impressive.
EM: Right? Now, if we suppose any rate of technological development, we have to conclude that the line between virtual reality and actual reality will grow thinner and thinner over time, so that, eventually, the two will become indistinguishable.
RD: So we won't be able to know whether we are in a game or reality, or as I like to put it, awake or dreaming?
EM: Something like that. But here is the real question. If we know it is possible that eventually virtual and actual reality will be indistinguishable because of technological advances, how do we know that we have not already arrived at that stage of technological development? Isn't it entirely possible that we are living in a computer-generated reality already? By my calculations, the probability that we are NOT living in a simulation is one in a billion, because there are likely billions of

---

[1] The argument was first formulated by the philosopher Nick Bostrom in his paper "Are You Living in a Computer Simulation?," *Philosophical Quarterly*, vol. 53, no. 211 (2003): 243–55.

computer games producing billions of simulated realities. Do you see anything wrong with this argument, René?

RD: I do see a flaw in your argument. Your argument assumes that we are disembodied minds, which is what I wanted you to experience in the first meditation, but that is not the whole story. Reality is a strange thing; it does not always conform to our concepts or expectations. Even if we are living in a computer-generated simulation, there must be a material machine to produce that simulation, and this would have to exist external to our minds. Now, any material object that exists independently of our minds will have its own qualities that produce sensations in us whether we want them to or not. For example, imagine that we are suspended in a pod of some kind, immersed in a fluid that preserves our bodies, and our minds are hooked up to a machine that produces the simulated reality you have described. That fluid has a temperature that will alter the temperature of our body causing sensations in our body, and these sensations can be pleasurable or painful. These experiences come to us against our will and would contradict the information from the simulation, giving rise to errors or "glitches." It seems to me, that we are not minds in bodies but embodied minds, and our bodies are constantly, and inescapably, impacted by an external world that is entirely real.

EM: I think I have seen this movie! I guess I need to finish reading the other five meditations.

RD: If you do, I hope you will see that reality is not a game. We can know reality; this is what makes science so important.

Summary

For Descartes, we have a clear and distinct idea in our minds of an infinite and perfect substance called God who is the source of our existence and cannot deceive us. Given that our minds are a modification of God's essence, and given that he gave us our faculty of judgment and cannot deceive us, we can have certain knowledge of reality when we confine our judgments to what we clearly and distinctly perceive. We can also know that objects in the external world actually exist because our bodily senses are passive to the activities of these objects in the world. There is an external world, and we can know it.

Questions

1. What would it mean to restrict your judgments to only what you clearly and distinctly perceive?
2. Is it possible to have certain knowledge about reality?
3. How can we know that we are not living in a simulation?

PART II EPISTEMOLOGY

HOW CAN WE KNOW WHAT IS REAL?
HUME AND KANT

Epistemology

The two philosophers we will read about in this section are David Hume and Immanuel Kant. Hume (1711–76) was one of the most important thinkers in the Scottish Enlightenment. He is best known for his empiricism and skepticism, by which he sought to overcome the speculative errors of rationalism. In contrast to Descartes, Hume claimed that our knowledge of reality begins in our sensory experience not through ideas in the mind. In order to know what is real, Hume argued, we have to verify our ideas in our sensory experience.

Immanuel Kant (1724–1804), like Plato, is one of the most important philosophers in history. His critical philosophy defines the limits of human reason and resolves the standoff between rationalism and empiricism, avoiding the dogmatism and skepticism that plagued both schools of philosophy. Unlike Descartes, Kant does not think concepts in the mind can be intelligible without sensory experience, but, unlike Hume, Kant does not think that our sensory experience can be intelligible without concepts. For Kant, our knowledge of reality is a synthesis of concepts and sensory experience, where objects in the world must conform to our concepts, and our concepts organize our experience of objects in an intelligible way.

While metaphysics asks about the nature of reality, epistemology asks how we can know this reality. Although Hume and Kant disagree about the scope and status of human knowledge, they are both concerned with the same epistemological question: How can we know what is real? This question seeks to identify the sources, faculties, and limits of human knowledge. As a result, both Hume and Kant will offer an account of the human mind and its capacity for knowing reality.

Our task in these chapters is consider how our minds and reality are related in order to determine whether we can have any objective knowledge of reality. If we can, what do we know when we know reality, and what are the limits of our knowledge? If we cannot, what are the implications for distinguishing between truth and falsehood? As we will see, answering these questions will have consequences for how we live.

5

Hume: The Mind is an Assemblage of Ideas
(An Enquiry Concerning Human Understanding, §I–§V)

Key terms

Impression – a sensory perception of reality
Idea – a mental copy of an impression
Rationalism – the view that we know reality through reason
Empiricism – the view that we know reality through experience

---

A conceptual revolution

The history of philosophy is often described as a "great conversation" between exemplary minds about the noblest ideas, but it is perhaps better described as mortal combat. Philosophers are more like revolutionaries than polite conversation partners; they storm each other's theoretical palaces to dethrone the reigning concepts, loot each other's intellectual wealth, create new concepts, and establish new theoretical regimes. The weapon of choice for philosophers is the question; questions destabilize long-held certainties and expose the weaknesses and vulnerabilities of concepts and systems. However, philosophical questions also reorient our thinking so that concealed aspects of reality can come into focus through the creation of new concepts that can help us better understand and navigate reality. Among the best philosophers, the destruction of concepts is followed by the creation of new ones. In this sense, philosophy is nomadic—it is always on the move.

Philosophers are notorious for shattering our conceptual lenses. The word *concept* comes from the Latin words *con* ("together with") and *capere* ("to take or capture"). The Germans also have a great word for *concept*: *der Begriff*; it is derived from the verb *greifen*, which means "to grasp." Concepts are the way we get a handle on reality; they also function like lenses through which we interpret reality. What this means is that we have to pay close attention to the concepts we employ to determine whether they are moving us closer to reality or further away from it. Our concepts need constant renewal and revision. If philosophy is the ongoing pursuit of wisdom that seeks to liberate us from falsehoods and delusions, so that we can come to terms with reality, then it requires a constant renewal of our theoretical lenses. Every philosopher must be prepared to destroy the old and outdated lenses of the past and create new ones to improve their understanding of reality. For Plato, this meant turning the mind from the constantly changing reality of our experience of the material world to the stable reality of immaterial forms. For Descartes, it meant turning the mind from the uncertainty of our sensory experience of the material world to the certain reality of the immaterial substances of our minds and God. Plato and Descartes were *rationalists*—they conceived our access to reality as being primarily through reason. This meant that our bodily experience of the world, including our sensations and emotions, was a diminished reality that had to be transcended. Hume disagreed and sought to challenge the empire of rationalism and show how the rationalist lenses distorted reality instead of giving us a clear and distinct perception of it.

Hume's clash with rationalism

In *An Enquiry Concerning Human Understanding*, Hume is engaged in a theoretical clash with rationalists, especially Descartes. Rationalism had not brought us closer to reality, Hume argued; it had estranged us from it. The rationalists had convinced us that reality was a stable, unified identity that could be known (e.g., Plato's forms or Descartes' substance), but for Hume this reality was a fabrication of the mind—a kind of freezing of the dynamic multiplicity of human experience. Hume was an *empiricist*—he conceived our access to reality as being primarily through experience and only secondarily through reason. He wanted to turn the world upside down by thawing out the reality of the rationalists to reveal the vibrant reality of human experience. To do this, however, he would have to destroy the three important concepts of Cartesian rationalism: the Cartesian ego, innate ideas, and clear and distinct knowledge. Hume replaced these concepts with three new ones. He replaces the stable Cartesian ego with a self that is a bundle of impressions; innate ideas with ideas that are copies of impressions; and clear and distinct knowledge with belief. In each of these destructive and creative moves, Hume redirects our thinking away from the *nature* of reality toward the external *relations* that make our knowledge of this reality possible. His intention is to help us see what is outside (relations) rather than what is inside (natures). This is Hume's most significant contribution to philosophy. To do this, however, Hume had to develop a new kind of philosophy.

A new kind of philosophy

For Hume, philosophy had become detached from reality and had lost its way, wandering among theoretical abstractions and unjustifiable superstitions. Philosophy needed to be reconceived as practical thinking, and this thinking had to be in the service of life, instead of life being in the service of thinking. For this reason, Hume conceived philosophy as a "science of human nature" (§I, 1).[1] Now, on the surface, this conception might suggest an essential core (nature) to human beings that we can know with our minds (science), but this is not what Hume meant. Hume understood philosophy as an inquiry into the fundamental operations of the human understanding, which include sensation, emotions, imagination, memory, and reason. For Hume, we are neither minds trapped in bodies, as Plato thought, nor immaterial minds linked with material bodies, as Descartes thought; human beings are simply material bodies in which mental operations are *activated* by the external world and everything in it. The world *affects* us; it makes impressions on us, and these impressions associate together in regular ways

---

[1] All quotations and references in these chapters will refer to David Hume, *An Enquiry Concerning Human Understanding*, second edition, ed. Eric Steinberg (Indianapolis: Hackett, 1993). The citations will refer to the section number followed by the page number. For example, the citation "§I, 1" indicates section I, page 1.

to produce a mind, so that there is a harmony between the reality of the world and our experience of it. For this reason Hume is best understood as philosopher of *immanence*—he wanted to return us to our bodily experience of reality and show us how this experience becomes a mind, and how our mind, in turn, becomes a person. Hume's new philosophy is therefore a kind of psychology of human nature insofar as it seeks to understand how the body and mind operate in their experience of reality.

Hume tells us that, historically, philosophy has approached the investigation of human nature in two ways. It has conceived it in either practical or theoretical terms: the human being is considered in terms of action or in terms of thought (§I, 1). This has given rise to two types of philosophy: the *easy* and the *abstruse*. The easy kind of philosophy is a kind of shallow thinking; it is simple, accessible, and useful for the person who never gets around to thinking about whether things are otherwise than they are. We encounter this kind of philosophy on bumper stickers, in memes, in popular songs, and in self-help books. This kind of philosophy is practical and does not require scholarly training or expertise to understand it, and so most people gravitate to this kind of philosophy. The abstruse kind of philosophy is not so accessible.

"Abstruse" is a strange and unfamiliar word to most people. It originates from the Latin word *abstrudere*, which means "to push away from sight" or "to conceal." Something is abstruse if it is "pushed away from" our everyday experience. Abstruse philosophy is obscure, abstract, and accessible only to the few intellectuals who have the training to understand it. Its meaning is hidden behind difficult terminology, which is intended to achieve greater precision; it is rigorous in its thinking and accurate in its conclusions. However, Hume also realized that the abstruse kind of philosophy, especially when it deals with metaphysical questions about reality, can be a cover for error and superstition when the abstract reasoning exceeds the capacities of human knowledge (§1, 5). To remedy this, Hume sought to synthesize the easy and the abstruse types of philosophy into a new kind of philosophical thinking that could "gradually diffuse itself throughout the whole society, and bestow a similar correctness on every art and calling" (§1, 5). This new way of thinking would replace abstract theorizing with practical inquiry; it would be clear, accurate, and useful for living. Hume thought that if we understood what a human mind is, how it works, and what its limits are, we could liberate ourselves from superstitions and errors and live wiser and more tranquil lives. In turning the world upside down with his new mode of philosophical thinking, Hume demystified reality and returned us to our immanent experience of the material world.

Hume's atomism and associationism

Hume's demystification of reality involves two theoretical principles: *atomism* and *associationism*. The first principle is *metaphysical* and demonstrates that reality is not a unified whole like a Platonic form or a Cartesian substance; it is a collection of simple, indivisible elements—like atoms. Consequently, we never experience or know the substance or essential nature of anything, but only how it affects the mind; we know reality through its effects—the sensory qualities of objects in our experience. For example, we see colors, hear sounds, feel textures, smell odors, and taste flavors, but we never experience the substance beneath these sensory qualities—all we experience is a collection of simple elements or qualities. As Hume puts it, "nature has kept us at a great distance from all her secrets, and has afforded us only the knowledge of a few superficial qualities of objects" (§IV, 21).

The second principle—associationism—is *epistemological* and demonstrates that our beliefs about reality are the result of the simple, indivisible elements of our experience being associated together in specific ways. This means that all of our ideas are constructed from the elements of our experience and held together, Hume argues, by three kinds of associations or relations: *resemblance*—elements resemble each other; *contiguity*—elements are in close proximity to each other in space or time; and *cause and effect*—one element appears to be the cause of another (§III, 14). With the principles of atomism and associationism, Hume dissolves reality into a collection of simple elements he calls impressions, and dissolves the ideas of the mind into a set of external relations. On his way to answering the question, "How can we know what is real?," Hume asks two preliminary questions: "How do we most immediately experience reality?" and "How does this experience become a mind that knows reality?"

The Cartesian ego vs the assemblage of the self

One of Hume's first targets for destruction was the Cartesian ego—the immaterial thinking substance that Descartes claimed to have discovered in his second meditation, and which was capable of knowing reality through innate ideas in the mind. In his earlier (and lengthier) work, *A Treatise of Human Nature*, of which *An Enquiry Concerning Human Understanding* is a shorter revision, Hume argued that this Cartesian self is an illusion, and that are no innate ideas in the mind. Descartes had claimed that when he turned inward, he found an enduring self—a thinking substance—that he could never doubt. However, when Hume followed Descartes along this inward path, all he found was a collection of perceptions, "For my part, when I enter most intimately into what I call myself, I always stumble on some particular perception or other, of heat or cold, light or shade, love or hatred, pain or pleasure. I never can catch myself at any time without a perception, and never can observe anything but the perception."[2] The self is not a *substance* that has these perceptions, according to Hume; it is an assemblage of ideas copied from sensory perceptions.

Assemblages are collections of parts that constitute a new whole that cannot be reduced to any of the parts. For example, the book you are reading is an assemblage. It is made of paper, ink, words, sentences, paragraphs, concepts, and arguments, but the book as a whole is greater than its parts. If we begin to strip away the various parts, we do not find a book underneath; there is not a book that has paper, ink, words, sentences, paragraphs, concepts, and arguments—these parts constitute the book; the book emerges from the collection and arrangement of the parts. Hume thought of the self in the same way. There is nothing like a soul or a self underneath our perceptions; these perceptions are organized in such a way that they produce what Descartes, and many others before him, took to be an enduring subject of these perceptions. Instead, Hume thought the collection of perceptions constituted the self—it was an inference of the mind not an underlying substance.

---

[2] David Hume, *A Treatise of Human Nature*, vol. 1, eds. David Fate Norton and Mary J. Norton (New York: Oxford University Press, 2011), 1.4.6, 164.

Innate ideas vs copies of impressions

Hume's second target for destruction is Descartes' claim that our minds contain innate ideas that we clearly and distinctly perceive and by which we know reality. Descartes and Hume both agreed that when we survey the contents of our mind, we find a collection of ideas, but they disagreed on the origin of these ideas—Descartes claimed they originated from God and were innate in the mind, but Hume claimed that all of our ideas are copies of sensory perceptions, or impressions (§II, 11). For Hume *ideas* are mental images of *impressions* produced by the imagination and saved in our memory to help us understand and navigate our experiences in the world. Impressions are our most immediate experience of reality. This means that all of our ideas originate in our experience, and that the mind is empty until furnished with ideas that we construct from our experience.

Our most immediate experience of reality is our sensory experience, wherein reality *affects* us. These simple affections—the way the world of things makes impressions on our bodies in the form of sensory qualities (e.g., sights, sounds, odors, flavors, textures)—are bundled together in complex arrangements by the imagination. These bundles of impressions are "copied" into the memory as *simple ideas* (e.g., red, round, sweet, hard), which are then assembled into more complex ideas (e.g., apple) by the three principles of "the association of ideas": resemblance, contiguity, and cause and effect (§II, 14). Every idea originates in our experience of reality, and this entails an important principle of verification for Hume: if every idea originates in an impression, then we can verify an idea by tracing it back to its original impression. If there is no corresponding impression, the idea is false and should be rejected; if there is a corresponding impression, the idea is true and should be accepted. Nevertheless, Hume says, it's not enough to find a single instance of an idea corresponding to an impression; we need to find this correspondence consistently and habitually (§III, 15). There are two kinds of thoughts that meet this criteria: *relations of ideas* and *matters of fact*. The former are undeniably certain; the latter can always be shown to be false upon further investigation (§IV, 15).

Relations of ideas are internally coherent deductions of the understanding that will always entail a self-contradiction if they denied. All mathematical, geometrical, and logical propositions are of this kind

(§IV, 15). For example, 2+2=4 is a proposition that is true because of the consistent relations between the quantities of 2 and 4—that 2 is half of 4 and 4 is the double of 2. These relations never change, and if the mind relies on these unchanging relations, it can consistently arrive at true propositions about quantities. It's important to note that this kind of deduction of the mind does not depend on discovering these quantities in our experience; their verification relies solely on the consistency of their internal relations, even though, Hume would admit, our idea of any quantity originates in an impression.

Matters of fact are conclusions reached by the mind based upon consistent and habitual experience, but because they lack the internal coherence of relations of ideas, it is always possible that the opposite of these conclusions will be true. This means that while we naturally base our beliefs upon past experiences, our past experiences cannot provide any certainty about future experiences—just because something *has happened* in the past does not mean it *will happen* in the future. To illustrate this point, Hume uses the example of the claim "the sun will rise tomorrow" (§IV, 15). Putting aside the fact that the sun does not "rise," this conclusion rests on the consistency of past experiences of the sun rising, and we infer (from the Latin word *inferre*, which means "to carry over into") future occurrences of this kind precisely because they seem to happen consistently. However, there is no logical guarantee that this will occur; the sun is a star after all, and it can always die, so that the sun may not "rise" at some point. Matters of fact are habitual conclusions that are always open to further verification.

Knowledge vs belief

Hume's third and final target for destruction was the rationalist conception of knowledge. Descartes had tried to show that we can have clear and distinct knowledge of reality through innate ideas in the mind, but as Hume shows, all of our ideas are the result of habitual associations of the mind, and the faculty that assembles and disassembles these ideas is the *imagination* not reason. Hume thought rationalists had too quickly dismissed the power of the imagination, which, he argued, "has unlimited power of mixing, compounding, separating, and dividing these ideas, in all the varieties of fiction and vision" (§V, 31).

The imagination is, for Hume, a mental activity that assembles ideas through the three principles of association—resemblance, contiguity, and cause and effect—and because its freedom is unlimited, the imagination can produce fictional ideas and believable ideas. The imagination is like an impressionistic painter, who looks at the world presenting itself in all of its sensory qualities, and renders an image of these impressions on a canvas. However, if the imagination is free to assemble ideas of phoenixes as well as pheasants, how can we know whether the paintings are accurate representations of reality? The answer is not, Hume argued, a correspondence between an innate idea of the mind and reality, as the rationalists contended, but rather *sentiment*—a feeling of the mind when it encounters the habitual arrangement of impressions (§V.II, 31). Understood in this way, belief is a judgment that human nature inclines us to make whenever we consistently find impressions we have encountered in the past repeated in our immediate sensory experience.

Hume argued that what distinguished fanciful ideas from believable ideas was a natural feeling that arose whenever we encountered the habitual conjoining of simple ideas. For example, we believe that when we see fire it will be hot. We believe this, Hume argues, because we have constantly encountered heat when we have encountered fire (cause and effect), and never found the contrary—cold as an effect of fire (§V, 30). Belief is a habitual *feeling* of the mind that arises when we consistently encounter sensory impressions arranged together in the same way. Fictions, on the other hand, do not provoke the feeling of belief (§V, 31). We can imagine a bird made from fire, and even conjure the idea that the fire is cold to the touch, but because we have never encountered these ideas together, we are not provoked to believe in the fiction of a phoenix. We only believe in what we experience habitually.

But wait a minute! Even if Hume is right, people sincerely believe in ideas that turn out to be false all the time. For example, stereotypes are false beliefs about groups of people that form because other people judge that they have habitually found certain qualities and characteristics constantly associated together in their experience and have made a generalization about all people of that group—stereotypes are habits of mind, but they do not necessarily correspond to reality. One of the most commonly held beliefs that philosophers held to be demonstrably certain was causation—the belief that every effect has a cause. For Hume, this belief was far from certain; it was merely an inference of the mind.

The fragile connection between cause and effect

Philosophers typically distinguish knowledge from belief. Plato, for example, held that knowledge is based on an account of the form of a given thing and beliefs are not—beliefs are part knowledge and part ignorance. His student, Aristotle, continued this tradition of distinguishing between knowledge and belief, but for him knowledge was based upon an understanding of the causes of a thing. There were, he argued, four basic causes of any given thing: the *material* cause, that explained what something was made of; the *efficient* cause, that explained who or what shaped the material into what it is; the *formal* cause, the design of a given thing; and the *final* cause, the purpose of a given thing. We have knowledge of a given thing if we can give an account of these four causes; that is, if we can explain the necessary connection between a thing (effect) and its four causes.[3] Aristotle called this explanation a *demonstration*. Consider a poem, for example: the material cause is the language (the letters and words), the efficient cause is the poet; the formal cause is the rhyme scheme; and the final cause is enjoyment. For Aristotle, the connection between a cause and its effect was necessary and demonstrably certain—every effect had a cause, and the aim of philosophy was to discover the ultimate cause(s) of things. Hume was not convinced.

As we have seen, causality—the view that every effect has a preceding cause—was one of the principles of association for Hume: linking an effect with a prior cause is a habit of the mind that tries to organize experiences in terms of this relation. But a cause—a poet for example—and an effect—a poem—are two different things; a poet exists independently of her poems, and unless a person knows what a poet is, it would be impossible for that person to infer that

---

[3] Aristotle, "Physics," in *The Complete Works of Aristotle*, vol. 1, ed. Jonathan Barnes (Princeton: Princeton University Press, 1984), 194b.1–37.

a poem is caused by a poet. According to Hume, the relationship or connection between a cause and an effect is based upon the experience of the constant connection of the two in our experience. However, as with all matters of fact, it could always turn out that the cause is not directly connected to the effect—the connection is an inference of the mind not intrinsic to the relationship between the cause and effect.

To illustrate his point, Hume asks us to imagine the Biblical character Adam—the first human being—encountering water for the first time. It would be impossible, Hume argues, for Adam to infer from the "fluidity and transparency of water, that it would suffocate him"; he could only discover this potential effect through his experience of the water (§IV, 17). Hume concludes from this thought experiment that the link between cause and effect cannot be established by reason alone, as Aristotle had argued, but only by way of experience. In fact, causal reasoning that is not subjected to critical observation and experimentation can lead us to adopt false beliefs and even superstitions. So how can we inoculate ourselves from false beliefs and superstitions? Hume proposes a new philosophical method for scrutinizing our beliefs, based upon skepticism and experimentation: the method of probability, which we will explore in the next chapter.

Summary

Hume created an experimental philosophy that was both theoretically accurate and practical, and he sought to demonstrate how our impressions of the world are copied into the mind as ideas. His goal was to overturn the rationalist philosophy of Descartes that prioritized reason over experience, because it led to superstitions and an estrangement from reality. In its place, Hume created an empirical philosophy that prioritized the immediacy of experience over rational speculation. He replaced Descartes' thinking substance with a self that is an assemblage of impressions; he replaced Descartes' innate ideas with ideas that are copies of impressions and held together by the principles of association; and he replaced Descartes' theory of knowledge with a theory of belief rooted in sentiment.

Questions

1. Are there ideas that are necessarily true but cannot be verified in our experience?
2. If there is no self, as Hume concludes, what are the moral implications of this?
3. If there is no necessary connection between cause and effect, what are the implications for scientific investigation?

6

Hume: Skepticism and Truth
(*An Enquiry Concerning Human Understanding*, §VI–§XII)

> **Key terms**
>
> Probability – principle for justifying beliefs by a superiority of evidence
> Skepticism – methodological doubt about the certainty of beliefs
> Necessary Connection – the belief that every effect *must* have a cause
> Compatibilism – freedom and determinism are not mutually exclusive

If the first half of Hume's *An Enquiry Concerning Human Understanding* is an attempt to dismantle the house that rationalism built and build a new one based upon experience instead of reason, the second half is an attempt to show new residents how to live in the new house. Hume disassembled Descartes' rationalist certainties about the self, ideas, and knowledge and reassembled a new psychological model of human nature that showed that the self, its ideas, and the beliefs it holds originate in our experience. We are not immaterial minds furnished with ideas that make us capable of knowing reality, as Descartes claimed; we are material bodies that are affected by the world, and these affections produce ideas, beliefs, and ultimately ourselves. Hume destabilized the knowledge of rationalism and replaced it with belief based on experience. Nevertheless, as we will see, it is possible to have false beliefs about our experiences—we can be sincerely wrong in the inferences we make about our experiences. This raises an important question about our ability to know reality: How can we know that our beliefs about reality are justified?

Hume recognized that if we relied only on sentiment to legitimize beliefs, we might believe things that are not true. Lying is a good example. Lies are only effective if they are believable, and in order for us to believe them, we have to *feel* that what we are being told is true because it corresponds to prior experiences and seems plausible. Van Meegeren, for example, was able to convince art critics and historians that his forgeries were genuine paintings by Vermeer because they had already inferred from their study of existing Vermeer paintings that the artist must have produced some works with Biblical themes during his career. Van Meegeren's forgeries were believable because they had a degree of plausibility—they resembled the style and composition of genuine paintings by Vermeer, and art historians inferred that the forgeries were authentic based upon their past experiences of Vermeer's work. Hume would say that the art critics and historians sincerely believed the paintings were authentic because of habitual associations between past and present experiences, but these associations were weak because they were not subjected to skeptical inquiry and experimentation. What this suggests is that in order for our beliefs about reality to be justified, they must be subjected to further scrutiny. So, how can a belief be justified?

Probability and belief

There are at least three ways to justify a belief, according to Hume. The first way is to *demonstrate* that something is true *a priori*—a Latin phrase that means that a proposition is based entirely on reason *prior to* experience. Demonstrations are self-evidently true and do not rely upon experience. Relations of ideas are justified in this way. The second way is to provide a *proof* that something is true by way of evidence derived from experience that "leaves no room for doubt" (§VI, footnote 24, 37). For example, we can prove that the Statue of Liberty is located on Liberty Island in New York Harbor by going to New York and verifying its location. Matters of fact can be justified in this way. The third, and final, way to justify a belief is to show it is more *probable* that a belief is true than not true based upon the amount of evidence gathered (§VI, footnote 24, 37). For example, we can justify our belief that cherries are sweet by appealing to our prior experiences of eating cherries and concluding that it is more likely that a cherry will be sweet than sour. Of course, it is always possible we will eat a sour cherry, and so our inference does not have the level of certainty that demonstration and proofs do. The principle of probability is an experimental form of justification that is essential to Hume's epistemology.

Hume argued that we should evaluate our beliefs that cannot be justified by either demonstrations or proofs by their probability. As he put it, "A wise man proportions his belief to the evidence" (§X, 73). To proportion our belief to evidence is to evaluate beliefs based upon whether it is more likely that a given belief is true or less likely, and we do this by weighing the evidence for and against a belief. Hume describes this method of evaluation as "a certain probability, which arises from a superiority of chances on any side; and according as this superiority increases, and surpasses the opposite chances, the probability receives a proportionable increase, and begets still a higher degree of belief or assent to that side, in which we discover the superiority" (§VI, 37). It is important to note that Hume thinks beliefs can be stronger or weaker based upon their degree of probability. Strong beliefs have a high degree of probability, and weak beliefs have a lower degree of probability. This means that to justify our beliefs, we must subject them to rigorous scrutiny and experimentation; we must evaluate the likelihood that they are true. If philosophy is the ongoing pursuit of the truth about reality, then the philosophical life must be skeptical and experimental.

The illusion of connection

Recall that Hume has shown that all our ideas originate in impressions—sensory experiences of the external world—and consequently, all of our ideas can be traced back to an impression. Causation is an idea, and so it must have originated in some impression. Hume thinks that if we begin to search for the source of our idea of the necessary connection between cause and effect, we will inevitably arrive at three possible explanations: *intrasubstantialism*—there is a causal power intrinsic to substances; *voluntarism*—our minds exhibit a volitional power; and *occasionalism*—God is the ultimate causal power. Let's consider Hume's example of a game of billiards to see if we can observe the necessary causal connection between two moving billiard balls, using each of the three explanations.

When we are playing billiards, and we see the cue ball in motion, heading toward another ball on the table, we assume that when the cue ball makes contact with the other ball it will cause it to move—hopefully into the pocket we have selected! The assumption we are making is that the ball in motion has a causal (kinetic) power within it sufficient to cause motion in another ball of equal size and weight. Hume thinks this assumption is not justified because all we actually experience with our senses is the motion of the two billiard balls; we never see or experience the causal power we attribute to the first ball. For Hume, we cannot have an impression of the causal power intrinsic to things (§VII, 39). Even if things possess causal power, it is not available to our senses, so *intrasubstantialism* cannot be correct.

But wait! Are not we the ones causing the cue ball to move in the first place by hitting it with our cue? Are not we the ones who chose to pick up the cue, line it up with the ball, and hit the ball? We assume, Hume argues, that "the motion of our body follows upon the command of our will," but this is an unjustified assumption for three reasons (§VII, 42). First, our bodies are complete mysteries to us, and we have little command over them. We simply are not conscious of all of the processes occurring in our bodies, and therefore cannot be conscious of our own volitional powers. Second, we cannot "move all of the organs of the body with a like authority" (§VII, 43). For example, we cannot will that our pancreas produce insulin to lower our blood sugar or produce glucagon to elevate it. In fact, we are only aware of our pancreas when it malfunctions. Sure, we can raise our hand, get up from a chair, walk across the room, and reach for another donut, but we have no experience of the causal chain in our bodies that leads to those movements. Finally, all of our bodily movements are preceded by the operations of our muscles, nerves, hormones, and chemicals that we are unaware of. Even more startling, studies of the brain, like the one conducted by Benjamin Libet (1916–2007), have demonstrated that unconscious brain activity is already occurring before we are conscious of making a decision, which suggests that at least some of our decision-making power is predetermined by other processes within the mind and body. For these reasons, the necessary connection between cause and effect cannot be discovered in us, and so *voluntarism* cannot be correct either.

There is, however, another possible source of the necessary connection: God. If there is, as Descartes argued, a single and infinite substance that exists necessarily, then it must be the ultimate cause of everything, and therefore the necessary connection between cause and effect is God. This view is called *occasionalism*, and it holds that each causal event—the motion of a billiard ball after being struck by another billiard ball—is an occasion where God intervenes causally. So, the first billiard ball does not cause the second ball to move, and neither do we—it only appears that way. God makes the ball move. Hume thinks this conclusion is unjustified. First, he thinks God is an idea conceived in "fairy land" because all of our ideas are derived from impressions, and we have never had a sensory experience of God. We have never experienced, for example, infinity or perfection. For Hume, any argument for God's existence is wholly speculative and cannot be empirically verified. Second, even if it God does exist, we cannot have any awareness of his causal power operative in the universe, just as we cannot have any awareness of the causal power in us or in things (§VII, 48). So, *occasionalism* cannot be correct either.

Let us further recall that our belief in causality is based upon our past experiences of effects following causes, from which we infer a necessary connection between causes and the effects that follow. However, Hume thinks we are not justified in making this inference because our past experiences do not offer us any certainty about future experiences. This means that the connection between cause and effect is not a *necessary* connection but merely an *inferred* connection. And this means that there is not sufficient evidence to warrant our belief in causal powers, whether of substances, our own will, or God. Nevertheless, our minds still organize our experience in terms of cause and effect, because of the strong feeling that accompanies our habitual expectation that an effect will always follow a cause. Therefore, it is important for us to realize that although causation is not theoretically justified, it is practically necessary. But if Hume is right, then all of our metaphysical claims about whether we are free or determined, or whether God exists, will need reconsideration in light of this new understanding of causation.

Are we free or determined?

Hume thought that if we are not justified in drawing a necessary connection between causes and effects, then we are also not justified in claiming we are absolutely free or absolutely determined. This is because to be absolutely free would mean we have certain knowledge of a free will that can cause us to act in any way we choose, independent of any outside influence, and we do not have this kind of knowledge. Similarly, to be absolutely determined means we would have certain knowledge of some external cause (e.g., God, nature, history, etc.) that causes us to behave in a particular way, contrary to our wishes. Philosophers refer to these views as examples of *incompatibilism*—the view that freedom and determinism are mutually exclusive. The first view is called *libertarianism*, and it holds that human actions are freely caused by the human will—we can act independently of external causes. The second view is called *hard determinism*, and it holds that human actions are caused by external forces or conditions. Both are absurd, Hume argues, because they attribute a causal power that we cannot have knowledge of either to our own will or to external forces. Instead, Hume argues, we can only rely on experience and the principle of probability, which leads us to infer that all our actions are freely determined. He points out that all of our actions are preceded by motives to act, which lead to decisions, and those decisions are influenced by thoughts, feelings, and expectations—without these prior, and necessary, causes, we would never reach a decision or take any action. Philosophers refer to this view as *compatibilism*—the view that freedom and determinism are not mutually exclusive. But how can this be true?

Hume argues that freedom, which he refers to as liberty, is "the power of acting or not acting, according to the determinations of the will" (§VIII, 63). On the surface, this definition seems like a libertarian claim—that we are free to choose our actions independent of external influences—but this is not what Hume argued. It is important to note that Hume attributes this liberty to everyone "who is not a prisoner"— everyone who is not restrained from acting as they will to act (§VIII, 63). But being free from restraints doesn't mean that our free actions are not determined by prior causes.

Consider the following example. I want to visit the Pergamonmuseum in Berlin, Germany. I had no desire to visit this museum until I read about it in the newspaper, but once I was aware of it, my desire to visit it motivated me to acquire a passport, purchase a plane ticket, reserve a hotel room in Berlin, and arrange transportation to and from the museum. Note the chain of causes and conditions that must be in place in order for me to visit the museum; until all of these conditions are in place, I am not free to visit the museum—these conditions are necessary and sufficient for me to freely visit the museum. Hume thought our *freedom* is always conditioned by *necessary* prior causes—we *infer* this necessity from the regularity of our actions always having prior causes even though we never experience the necessary connection between the prior causes and our action. Consequently, freedom and necessity are compatible. For Hume, everything in nature follows regular and necessary laws, and human beings are no different. We are natural creatures whose bodies and minds follow natural laws just like everything else in the universe, and this has an important implication for religious belief.

Should we believe in God or miracles?

As Hume has made clear, our beliefs must always be proportionate to the evidence, and when it comes to beliefs about God and miracles, he argues, the evidence does not warrant our belief. Recall that our judgments should be measured by probability (§X, 73). Consider the Biblical miracle of the parting of the Red Sea. Hume argues that the splitting of a large body of water like the Red Sea would require a violation of the natural laws that govern that body of water. Applying the principle of probability, we should ask both about the credibility of the witness of the supposed miracle and whether it is more likely or less likely that the laws of nature could have been violated. If we examine our experience, we are unlikely to find prior instances of such violations, which leads us to conclude that the occurrence of the miracle is improbable. Hume evaluates testimonies about people resurrected from the dead in a similar way:

> When any one tells me, that he saw a dead man restored to life, I immediately consider with myself, whether it be more probable, that this person should either deceive or be deceived, or that the fact, which he relates, should really have happened. I weigh the one miracle against the other; and according to the superiority, which I discover, I pronounce my decision, and always reject the greater miracle. (§X, 77)

Miracles are violations of natural laws, and these violations are inconsistent with our experience, so, Hume argues, we should not give our assent to belief in them.

But if we rule out everything that isn't consistent with our prior experiences, won't we rule out new discoveries that enlarge our understanding? Hume does not think so. He recognizes that we can have novel experiences that violate our expectations, but these are merely *contrary* to expectations. For example, if you do not know that water freezes at 32°F, then you will be surprised when your dog's water freezes in the bowl when the temperature drops below freezing. In this experience, you learn something new about the laws of nature—a matter of fact—but the event of water freezing does not *contradict* any prior experience. You have not experienced water freezing at 42°F or not freezing at 32°F. The experience is a novel experience, and so this new experience is believable. However, miracles are violations of the laws of nature—they contradict our experiences and expectations, and therefore they are improbable, and so should not be believed. Moreover, if miracles are improbable and cannot be believed, then they cannot be used as evidence in arguments for the existence of God either.

Philosophical arguments for the existence of God typically rely upon the principle of causation by inferring an ultimate cause to explain a long chain of effects. Hume, as we have already seen, challenged the necessary connection between cause and effect, and in so doing undermined all arguments for the existence of God that rely upon causation. If we cannot have any knowledge of the causal powers of material objects, we certainly cannot have a similar knowledge of immaterial objects. Hume saw very clearly that arguments for the existence of God that begin with effects and work their way back to an ultimate cause are empirical arguments; that is, they begin with our impressions, and our ideas must always be in proportion with our impressions (§XI, 93). Hume asks his readers to consider what our impressions allow us to infer about the causes of any given effect. For example, if we examine our impressions of an oak tree, we find colors, odors, textures, sounds, and flavors. The cause of these qualities must certainly be great enough to produce them, but, Hume argues, these qualities do not authorize us to attribute to this cause qualities like omnipotence, omnipresence, or omniscience (§XI, 94). Arguments of this kind cannot succeed in proving God's existence. Instead, Hume writes, "Let your gods, therefore, O philosophers, be suited to the present appearances in nature" (§XI, 95)—in other words, confine your inferences within the limits of experience.

Skepticism as philosophical therapy

It may seem that, in challenging so many of our most cherished beliefs in causation, God, and miracles, Hume is simply a skeptic who thinks we cannot know reality at all, and who recommends that we cease making any claims whatsoever. However, this would be a misunderstanding of Hume's purpose. He wanted philosophy to sober up from its intoxication with metaphysical speculation, so that it could become useful for living. For this reason, his skepticism is not total; he thinks we can know reality within the limits of human understanding. He recommended an academic skepticism as a model for living an intellectually honest life in the world. This kind of skepticism makes room for uncertainty and ambiguity; it challenges us to be sober-minded and cautious in our reasoning, so that we are not led astray by superstition and wild speculation. What Hume proposed was a more scientific and experimental approach to human knowledge. This approach began "with clear and self-evident principles, to advance by timorous and sure steps, to review frequently our conclusions, and examine accurately all their consequences; though by these means we shall make both a slow and short progress in our systems; are the only methods, by which we can ever hope to reach truth, and attain a proper stability and certainty in our determinations" (§XI, 103). Hume's academic skepticism was proposed as a kind of philosophical therapy for a world intoxicated by superstition and unjustified beliefs. Sadly, Hume did not apply this therapy consistently in his own thinking.

Hume and the idea of race

In the same year Hume published *An Enquiry Concerning Human Understanding* (1748), he published a short and disturbing essay titled "Of National Characters," to which he added a footnote five years later where he expressed a belief in biological racism—the belief that physical differences like skin color, hair type, or facial structure were produced by differences in innate biological traits that also produce differences in characteristics like intelligence and morals.

> I am apt to suspect the negroes to be naturally inferior to the whites. There scarcely ever was a civilized nation of that

complexion, nor even any individual eminent either in action or speculation. No ingenious manufactures amongst them, no arts, no sciences. On the other hand, the most rude and barbarous of the whites, such as the ancient Germans, the present Tartars, have still something eminent about them, in their valour, form of government, or some other particular. Such a uniform and constant difference could not happen, in so many countries and ages, if nature had not made an original distinction between these breeds of men. Not to mention our colonies, there are Negroe slaves dispersed all over Europe, of whom none ever discovered any symptoms of ingenuity; though low people, without education, will start up amongst us, and distinguish themselves in every profession. In Jamaica, indeed, they talk of one negroe as a man of parts and learning; but it is likely he is admired for slender accomplishments, like a parrot, who speaks a few words plainly.[1]

In this infamous footnote, Hume claimed there are distinct "breeds of men" (a synonym he used for the concept of "race"), each having a unique nature that expressed itself in physical characteristics (i.e., skin color, facial structure) and cognitive capabilities. Some natures are capable of higher cognitive abilities (i.e., eminence in the arts and sciences) and some, as Hume would argue about animals (§IX), possess only limited cognitive abilities, diminishing, for Hume, their status as human beings. Philosophers call this view *racial naturalism*—the belief that there are racial essences or natures that are biologically based and give rise to traits and capacities.

The historical context for Hume's racist remarks was the expansion of European economic and political power through colonization, and the accompanying slave trade that began in the mid-seventeenth century and involved the capture, enslavement, and sale of inhabitants of West Africa to plantation owners in the Americas and the Caribbean. In order to justify this treatment of people from Africa, a new scientific category was created by a physician named François Bernier

---

[1] David Hume, "Of National Characters," in *David Hume: Selected Essays*, ed. Stephen Copley and Andrew Edgar (New York: Oxford University Press, 1993), footnote 120, 360.

(1620–88), to establish a hierarchy among the various groups of human beings on the planet based on physical characteristics that were rooted in their biology—it was called "race." Bernier divided the human species into four distinct races arranged in a hierarchy with white Europeans at the top. Later theorists like Carolus Linneaus (1707–78) and George-Louis Leclerc (1707–88) expanded these racial hierarchies to provide a scientific justification for the racism that motivated the slave trade. (It is important to note that the idea of *race* was created to justify *racism*, not the other way around). These scientific theories tried to establish that race was natural and biological, and that the physical differences between human beings were expressions of innate and unchanging differences in their biology. Instead of affirming the Biblical idea that all human beings were descended from a single progenitor like the biblical Adam—a view called *monogenesis*—the new science of the Enlightenment sought to demonstrate that there were in fact multiple species of humans, all descended from unique progenitors—a view called *polygenesis*. Hume's ideas about race were deeply influenced by the colonialism of his day and the emerging science of race, and this raises an important question: is Hume's empiricism inherently racist?

Recall that for Hume, all of our ideas are copies of impressions that are held together by the three principles of association—resemblance, contiguity, and cause and effect—and our ideas are verified by tracing them back to their originating impressions. If Hume's idea of race is true, it should be possible to discover the originating impressions that gave rise to it; that is, if there are indeed "racial essences," as Hume believed, it should be possible to discover these essences. The evidence Hume uses to justify his belief in racial essences is his perception of a lack of intellectual excellence among people with darker complexions. However, Hume was wrong about this perception. One of the impugned "slaves dispersed all over Europe" was Anton Wilhelm Amo, who, with his parents' permission, was taken from his Native Ghana at three years of age by a missionary and raised by a German Duke who gave him an aristocratic education that allowed him to learn multiple languages and study philosophy and medicine. He eventually completed two doctorate degrees, one in philosophy and the other in medicine. In his philosophy dissertation—published five years before Hume's *Treatise of Human Nature*—he developed an empiricist philosophy that understood ideas to be mental compositions of bodily sensations—a view similar to Hume's. Amo was not an exception, either. Zera Yaquob, a seventeenth-century Ethiopian philosopher, had developed a rationalist philosophy not unlike Descartes' in a book titled *Treatise* in 1667; and Kocc Barma, a seventeenth-century pre-colonial Senegalese philosopher, had composed an ethics and a political philosophy.

But that's not the only problem with Hume's belief in "race." It turns out that there is no biological basis for the category of race. As the Human Genome Project would eventually demonstrate, we as human beings share 99.9% of our DNA, and our physical differences are miniscule by comparison. The idea of "race" is, as Hume should have concluded, a socially constructed category that cannot be empirically verified and should be rejected as a pernicious fiction. This view is called *racial eliminativism*—the view that since race is a social fiction that cannot be empirically verified by science, it should be eliminated from our thinking and discourse just as we abandoned our beliefs in witchcraft and a flat Earth. Hume's empiricist philosophy could have liberated him from the fiction of race, but he failed to apply his skepticism consistently, and succumbed to the moral disease of racism. Race was a forgery painted by Enlightenment scientists. Unfortunately, just as the best art critics at the Rijksmuseum in Amsterdam were duped by van Meegeren's forgeries, Hume was duped by the concept of race.

Summary

Hume argued that our beliefs about reality should be justified by the principle of probability, and that we should suspend our judgment regarding claims that lie outside the limits of human understanding. These include claims about causation, miracles, and God, all of which rely upon improbable evidence. Hume argued that, since we cannot verify the connection between cause and effect, we cannot know whether we are free or determined. Instead, Hume held a compatibilist view and argued that we are freely determined. Hume's empiricism, unfortunately, did not prevent him from adopting the unjustifiable belief of racism.

Questions

1. Is the theory of probability sufficient for evaluating beliefs?
2. If our free actions are determined by prior unconscious influences, as Hume argues, can we be held morally accountable for our actions?
3. Is Hume's empirical view of human nature inherently racist?

7

Kant: The Architecture of the Mind
(*Prolegomena to Any Future Metaphysics*, Preface–II)

> **Key terms**
>
> *a priori* – a type of knowledge before experience
> *a posteriori* – a type of knowledge after experience
> Analytic – a judgment in which the predicate is contained in the subject
> Synthetic – a judgment in which the predicate expands the knowledge of the subject
> Fallibilism – the view that absolute certainty about reality is impossible

If Hume was an empiricist revolutionary who declared war on the rationalist regime, then Immanuel Kant was the new philosopher king who attempted to bring about a perpetual peace between these rival factions. However, the peace Kant forged turned out to be more revolutionary than anyone could have imagined. Kant agreed with Plato that universal conditions are necessary to make our experience intelligible and our knowledge of reality possible, but he disagreed that these conditions were mind-independent *forms* accessible to the human mind. Instead, Kant understood these conditions as Aristotelian *categories* within human understanding that provided the formal conditions of thought for any possible experience. He also agreed with Descartes that the human mind plays an active role in constituting knowledge through these formal categories. However, Kant also realized that the capacities of the human mind were limited and could not go beyond what was given in the basic qualities of objects; consequently, we could not have direct knowledge of the essence of any object or the nature of reality. Like Hume, Kant understood that objects in the world affect us, and that we are passive to these affections, but Kant thought empiricists like Hume had failed to see that in order for our sensory experience to be intelligible, it must be structured by principles and operations of the mind prior to our experience. As Kant surveyed the views of the rationalists and empiricists on the nature of reality (metaphysics) and our knowledge of it (epistemology), he realized that all their philosophizing had resulted in speculations beyond the reach of the human mind. For him, their debates "constantly move around the same spot, without gaining a single step," and this left him wondering whether metaphysics—the study of the nature and structure of reality—was even possible. If it was possible, and if philosophy had any hope of making progress on metaphysical questions, it would need to confront two problems: the limitations of human reason and the skepticism of Hume (Ak. 4:255).[1]

Hume's problem and Kant's awakening

The first problem concerns our ability to know reality through purely rational concepts. In the Preface to his *Critique of Pure Reason*, to which the *Prolegomena* is intended to be an introductory guide, Kant wrote that "human reason has a peculiar fate in one kind of its cognitions: it is troubled by questions that it cannot dismiss, because they are posed to it by the nature of reason itself, but that it also cannot answer, because they surpass human reason's ability" (Ak. 4:Avii).[2] Kant saw that our minds naturally, and inescapably, seek answers to questions our minds cannot answer—questions like "Does God exist?," "Is the soul immortal?," and "Is the universe eternal?" Our minds are not satisfied, for example, by

---

[1] All citations for Kant in these chapters are based on the standard critical edition of his work, the *Preussische Akademie* edition. Each citation will include an abbreviation for the *Akademie* edition (Ak), followed by the volume number, and then the page number, which is located in the margins of the English translations of his work. All quotations from Kant's *Prolegomena* in these chapters will refer to Kant, *Prolegomena to Any Future Metaphysics*, second edition, trans. James W. Ellington (Indianapolis: Hackett, 2001).

[2] All quotations from Kant's *Critique of Pure Reason* will refer to Kant, *Critique of Pure Reason*, trans. Werner S. Pluhar (Indianapolis: Hackett, 1996).

knowing the immediate cause of some event; we must know its ultimate cause. Plato and Descartes had capitalized on this tendency of reason and argued that the mind has the ability to know the reality it seeks either naturally or with divine assistance. The human mind, they claimed, has access to ideas that are demonstrably certain (e.g., forms or innate ideas), and we can use these ideas to make our sensory experiences intelligible, so we are not deceived about reality. However, Hume was less confident in the natural ability of the human mind to discover reality. Hume realized that the human mind has a tendency to arrive at judgments about reality that cannot be justified because they cannot be shown to accurately represent our experience; human reason, he argued, can lead us astray, and Kant agreed with him for the most part.

Kant acknowledged that Hume's critique of rationalism and causality had awakened him from a "dogmatic slumber"—the intellectual complacency of rationalist certainty (Ak. 4:260). Nevertheless, Kant could not follow Hume in concluding that there were no concepts in the mind prior to our experiences, especially the principle of causality. This seemed absurd to Kant because the intelligibility of any experience seemed to require some logical structure not provided in the experience itself. This insight, however, created a second problem for him. If Hume was right, then we could only have two types of knowledge about reality: *relations of ideas* and *matters of fact*. The former kind was demonstrably certain because any denial involved a contradiction, but the latter kind could never be certain because the contrary was always possible. Philosophers call this *Hume's Fork*, because along the path to knowledge about reality we come to a fork in the road—we can have certainty about relations of ideas, which have no connection to objects external to the mind, but never any certainty about matters of fact, which do concern objects external to the mind. This is the problem of the relationship between *thinking* and *being*—between our minds and reality. Moreover, if all our ideas are derived from our sensory experience, as Hume claimed, and we cannot have any certainty that these ideas accurately represent reality, then we cannot have any certainty in the disciplines of mathematics and natural science. Hume's skepticism about our ability to have objective knowledge about reality seemed to go too far for Kant.

Think about it. If we can never have any objective knowledge of causation—if it's merely a probable inference based on prior experiences—then the mathematical calculations about the motion of the planets deduced by Johannes Kepler and the subsequent laws of gravity and motion discovered by Isaac Newton are as uncertain as our claims about the sun rising tomorrow. This, Kant thought, left mathematics, science, and our basic knowledge about the external world, as well as our metaphysical claims about God, the soul, and the world, on very shaky ground. Against Hume's skepticism about causation, Kant argued that whenever we experience an event, like the collision of two billiard balls and the subsequent movement of the second ball (à la Hume), we can know objectively that something caused the second ball to move, even though we cannot know the specific nature of that cause. Philosophers call this epistemological view *fallibilism*—the view that we can have sufficient knowledge of reality without certain knowledge of the nature of reality. Hume's skepticism seemed to have opened a gulf between our minds and reality, with rationalists on one side and empiricists on the other. Kant wanted to build a bridge over this gulf, to bring a perpetual peace to the war between rationalism and empiricism, and so he set out to move beyond both of them by setting aside their errors and preserving their insights in a new philosophical approach that would revolutionize the way we think about reality—he called this way of thinking *critique*.

Critical philosophy

In the *Critique of Pure Reason*, Kant likened himself to Copernicus, who revolutionized the way we understood the motion of the planets by changing our perspective from one in which the planets revolve around the earth to one in which the earth revolves around the sun. Similarly, Kant sought to revolutionize the way we understand reality by changing our perspective from one in which our minds must conform to reality to one where reality must conform to our minds. He called this philosophical approach "critical idealism" (Ak. 4:294).

Critical philosophy, as Kant understood it, involved asking a fundamental question: Given our experience, what are the universal and necessary conditions that make it possible? When, for example, we inhale the aroma of a vanilla latte, what principles and operations of the mind have to be in place for us to have that experience? Kant thought if he could answer questions like this, then he would discover the universal and necessary grounds for knowledge about reality.

Let's think about this question for a moment. Kant starts with what is *given*—our sensory experience of the external world of things. To say that it is *given* is to admit that our minds are passive or receptive to the effects of objects in the world. Taking his lead from Hume, Kant wanted to begin with our immanent experience of the world of objects and work his way backward into the subject who knows these objects in order to discover what conditions and categories had to be in place for that experience to be intelligible. What he discovered, or better, deduced, was the intellectual architecture of the human mind that spanned between two poles: the *subject* (the "I" who perceives) and the *object* (the thing the "I" perceives). Now let's consider what Kant meant by the *universal* and *necessary* conditions of our experience. Something is universal if it applies constantly and consistently to every situation; something is necessary if it must precede the occurrence of something else. What Kant is looking for are the conditions or principles that are constantly, consistently, and necessarily at work whenever we experience anything.

When Kant tried to solve Hume's problem—the problem of how cause and effect can be known prior to our experience—he applied his critical approach and asked if we could have any experience at all without the principle of causation. The answer was "no." The principle of causation organizes our experience into a logical sequence in which one event is followed by another; without this principle in place, we would simply be drowning in sensory data like light waves, sound waves, gravity, odors, and sensations without any way to organize them. This would be maddening and unintelligible. Kant realized that causation wasn't the only principle we know *a priori*; he deduced that the human mind contains twelve basic concepts (or "categories," as Aristotle liked to call them) that organize our experience, and these concepts are part of the pure understanding (Kant used the term *pure* to indicate that a faculty of the mind or a concept is independent of sensory experience).

Knowledge and Judgments

Kant agreed with Hume that there are two basic kinds of knowledge: knowledge we derive from experience, and knowledge we arrive at prior to experience. Hume referred to the former as matters of fact and the latter as relations of ideas, but Kant used more precise language; he called these two types of knowledge *a posteriori* knowledge (after experience) and *a priori* knowledge (prior to experience). On the basis of these two types of knowledge, we make two kinds of judgments: synthetic and analytic judgments (see Figure 7.1). Synthetic judgments enlarge our knowledge of a concept through our experience of an instance of that concept. For example, imagine that I have only had Folgers coffee made from a drip coffee maker all my life, and I always drink it black. Now imagine that I visit an artisan coffee house in Brooklyn, New York for the first time, and I order a vanilla latte. The concept of "coffee" will take on a whole new meaning for me because I now know that coffee can be more than simply thin, black, and bitter. Analytic judgments are different; they are self-validating claims where what is said about a concept (predicate) is already expressed in the concept itself (subject). For example, the claim "All bachelors are unmarried men" is an analytic claim because the predicate "unmarried men" is contained in the subject "bachelors." We don't need to interview bachelors to discover they are unmarried or male; we know that from the concept itself.

		Sources of Knowledge	
		A priori	A posteriori
Types of Judgments	Analytic	All bachelors are unmarried men	N/A
	Synthetic	Every event has a cause	This coffee is cold

Figure 7.1

Kant and Hume both agreed that all analytic judgments rest on *a priori* knowledge (relations of ideas) and all synthetic judgments rest on *a posteriori* (matters of fact) knowledge. But this is where they part company. Kant realized that the only way mathematics, science, or even metaphysics could be shown to be objectively valid would be if they rested on what he called *synthetic a priori* judgments. These are judgments based on knowledge that is prior to experience (*a priori*) but is also enhanced by experience (synthetic); Kant thought the judgment that "Every effect has a cause," upon which Newtonian physics rested, was an example of this kind of judgment. Nothing in the concept of "effect" tells us anything about it having a prior "cause," but whenever we think about causality, we also think about the effects produced by causes, because, Kant argued, "cause and effect" is a logical structure of the human mind that we bring to every experience. The same can be said of mathematical statements like "The shortest path between two points is a straight line." Nothing in the concept of "shortest path between two points" gives us the predicate "straight line," and yet the statement is only possible because we have the concept of "shortest path," which allows us to reach the conclusion of a "straight line" (Ak. 4:269). Kant knew synthetic *a priori* statements existed, but he wanted to know *how* they were possible; so, the question he poses in the *Prolegomena* is: How are synthetic *a priori* judgments possible? If he could answer this question, Kant thought, he could overcome the conflicts between rationalists and empiricists and develop a science of metaphysics that would serve as a foundation for mathematics and physics.

Mathematical judgments are synthetic *a priori* judgments

Most people think that the judgments of pure mathematics are *analytic*—demonstrably certain—and *a priori*—known prior to any experience. For example, consider the mathematical proposition 7+5=12. If this were an analytic statement, the predicate (12) would be contained in the subject (7+5); much like the concept of "bachelor" containing the concepts of "unmarried" and "male," the concept of "7+5" must contain the concept of "12," but as Kant points out, it doesn't. No matter how much we analyze the concepts of "7," "5," or the sign of addition, we will never discover the concept of "12" (Ak. 4:268). The only way we discover the concept of "12" is if we go beyond the concept and make use of some sensory aid like counting fingers or making marks that can be visually counted. This suggests that there is a synthetic aspect to mathematical judgments; that is, our experience expands our knowledge of mathematical concepts like "7" and "5." At this point, it seems that Kant and Hume are on the same page—all of our ideas, like numbers, are derived from counting objects in our sensory experience. However, Kant notes something important about counting: counting requires principles for distinguishing and sequencing the objects we count. These principles have to be in place before we can count anything, and so they must be *a priori*. He calls these principles the *pure intuitions* of *space* and *time*—these are the general conditions that make it possible to experience anything sensible (Ak. 4:281).

Space and time

According to Kant, the human mind represents reality through the use of concepts and intuitions that are either pure or empirical. Recall that concepts are the way we get a handle on phenomena, but they are like the empty outlines in a coloring book that need to be filled in with colors from our experience. Concepts can be *pure* (not contaminated by experience) or *empirical* (derived from experience). Substance is an example of the former, and vanilla latte is an example of the latter. The German word translated as *intuition* is *der Anschauung* and it is derived from the German verb *schauen*, which means "to look." Intuitions are the way things are represented so we can apprehend them. Intuitions can also be pure or empirical. Space and time are examples of the former, and the immediate presence of this particular book to your mind is an example of the latter.

Kant claimed that mathematical knowledge is based upon the pure intuitions of space and time. Space provides an external framework within which objects can appear—which allows you to distinguish each of your five fingers. Time provides an internal framework for sequencing the objects that appear—which allows you to count each of your five fingers. If we cannot arrive at the synthetic statement of "12" without counting, and we cannot count without the pure (*a priori*) intuitions of space and time, then all mathematical knowledge is synthetic *a priori* knowledge, Kant claimed. And this leads to an important point about knowledge. Knowledge is not simply based on concepts, as the rationalist would have it, nor solely on intuitions, as the empiricists would have it. Instead, knowledge is comprised of concepts and intuitions—our minds and reality are correlated in knowledge. As Kant wrote in the *Critique of Pure Reason*, "Thoughts [concepts] without content [intuitions] are empty, and intuitions without concepts are blind. Hence it is just as necessary that we make our concepts sensible (i.e., that we add the object to them in intuition) as it is necessary that we make our intuitions understandable (i.e., that we bring them under concepts)" (Ak. 4:51). So, if mathematical knowledge is synthetic *a priori*, what about natural science?

Natural science judgments are synthetic *a priori* judgments

Natural science is the study of *nature*, which, Kant claims, "is the existence of things, so far as it is determined according to universal laws" (Ak. 4:294). For Kant, we cannot understand the nature of any object through concepts alone or through our experience of that object. Imagine you are walking through your house in the middle of the night and step on something that has sharp edges causing you to experience pain in your foot. There is nothing in the pain of that experience that tells us anything about the essence of the object causing the pain, and there are no concepts in our mind that can tell us what the essence of the object is. Even if we turn on the light and look directly at the object, our experience of it is made possible by the pure intuitions of space and time, which allow the object to appear, but additionally, all of the sensory qualities are being organized by what Kant calls the *concepts of the understanding*. These concepts are the "universal laws" that determine the existence of objects for us and render them intelligible. They are *universal* because they apply for everyone, everywhere, and always, and they are laws because they provide the rules by which we can understand any object. Without these concepts in place, we cannot organize the multiple sensory qualities we experience into anything intelligible (see Figure 7.2). In fact, if we did not have these concepts, we would be overwhelmed with meaningless sensory data. The concepts of the understanding render the objects encountered in our experience in an intelligible representation. However, this does not mean we know these objects as they are in themselves; it is impossible to know the essence of any object, according to Kant.

We can know that natural objects exist because they affect us—they impact our sensory organs with their material qualities. We can see colors, smell odors, hear sounds, feel textures, and taste flavors because we are open to the material world through our bodies—we are receptive to the objects of our experience. The essence of an object—what it is in itself—is not communicated to us through those experiences.

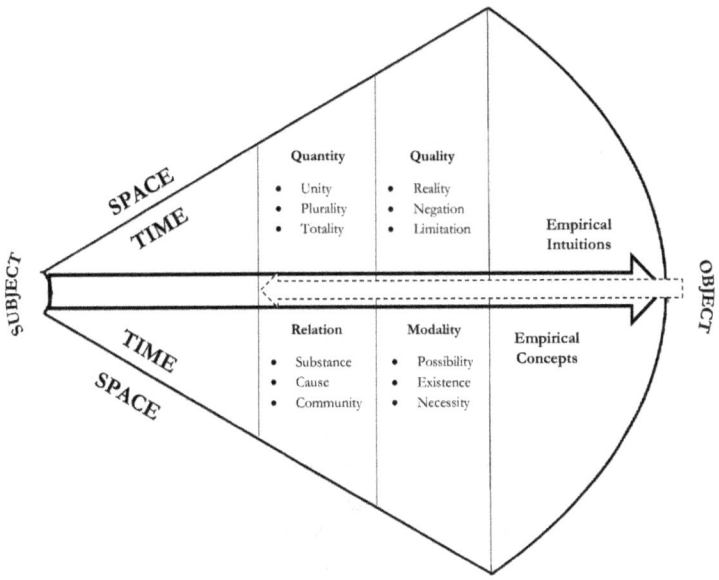

Figure 7.2

But wait! If we cannot know what an object is, how can we be sure that our understanding of the object is accurate; that is, how can we be sure that what we know is real and not an illusion? Kant's answer is that all human beings who are rational possess the same *a priori* concepts of the understanding to which every possible object must conform to be intelligible (Ak. 4:296). This means that we possess the formal conditions for any object prior to experiencing it, and when we do experience it, it is organized according to these conditions. To understand what Kant means, we need to return to Aristotle for a moment.

Aristotle argued in his *Categories* that whenever we try to articulate what something is, we make use of one or more of ten categories: substance, quantity, quality, relation, place, time, position, state, action, and affect (Aristotle, *Categories*, 1b.25). For example, we can make a variety of statements about Socrates using these categories: "Socrates is a man" (substance); "Socrates is one" (quantity); "Socrates is speaking" (action); "Socrates is lying down" (position). In each of these statements, we make judgments about Socrates by organizing our experience of him in terms of a category. Kant thought Aristotle was on to something in identifying these ten universal categories, but he thought Aristotle was wrong to claim that these categories were derived from our sensory experience of objects. Instead, Kant argued that the pure categories of the understanding were produced by a necessary and spontaneous synthesis in the human mind: our experiences must conform to space and time to be possible, and they must be logically organized to be intelligible. The categories are the logical requirements for any intelligible experience (Ak. 4:B114). By examining all of the possible judgments we can make about reality, Kant created a table of twelve general types of judgments, and grouped them into four basic categories, which he borrowed from Aristotle: *quantity*, *quality*, *relation*, and *modality* (see Figure 7.3). These categories represent the four basic logical functions of human thought in any given judgment about objects (Ak. 4:302–3). For example, in the judgment "All painters are artists," the term "all" designates a universal *quantity*, the equation of painters and artists indicates an affirmative *quality*, the designation of "all painters" as "artists" indicates a categorical *relation* between painters and artists, and the judgment is formulated in the *modality* of an assertion. All judgments contain these four logical functions.

Quantity	Quality	Relation	Modality
Universal	Affirmative	Categorical	Problematic
Particular	Negative	Hypothetical	Assertoric
Singular	Infinite	Disjunctive	Apodeictic

Figure 7.3

When he listed these judgments, Kant noticed that each of them made use of a universal concept that served as the objective basis for the judgment. So, he listed out these concepts in a table as well (see Figure 7.4).

Quantity	Quality	Relation	Modality
Unity	Reality	Substance	Possibility
Plurality	Negation	Cause	Existence
Totality	Limitation	Community	Necessity

Figure 7.4

These concepts function as the universal rules for all thinking; they are prior to any experience and make all experience possible. Nevertheless, it is important to note that they are neither innate in the mind like Descartes' ideas, nor derived from our experience like Hume's ideas; they are spontaneously produced when the mind tries to render an experience intelligible. One way of understanding these concepts is to think of them as a universal code that underlies all of our experience. Consider what you see when you open up a web browser on your computer. You see a search box, a colorful logo for the search engine, and icons for various tools. These visual images (experience) are made possible by the HTML, CSS, and JavaScript codes (concepts) that are concealed behind the webpage. The concepts of the understanding work in a similar way—they render our experience intelligible.

It's important to note that causality is one of the categories of the understanding. Kant was startled by Hume's claim that causality was merely an inference that can never be verified in experience. Kant certainly agreed that we will never have an empirical intuition of causality, but disagreed with Hume's claim that causality was simply a matter of fact. What Kant's deduction of the concepts of the understanding shows is that causality is a necessary concept of the understanding without which we cannot have any experience at all. Experience for Kant "consists of intuitions, which belong to the sensibility, and of judgments, which are entirely a work of the understanding" (Ak. 4:304). This means that our experience of natural objects is at once *synthetic* (empirical intuitions) and *a priori* (concepts of the understanding)—our minds are correlated with reality. The mind casts a kind of intellectual net over our experiences in order to render them intelligible. So, when we make judgments about nature, we are making what Kant calls *judgments of experience*, where our minds take the data we receive in a given sensory experience and organize it by means of the concepts of the understanding (e.g., "Fire is the cause of heat") (Ak. 4:298). These judgments are objectively valid because they make use of universal and necessary categories that every rational human being has to use in order to make their judgments; that is, everyone will agree to them—they are not mere opinions. By contrast, *judgments of perception*, where our imagination tries to fit a given sensory experience into an empirical concept or schema (e.g., "Cilantro tastes like soap"), are only subjectively valid because they do not make use of universal or necessary categories, but rely simply on personal perceptions (Ak. 4:298). With these insights, Kant realized that natural science is based upon synthetic *a priori* knowledge, and this knowledge is possible because of the pure intuitions of space and time and the universal and necessary concepts of the understanding, which organize our sensory experience of nature in a consistent way, giving us objectively valid knowledge of nature. Notice, however, that objectively valid does not mean we have objective knowledge of the essence of nature or complete knowledge of ultimate reality. On the contrary, objectively valid means that we know nature and reality within the objectively valid structures of the human mind. The reality we know is *virtual*, you might say.

Summary

Kant moved beyond the impasse of rationalism and empiricism in what he called critical idealism, which deduced the universal and necessary conditions for any possible experience from human cognition. Kant argued that there were two sources of knowledge—*a priori* and *a posteriori*—from which we make two kinds of judgments, analytic judgments that are *a priori* and synthetic judgments that are *a posteriori*. Kant notes that a third kind of judgment exists—*synthetic a priori* judgments—which mathematics and natural science use. Kant sought to discover how these judgments are possible, and he concluded that the pure intuitions of space and time provide the formal framework for any experience, and the pure concepts of the understanding provide the logical organization for any experience, making synthetic *a priori* judgments possible.

Questions

1. Is it possible to have objectively valid knowledge of reality?
2. Why is metaphysical knowledge important for math and science?
3. Does Kant overcome Hume's skepticism about reality?

8

Kant: Virtual Reality and the Limits of Reason
(*Prolegomena to Any Future Metaphysics*, III–Solution)

> **Key terms**
>
> Transcendent– knowledge beyond possible experience
> Transcendental – knowledge restricted to *a priori* conditions of possible experience
> Ideals of Reason– unconditioned aims of rational inquiry
> Antinomies of Reason– paradoxes of rational inquiry

Kant's account of reality has a serious problem. One of his central claims is that we cannot know the essence of anything, a thing as it is in itself; we can only know our representations of a thing, its virtual appearance (Ak. 4:314). Like Plato, Kant divided the world into two realms: the sensible realm of *phenomena* (Greek, *phaino*, "to appear") and the intelligible realm of *noumena* (Greek, *nous*, "mind"). Rationalists like Plato and Descartes had viewed the sensible realm as untrustworthy when it came to reporting reality, and sought certainty in the intelligible realm. Empiricists like Hume viewed the intelligible realm as untrustworthy and sought to return to the immediate experience of reality in the sensible realm. Idealists like George Berkeley (1685–1753), who was also, simultaneously, an empiricist, denied the existence of material substance, and claimed that all our perceptions were caused by ideas in the mind, thereby collapsing the two realms into one. When Kant sought to bring the two realms together in what he called critical or *transcendental idealism*, most of his early readers interpreted him as making an argument similar to Berkeley's—an interpretation that Kant explicitly rejected (Ak. 4:294). However, this interpretation has an important implication for our knowledge of reality: if all we can know are the appearances that the forms of sensibility (space and time) make possible and the concepts of the understanding render intelligible, how can we know we are not being fooled? This is the problem of *subjectivism*—the view that knowledge is constituted by the individual knower and cannot be objective. More importantly, if we cannot know things as they are in themselves, how can we have any certainty in the disciplines of mathematics or science? Kant was faced with the same problem as Plato—the problem of being and appearance.

The problem of reality and appearances

To understand why Kant thinks his epistemology does not lead to subjectivism, we need to understand his distinction between *transcendent* and *transcendental* objects of knowledge. For Kant, objects of knowledge are *transcendent* if they go beyond (Latin, *transcendere*, "to climb over or beyond") what it is possible for us to experience empirically, while objects of knowledge are *transcendental* if they are concerned with the *a priori* concepts that makes our experience possible (Ak. 4:373, footnote 48). What is important to keep in mind is that whenever we have a sensory experience—the smell of a vanilla latte, for example—that experience is of something objectively real even though we cannot know its essence. The concepts of the understanding provide the formal conditions under which that real object—the vanilla latte—can appear for us. So, our knowledge is objective, insofar as it is the result of subsuming our sensory experience of real objects under the concepts of the understanding. The concepts cannot represent the real object without the input from the object in our sensory experience. Recall that for Kant knowledge is a synthesis of our concepts and intuitions, which are the two primary ways our minds represent reality—concepts represent reality logically and intuitions represent reality aesthetically (Greek, *aesthesis*, "perception"). Prior to Kant, rationalists had claimed our knowledge of reality depended on concepts, while empiricists had claimed our knowledge of reality depended on intuitions.

Rationalists
Concepts = Knowledge

Empiricists
Intuitions = Knowledge

Kant
Concepts + Intuitions = Knowledge

According to Kant, the pure intuitions of space and time combined with the pure concepts of the understanding are universal and necessary conditions of the human mind that make all our experiences possible and intelligible, and without these *a priori* conditions, we cannot have any experience at all. However, the transcendental architecture of our minds is like an empty coloring book that must be filled in by our intuitions—the representations of our sensory experience—which in turn must be organized by the concepts of our understanding. This means that human knowledge is the product of these two forms of representation—concepts and intuitions—and therefore all human knowledge is empirical, insofar as the transcendental categories of the understanding are used to render empirical objects of our experience intelligible. But human knowledge can never be transcendent—it can never go beyond the experience made possible by our pure concepts and intuitions, even though, as we will see, human reason seeks transcendent knowledge. Kant's transcendental idealism (metaphysics) is therefore the basis for his empirical realism (epistemology).

Kant's distinction between concepts and intuitions, and his claim that knowledge is a synthesis of the two, was his unique contribution to philosophy. Rationalism installed concepts as a dictator to rule over the senses, and thereby slipped into a rigid dogmatism. Empiricism liberated sensory experience from the tyranny of concepts, but slipped into skepticism. Kant tried to resolve the impasse between rationalists who "intellectualized appearances" and empiricists who "sensualized all of the concepts of the understanding" by distinguishing between concepts that actively organize our experience and intuitions that we receive from experience.[1] This distinction had important implications for the history of philosophy.

---

[1] Kant, *Critique of Pure Reason*, Ak. 4:A271.

Kant certainly resolved the conflict between rationalism and empiricism, but his distinction between concepts and intuitions gave rise to another conflict—a war between philosophers who emphasized the active role of our concepts in constructing our knowledge of reality, and those who emphasized the mind's receptivity to intuitions. The former tradition became known as the *analytical* school of philosophy and the latter the *continental* school of philosophy. Analytic philosophy claims that the truth about reality is disclosed in logically consistent statements about the facts of the empirical world. Given that the facts of the empirical world have a logically consistent structure, they can be described in language. However, we make false claims about reality when we get the facts about the empirical world wrong and make statements about it that are logically inconsistent with these facts. Consequently, analytic philosophers focus almost exclusively on the logical analysis of language and scientific investigation of the empirical world.

Continental philosophy claims that the truth about reality is disclosed aesthetically and cannot be reduced or confined to language—reality, you might say, is always more than words can say. Consequently, continental philosophers focus, almost exclusively, on art, literature, and politics. This does not mean, of course, that continental philosophers are not concerned with linguistic analysis or science, or that analytic philosophers are never concerned with art, literature, or politics. It means that analytic philosophy privileges concepts over intuitions and understands reality as a logically stable state of being, and continental philosophy privileges intuitions over concepts and understands reality as a dynamic state of becoming. This results in two very distinct approaches understanding reality. To better understand how these two philosophical approaches developed, we need to understand Kant's understanding of the threefold synthesis.

The threefold synthesis

In the *Critique of Pure Reason*, Kant described the process by which we come to know reality as a threefold synthesis of *apprehension*, *reproduction*, and *recognition* (Ak. 4:A97–103). We *apprehend* objects in the world through the five senses of our bodies—our bodies are receptive to objects in the world that act upon us—but we cannot go beyond our sensory experience to grasp objects as they are in themselves, so we must reproduce the objects of our experience in a virtual representation. The imagination *reproduces* our sensory experience in a representation by taking all of the sensory data we receive in our experience and bundling it together in what Kant calls a *schema* (Greek, *skhema*, "figure"), which can then be *recognized*—made intelligible—through the pure concepts of the understanding. When we recognize an object, we subsume its appearance, made possible by the concepts of the understanding, under an empirical concept that includes all of its sensory qualities, thus synthesizing the concept with our experience. What is important to note about this threefold synthesis is that our minds are simultaneously receptive to the world and actively constructing it. In fact, Kant claims that all "objects must conform to our cognition"; that is, our minds give orders (concepts of the understanding) to objects that they must obey (Ak. 4:Bxvi). It's also important to remember that when the imagination schematizes our experience it is doing so within the framework of the formal conditions of space and time, so an order is already in place prior to any apprehension of an object—objects are already conforming to spatial and temporal constraints—something Kant thought Hume had overlooked. But why aren't our virtual constructions of the world simply subjective opinions? How can we be sure that our apprehension, reproduction, and recognition of reality is true? To understand why and how Kant thinks we know reality, we need to review his architecture of the mind.

Kant referred to the operations of the human mind as *cognitions*, and he claimed that the two primary forms of cognition were *concepts* and *intuitions*, which constitute the two ways that reality is given and represented to us in our experience. Intuitions represent objects given in our sensory experience, but never objects as they are in themselves, and concepts organize our intuitions in a logical representation, so that we can make sense of our intuitions. These two forms of cognition have two sources. The source of our intuitions is *a posteriori* (after experience), and the source of our concepts is *a priori* (before experience). Our experience of reality begins in our *a posteriori* receptivity to objects in the world, to which our minds apply the *a priori* concepts of the understanding, making our experience intelligible. These forms and sources of cognition allow us to make two kinds of judgments, *analytic* judgments, in which the predicate is contained in the subject

("All bachelors are unmarried men"), and *synthetic* judgments, in which our knowledge of the subject is enhanced through our experience ("The table is red"). Analytic judgments are true *a priori*, but synthetic judgments can only be true *a posteriori*. What Kant would have us realize is that although the mind spontaneously orders our experience of objects, it does so in a way that is *universal* (all human beings order their experience in this way) and *necessary* (objects must conform to this order to be apprehended). The formal intuitions of space and time and the concepts of the understanding, then, are the conditions for our knowledge of reality.

Understood in this way, we do not create reality; instead, there is a harmony between our minds and reality—any object of our experience must be apprehended according to the conditions of our minds. Consider the sweetness of maple syrup. We cannot hear the sweetness of maple syrup because our ears do not have the conditions for apprehending taste. We can hear the maple syrup being poured over pancakes perhaps, but we cannot hear how it tastes. In the same way, our minds can only apprehend objects that can appear within the framework of space and time and can be organized according to the logical concepts of the understanding. But what about objects that can't be apprehended in this way? For example, God is conceived as being omnipresent and eternal, which means God is neither spatial nor temporal. Can we have knowledge of God's existence in the way Descartes claimed we could? Kant does not think so, but in order to understand why he is skeptical, we need to understand a final faculty of our minds: reason.

Reason and the three dialectical illusions

Kant has demonstrated in the first two sections of the *Prolegomena* that the judgments of mathematics and natural science are synthetic *a priori* judgments—they make use of concepts and intuitions. However, Kant's stated goal in the *Prolegomena* was to address the problem of metaphysics, namely, whether we can have any metaphysical knowledge at all, or whether all metaphysical judgments about reality are speculative illusions. To answer this question, Kant maps out a separate domain of the human mind: *reason*. Reason is the faculty of mind that draws inferences from the premises of the concepts of the understanding. Reason naturally and inevitably seeks ultimate reality, and, consequently, it goes beyond the virtual limits imposed upon our experience by the concepts of the understanding. In doing so it falls into three dialectical illusions: paralogisms, antinomies, and ideals of pure reason (Ak. 4:329–330). Like van Meegeren's forgeries, these dialectical illusions take their cue from existing representations (concepts of the understanding) but go beyond them and attempt to create idealized representations of reality that can never be the object of our sensory experience. These illusions are forgeries of reality.

Paralogisms

Paralogisms are logical errors made by reason that lead to illusions that are taken to be real. In the *Critique of Pure Reason*, Kant argued that Descartes' *Cogito* ("I think, therefore, I am") was an example of this kind of illusion (Ak. 4: A348). Kant claimed that Descartes erred when he inferred the essence of the self to be a "thinking substance." Substance is one of the pure categories of the understanding that indicates something that can be described in terms of its accidents or attributes—a table (substance) that we describe as brown (accident), for example. However, as Kant has explained, concepts are empty until they are filled in by experience, so in order for Descartes to infer that he is a substance that thinks, he would have to have an empirical intuition of himself as an object, but this is precisely what he never has. Descartes is always the subject of his experience, who experiences himself within the pure intuition of time, but never as an object of empirical intuition. When Descartes claims that he is a "thinking substance," he commits the logical error of *equivocation* by treating the absolute *subject* "I" and the substantial *object* "I think" as the same thing. Given that Descartes is always the subject of his thinking, he can never become the object of his thinking, and so to infer that he is a thinking substance is a logical error of reasoning. Interestingly, Kant thought that reason naturally falls into paralogisms of this kind because reason seeks the unconditioned condition of reality, which is beyond the limits of the human mind. Whenever philosophers are convinced by these *illusions*, as Descartes was, they fall into metaphysical *delusions*. For Kant, the way to avoid these delusions is to restrain one's reasoning within the limits of human cognition.

Antinomies

The second kind of dialectical illusion that reason falls into are what Kant called the *antinomies of reason*. He discovered these antinomies through his analysis of the contradictory metaphysical claims of rationalists and empiricists about the connection between the totality of conditioned things and their ultimate conditions, which he called the *cosmological idea*. Descartes, for example, concluded that there must be an unconditioned and necessary condition that is the cause of our existence and everything else in the world, but Hume denied the existence of such an unconditioned and necessary condition, and claimed that the self and everything in the world were unconditioned and contingent multiplicities. Who is right? Kant saw that while the paralogisms involved a logical error, the antinomies are neither invalid nor do they involve a logical fallacy. However, he also saw that both approaches assume that space and time are transcendent objects of our experience rather than transcendental *conditions* of our experience—remember, Kant claims that space and time are the formal conditions of our experience. Kant argued in the *Critique of Pure Reason* that these arguments rely upon a faulty premise: "If the conditioned is given, then the entire series of all its conditions is also given; now objects of the senses are given to us as conditioned; consequently," the entire series of its conditions must be given to us as well (Ak. 4:A497). The problem, Kant argued, is that objects are never *given* to us in our experience, objects *appear* to us in conformity with the pure intuitions of space and time and the categories of the understanding. All empirical objects of our experience are appearances and must conform to the transcendental conditions of our mind (space and time; concepts of the understanding). The faculty of reason, by its very nature, tries to go beyond our experience to apprehend the chain of preceding causes and conditions, looking for the ultimate cause or the unconditioned condition of everything (e.g., the beginning of the world, its creator, etc.), but it ends up in conflict with itself. It is impossible for contradictory theses to both be true or false, so reason finds itself trapped in an unsolvable contradiction (Ak. 4:341). Each of the four antinomies arises from the inferences about the cosmological idea that reason draws from the four main concepts of the understanding: quantity, quality, relation, and modality. The first two antinomies are mathematical in nature and concern quantity and quality. The second two antinomies are dynamical in nature and concern relation and modality (Ak. 4:343). Let's examine each one to see how they arise.

The first antinomy concerns whether the world is a limited quantity or an infinite quantity. If the world is a limited quantity, then it had a beginning in time and is confined within temporal and spatial boundaries, but this would mean that there is an empty time before the beginning of the world, and empty space beyond the boundaries of the world, and it is impossible for us to experience either of these limits (Ak. 4:342). Think, for example, of looking up into the sky at night and seeing the stars above you. You could ask, "Is all that I see bound within some limited framework of matter, or does all that I see extend infinitely within space and time?" If all that you see is fixed within some framework, then what lies outside of that framework—that is, what is that framework *in*? If it is in something, then the universe is finite, but if the universe extends infinitely, then there must have been an infinite series of events extending in infinite space, both of which our minds cannot grasp. So, it would seem that neither the claim that the world is limited nor the claim that the world is infinite can be demonstrated to be true or false.

The second antinomy concerns whether the quality of substances in the world is simple or composite. When we experience any object, we take it to be a whole comprised of a finite set of parts because a whole without parts is impossible. For example, water is comprised of two hydrogen molecules and one oxygen molecule—water is a whole made from simple parts without which there could not be water. Nevertheless, the contrary can also be shown to be true, namely, that all simple parts can be reduced to an infinite series of other parts because all parts have to exist in space and space can always be divided. So, objects of our experience can be shown to be both simple and composite. Kant claims that these first two antinomies rely on the false assumption that an object of appearance (the world or a substance) is a thing in itself instead of an appearance conditioned by space and time and organized by the concepts of the understanding (Ak. 4:343).

The third and fourth antinomies are dynamical, which means that they are concerned with the causal power in us (freedom) and in an ultimate and necessary cause outside of us (God). The third antinomy involves a thesis and antithesis about whether we are free or determined in our actions; both propositions could be true, but reason cannot verify either one, and consequently becomes mired in a contradiction (Ak. 4:339). The thesis claims there has to be freedom in the world to initiate a chain of causes that leads to the appearance of anything; that is, there must be some initial cause that acts spontaneously to bring about all the succeeding causes, and this requires that the cause be free. However, if this is true, and Kant thinks it could be, then that cause must have some prior cause that explains its existence, and this means that there cannot be any freedom in the world, because every cause requires a prior cause, and therefore, everything in the universe is determined.

The fourth antinomy is concerned with the existence of a necessary cause of the world and of everything in it—an important metaphysical controversy among philosophers. Kant demonstrates that it is possible to offer well-reasoned arguments for and against the existence of a necessary cause like God. On the one hand, we can reasonably argue that every effect must have a cause, and that there cannot be an infinite regress of causes—because if there were, we would never arrive at an explanation of the effect—so there must be an ultimate cause that is itself uncaused. On the other hand, we can reasonably argue that if every effect has a cause, then the ultimate cause must have a cause, otherwise we cannot explain its existence (if God created the world, who created God?), and this would lead to an infinite regress, so we can never have any knowledge of the ultimate cause.

Reason, Kant argues, reaches its limits in the mathematical and dynamical antinomies because it assumes that space and time are transcendentally *real*, but as Kant has demonstrated, space and time are transcendentally *ideal*—they are the formal conditions of the mind that make our experience of the world possible. Once this is realized, it becomes clear that neither the spatial and temporal limits of the world, nor the simple or composite natures of things in the world, can be rationally determined. Both the theses and antitheses of the first two antinomies are therefore false. Conversely, both the theses and antitheses of the third and fourth antinomies can be true because knowledge of freedom and of a necessary being can be posited as transcendental ideas and denied as transcendent realities. Once the four antinomies are resolved, reason can be reestablished within its proper limits, or, as Kant put it in the *Critique of Pure Reason*, reason is made "its own pupil" (Ak. 4:Bxiv).

Ideals of pure reason

Reason, Kant argues, takes the judgments of the understanding that organize our experience by the pure concepts of the understanding and tries to deduce their unconditioned condition—ultimate reality. For example, when we watch a game of billiards and see one ball strike a second, we organize this experience in terms of cause and effect—the cause of the second ball's motion is the movement and impact of the first ball. Reason takes the judgment of the understanding—every cause has an effect—and tries to determine what the ultimate cause of motion is. What for example, caused the first ball to move? Certainly, the billiards player, but what caused him to move—or more importantly, what caused the billiards player? Reason is insatiable—it can only be satisfied by discovering the ultimate cause of everything. Kant thinks that reason is the cause of our metaphysical mistakes about reality. When we allow reason to extend beyond the limits of the concepts of the understanding, we end up with illusions instead of reality. So, Kant argued, if we want to avoid these illusions, we must restrain reason within the limits of possible experience.

It is important to note that Kant deduced the concepts of the understanding from the judgments we make about our experience. He grouped these judgments into four categories: judgments of quantity, judgments of quality, judgments of relation, and judgments of modality (Ak. 4:303). The judgments we make about our experience are conclusions drawn from premises supplied by the understanding. These premises and conclusions are logically organized in what Kant calls a syllogism. A *syllogism* is a deductive (Latin, *deducere*, "to bring down from") argument, in which a conclusion follows down from minor and major premises or statements. The minor premise is the subject of the argument and the major premise is the predicate of the argument. In deductive arguments, the conclusion must follow from the premises. Consider the following example of a syllogism:

Minor Premise: All humans are mortal.
Major Premise: Socrates is a human.
Conclusion: Socrates is mortal.

In the minor premise, a universal (quantity) statement is made about the mortality (quality) of humans. In the major premise, the subject of the minor premise is logically linked to a particular (quantity) human being, Socrates. This allows for a conclusion to be drawn from the two statements. If every human being will die, and Socrates is a human being, then it follows that Socrates will die. Kant claimed that the inherent logic of the human mind makes use of three types of syllogisms when we organize our experience: categorical syllogisms (like the one above), hypothetical syllogisms, and disjunctive syllogisms. Hypothetical syllogisms follow an "If ..., then..." pattern, and disjunctive syllogisms follow an "Either ..., or ..." pattern. Kant argued that the pure concepts of the understanding were derived from the logical structure of judgments that all human beings make about their experiences. Consequently, they provide the universal and necessary conditions for all possible experiences. Reason takes the concepts of the understanding and tries to deduce the pure ideals from the logical structure of categorical, hypothetical, and disjunctive syllogisms. These ideals of reason are higher premises, derived from the initial premises of the syllogisms of the understanding, that make further inferences about the ultimate nature of reality by referring the understanding to transcendent objects (e.g., God, soul, world) rather than to objects of possible experience. It is this that leads to illusions about reality.

Kant claimed that reason inferred three ideals from the concepts of the understanding in the mode of relation. From the concept of substance, reason infers a *psychological* idea that there must be a soul that is the subject of our experience. From the idea of causality, reason infers a *cosmological* idea that there must be a world that is the sum of everything we experience, as well as the practical idea of freedom. From the concept of community, reason infers a *theological* idea that there must be a God (Ak. 4:330). The problem with each of these inferences is that none of these ideals can be experienced; that is, they are ideas that have no corresponding intuition, and therefore we cannot be said to have knowledge of a soul, the world, or God. These ideals refer to objects that transcend our experience.

Metaphysical judgments are synthetic a priori

It turns out that all metaphysical judgments about the origins of the universe, the nature of reality, human freedom, and the existence of God, are synthetic *a priori* judgments, like those of mathematics and natural science—they are inferences that are made possible by the formal conditions of space and time and that make use of the *a priori* concepts of the understanding. The problem is that both space and time, and the concepts of the understanding, are the organizing principles of our experience, but the ideas of the world, our own soul, our freedom, and God, are all beyond our experience. We do not experience the world; we only experience discrete objects in the world at a given moment in time. We do not experience our soul or essential self, either, because to do that, we would need to stand outside of ourselves and observe ourselves from an objective point of view, but this is impossible because we are always the observer and observed. We do not experience our freedom either; we can only act *as if* we are free. And, we have never had a sensory experience of God which could be organized in a concept of the understanding. But why doesn't this lead to skepticism? Kant claimed that in denying the possibility of our having knowledge of ultimate realities like God, soul, or world, he made "room for faith" (Ak. 4: Bxxx). By setting limits on reason's boundary-crossing tendencies, Kant was not seeking to become a complete skeptic; he was seeking to foster some intellectual humility—to remind us of our limitations in our attempts to know reality. We are better served, Kant argues, when we restrict our knowledge to what we can know and leave the rest to faith.

Summary

Kant used his transcendental idealism (metaphysics) as the basis for his empirical realism (epistemology). He claimed that the transcendental conditions of the mind (pure intuitions of space and time and categories of the understanding) were universal to all human beings and, therefore, we could have objective knowledge of reality. The faculty of reason, Kant argued, has a natural tendency to seek the unconditioned conditions of reality, and arrive at ideas like God, soul, world, and freedom that can never be an object of our experience, and consequently, reason becomes entangled in metaphysical contradictions. Kant argued that all metaphysical claims are synthetic *a priori* judgments, and that they must be restrained within the limits of possible experience.

Questions

1. Is our knowledge of reality merely subjective?
2. If we cannot have knowledge of God's existence, what is the justification for faith in God?
3. Is it possible to have metaphysical knowledge given Kant's account?

PART III ETHICS

HOW MIGHT WE LIVE AUTHENTICALLY?
NIETZSCHE AND ARENDT

Ethics

The two philosophers we will read about in this section are Friedrich Nietzsche and Hannah Arendt. Nietzsche (1844–1900) is best described as an anti-philosopher because he sought to shatter the metaphysical and epistemological concepts enshrined in the history of philosophy and move beyond them. His iconoclastic character and his focus on the "will to power" made him appealing to the Nazis of the early twentieth century, but, as we will see, Nietzsche was opposed to oppressive systems that curtailed freedom and creativity. For Nietzsche, every human being has the capacity to live an exemplary and authentic life, but not everyone has the courage to do so.

Arendt (1906–75) can also be described as an anti-philosopher but for very different reasons than Nietzsche. Arendt was a German-Jewish immigrant who fled Nazi Germany for France in 1933, eventually settling in the United States, where she became a citizen in 1951. She had studied philosophy with Edmund Husserl, Martin Heidegger, and Karl Jaspers, but her experience as a stateless refugee and the unprecedented horrors of totalitarianism in the twentieth century caused Arendt to turn her thinking toward the importance and fragility of political life. Arendt famously rejected the title of "philosopher" in favor of "political theorist," because in her view philosophy had tried to escape the world of human affairs into the solitary contemplation of ideas. Arendt sought to return to the world and the immanent experience of political life. The world, Arendt argued, was a shared space where we appear with others and communicate who we are through our words and deeds. For her, we live fully human lives when we speak and act with others in a common world.

Arendt and Nietzsche were both concerned with our immanent lives in the world, and they were both concerned with the ethical question: How might we live authentically? Their starting points for answering this question were very different and led them to different conceptions of the authentic life. Nietzsche begins with the singularity of human life that must be liberated from social conformity and creatively fashioned like a work of art. For Nietzsche, we live authentically when we resist the demand of others to conform and affirm our lives to become who we are and make creative contributions to culture. Arendt begins with human plurality, which must be preserved by creating public spaces where individuals can appear and communicate who they are with others though speech and action. For Arendt, we live authentically human lives when we speak and act in concert with others to build and preserve a common world.

This final question allows us to further develop our own philosophy by integrating our conceptions of reality into our lives. It requires us to consider what reality is and how we know it in order to live consistently with this reality. It is only when we interrogate and clarify our metaphysical and epistemological assumptions that we can live authentic lives, and this means that our conceptions of reality directly impact our way of life.

9

Nietzsche: Become Who You Are!
(Schopenhauer as Educator, 1–3)

Key terms

True Educator – one who liberates you to become your authentic self
Apollonian – the drive toward order
Dionysian – the drive toward disorder
Unfashionable – out of sync with the common order of things

We have seen that philosophy is a *theoretical* practice concerned with the nature of reality (metaphysics) and our knowledge of it (epistemology). However, philosophy is also a *practical* endeavor. It is not just concerned with knowing reality but also with living a real and authentic life. Friedrich Nietzsche thought philosophy should be in the service of life, not life in the service of philosophy. Instead of withdrawing from the world into a transcendent realm of forms or divine contemplation, Nietzsche sought to bring philosophy down to earth by emphasizing our immanent experience; he wanted to affirm *this* life instead of denying it by seeking a life *beyond* this one. Philosophers, he argued, had become intoxicated on otherworldly illusions. The more they explored the nature of reality, the further they got away from it; instead of discovering reality, they had abandoned it. In his book *The Twilight of the Idols*, Nietzsche wrote that philosophers have a peculiar trait: "They put what comes at the end—unfortunately! for it should not come anywhere—the 'highest concepts,' i.e., the most general emptiest concepts, the last wisp of evaporating reality, at the beginning as the beginning."[1] All the concepts philosophers had developed—being, non-being, forms, substances, God—were simply "evaporating reality" instead of reality itself. Plato had mistaken reality for empty and immaterial forms, and Descartes had mistaken it for God. To live in accordance with these unrealities was to live an unreal life, according to Nietzsche. Contrary to all the philosophers who preceded him, Nietzsche argued that the path to reality was not through abstraction, moving further and further away from the particulars of our lived experience, but through immersion into life—the creative power expressed in our will, instincts, and desires. For Nietzsche, the task of philosophy is not to know some abstract reality but to know the reality of ourselves, so that we can live authentically. But in order to live authentically, we need to understand what and who we are.

How to know yourself

When Nietzsche was twenty-nine years old, just after publishing his first book *The Birth of Tragedy*, he published four essays that he grouped together under the title *Unfashionable Observations* (*Unzeitgemässe Betrachtungen*), which took a critical look at European culture. Nietzsche railed against an education system that turned students into obedient drones, music and art that trafficked in clichés, and a culture that was slouching toward mediocrity. These "observations" were a kind of inversion of Descartes' *Meditations*; instead of directing our gaze toward a transcendent God through reason, Nietzsche sought to direct our gaze toward the immanent experience of life, where he sought to illuminate exemplars of excellence—models for overcoming the conventions of one's time and living more authentically. He called these exemplars "true educators," because, instead of indoctrinating you with their ideas in order to make you in their own image, they

---

[1] Friedrich Nietzsche, *Twilight of the Idols: Or How to Philosophize with a Hammer* (*TI*), trans. Duncan Large (New York: Oxford University Press), *TI* III.4, 17. There is no standard reference system for Nietzsche's works, but there is a typical citation practice of indicating the abbreviated title, part, section, and page number of each work. These chapters will follow this practice. So, in this citation, *TI* is an abbreviation for *Twilight of the Idols*, "III" indicates the part, "4" indicates the section within Part III, and "17" indicates the page number.

liberated you to become yourself (*UO* III.1, 174).[2] Nietzsche found this kind of true educator in the philosopher, Arthur Schopenhauer.

In the first section of Nietzsche's third "unfashionable observation," titled *Schopenhauer as Educator*, Nietzsche argues that all human beings share a common trait: they hide who they are out of fear of the judgment of others (*UO* III.1, 171). Everyone has experienced a moment when they chose to remain silent rather than voice their opinion, because they knew if they shared their opinion they would find themselves out of harmony with the common opinions of most people—they would be different, weird, or odd. Nietzsche calls the repression of who we are "bad conscience"; when we masquerade as someone else—the person our society, families, or peers want us to be—then we speak and act in bad faith: we are unfaithful to who we are. We become like Han van Meegeren, forging our lives in the style of someone else instead of creating our lives in our own unique style. We notice this bad conscience in others but rarely in ourselves, because we have become habituated to acting like everyone else—we accept the roles we are given and play them faithfully. The more we live like this the more we become alienated from ourselves, Nietzsche argues. Consequently, we begin to understand ourselves only through the roles we are assigned, and we lose touch with ourselves and convince ourselves that we *are* what others want us to be. The reason for this is that our lives run smoother when we "fit in."

The demand to "fit in" exists prior to our birth in the form of concepts and categories that govern who we should be and how we should act. These concepts and categories are the molds into which our lives are poured, the frames in which we are viewed and understood. The more we are viewed and understood in these frames, the more we come to understand ourselves in them. By understanding ourselves this way, we repress our will, instincts, and desires, and conform to the conceptions of other people; which leads Nietzsche to say, "You are none of those things that you now do, think, and desire" (*UO* III, 172).

---

[2] I am using the English translation of *Schopenhauer as Educator* in *The Complete Works of Friedrich Nietzsche, Vol. 2: Unfashionable Observations*, trans. Richard T. Gray, Stanford: Stanford University Press, 1998. The citation indicates that the quotation is on page 174 in the first section (1) of *Schopenhauer as Educator*, which is the third essay (III) of Nietzsche's four *Unfashionable Observations* (*UO*).

But, as Sigmund Freud, the founder of modern psychoanalysis, would later explore in depth, everything that is repressed comes back with a vengeance.[3] Understanding ourselves through the lens of others creates a tension in us between who we might become through the expression of our will, instincts, and desires, and who others want us to be. This tension can lead to a war within us that leaves us psychologically torn apart when we fail to become ourselves, or when social structures prevent us from doing so.

In *The Souls of Black Folk*, W. E. B Du Bois described the experience of African-Americans in the early part of the twentieth century as being torn between two selves, a psychological condition he called "double consciousness"—seeing oneself through the eyes of another.

> It is a peculiar sensation, this double-consciousness, this sense of always looking at one's self through the eyes of others, of measuring one's soul by the tape of the world that looks on in amused contempt and pity. One ever feels his twoness—an American, a Negro; two souls, two thoughts, two unreconciled strivings; two warring ideals in one dark body, whose dogged strength alone keeps it from being torn asunder.[4]

These Americans were descendants of slaves who were brought to the early American colonies, and although they had been emancipated from slavery, they were forced to live under strict and often brutal segregation laws that left them mired in poverty and subject to racial prejudice and violence. Under these conditions, fitting into society was not a matter of laziness, as Nietzsche's "traveler" observed in the first section of *Schopenhauer as Educator*, but rather of survival. African-Americans were born into a world already permeated by the pernicious concept of race—the mold into which their lives were poured—that categorized them as inferior; a categorization enforced by law and state violence. Unable to see themselves through their own eyes, African-Americans viewed themselves through the eyes of others, adopting the contempt for themselves that others directed at them. Consequently, African-Americans were alienated from themselves, and

---

[3] Sigmund Freud, "Repression" (1915) in *The Complete Psychological Works of Sigmund Freud*, Vol. XIV, trans. James Strachey (London: The Hogarth Press, 1981), 154, 157.
[4] W. E. B. Du Bois, *The Souls of Black Folk* (New Haven: Yale University Press, 2015), 5.

yet they continued to hear the call to "Be yourself!," echoing in the conflicting voices within them, and, as Du Bois knew, answering this call would lead to their liberation.

Society, Nietzsche claimed, wants us to conform to its standards; society demands that we be "normal" and suppress our differences, our uniqueness. However, as Nietzsche reminds us, we have a natural desire within us to become who we are, and until we answer this call, we will never be happy (*UO* III.1, 172). In our will, instincts, and desires, we know who and what we are, and we know that we can only be free if we live in way that is consistent with these natural impulses. Nevertheless, Nietzsche claims that most of us choose to conceal who we are out of fear—we lock our uniqueness away in a dungeon and choose to live as slaves to social norms. Still, like all desires that are repressed, they return in other symptoms that can make our lives miserable. Until you know who you are and begin to live authentically, Nietzsche claims, you will never be happy. So, who and what are we? It might seem strange for a philosopher to ask such a question, given philosophy's preoccupation with the intellectual life, but for Nietzsche, the philosopher is primarily a *psychologist* not an intellectual. So, he begins this essay by examining our symptoms—our misery and conformity—and traces them back to the neurosis that produces them: our fear of others.

In contrast to Plato, who was a philosopher of identity, Nietzsche was a philosopher of *difference*. Instead of conceiving reality in terms of being—a static and unchanging reality—Nietzsche conceived reality in terms of becoming. What is real is *life*, the natural and vital power that is constantly unfolding in nature and in us; it is a dynamic process of becoming. *What* we are is a complex of natural drives that are seeking to express themselves, and *who* we are is the unique and creative expression of those drives in our lives. In *The Birth of Tragedy*, Nietzsche described two fundamental drives in nature, which he named after the Greek gods Apollo and Dionysus. The *Apollonian* drive seeks to establish an identity within strict limits, like the columns of an ancient Greek temple. Nietzsche equates this drive with the experience of dreaming, because it seeks to create the appearance of order out of the chaos of our experience.[5] Nietzsche's conception of the

---

[5] Friedrich Nietzsche, *The Birth of Tragedy* (*BT*), trans. Douglas Smith (New York: Oxford University Press, 2000), *BT* I.4, 30.

Apollonian drive recasts Kant's pure concepts of the understanding as a psychological principle. Just as the concepts of the understanding organize our experience, the Apollonian drive strives to bring order to the chaos within us. In contrast, the *Dionysian* drive seeks to unleash difference by shattering all limitations, transgressing all boundaries, like a mighty river overflowing its banks. Nietzsche equates this drive with the experience of intoxication—Dionysus was, after all, the god of wine and dance (*BT*, I.3, 24). With this drive Nietzsche converts Kant's intuitions into a psychological principle. Just as the intuitions are the unorganized appearances of the multiplicity of our sensory experience, the Dionysian drive is the torrent of desire within us.

The two drives represent the psychological principles of order and chaos within us, and according to Nietzsche they are locked in a primordial struggle. Freud, who was likely influenced by Nietzsche, had a similar conception of these principles of order and chaos in what he conceived of as two aspects of our personality (ego), the *Superego* (Apollo) and the *Id* (Dionysus). For Freud, the Superego was the repository of social and parental norms that functioned to keep our wild and lawless Id in check, producing an ego torn between passionate urges and social constraints.[6] When Nietzsche says that most people conceal who they are, he is saying that we repress our Dionysian drive in favor of the Apollonian drive; in Freudian terms, we allow the Superego to dominate the Id.

You might think that Nietzsche would conceive the authentic life as the free expression of the Dionysian drive and the destruction of the Apollonian drive, but this was not what he recommended. Instead, he argued that the two drives must be held together in a creative dissonance, like opposing notes in a musical chord. We are, he argued, the composers of our lives—we must treat our lives as works of art. Artists, Nietzsche would have us understand, reject the common, mass-produced identities that society seeks to impress upon them, as if their lives were like warm wax ready to receive a form. Instead we give form to our own lives. Most people, Nietzsche writes, live passive lives and allow themselves to be created by forces

---

[6] Sigmund Freud, *The Ego and the Id*, in *The Complete Psychological Works of Sigmund Freud*, vol. XIX, trans. James Strachey (London: The Hogarth Press, 1986), 25, 34.

outside themselves—life circumstances, family influences, religious traditions, political forces, cultural trends, etc. Others try to imitate those they admire, but in doing so they end up living someone else's life and never their own. He called those who live passive lives like this "pseudo-human beings" (*UO* III.1, 172). To be the artist of one's life one must find the courage to live according to one's own unique nature—to walk one's own path: "No one can build for you the bridge upon which you alone must cross the stream of life, no one but you alone. To be sure, there are countless paths and bridges and demigods that want to carry you through this stream, but only at the price of your self; you would pawn and lose yourself" (*UO* III.1, 173). The work of creating oneself as a work of art is an individual task; only the artist can give form and direction to the materials of his existence. The temptation for many will be to seek "demigods" to guide them. These are the people we admire and are tempted to imitate. However, if we walk the paths and bridges that others have built for themselves, we will never live *our* lives, we will only live forgeries of *their* lives. Instead of becoming a Johannes Vermeer, we will become a Hans van Meegeren. You can ride someone else's boat down the stream of your life, but the cost of the ticket will be your own self. We must build our own bridges to walk on and become our own guides. But how might we do this? Nietzsche's answer is twofold: *self-knowledge* and *self-education*.

Self-Knowledge

Before we can become the artists of our lives, Nietzsche thought, we need to understand the materials we will be working with; that is, we need to come to know ourselves. Have you ever wondered who you really are? You have probably lived most of your life with some vague knowledge of who you are based upon the variety of roles you occupy: daughter, student, boyfriend, wife, barista, etc. However, Nietzsche would have us understand that these are merely roles we occupy for others; they are not who we truly are. Let's recall that reality for Nietzsche is a dynamic process (becoming) not a static nature (being). *What we are* is a complex of drives—the Apollonian drive toward order and the Dionysian drive toward chaos. *Who we become* will be the result of weaving these dissonant drives together into a unique existence. To "Be yourself!" means to create yourself. Do not be the echo of someone else's music; compose your own!

Nietzsche says that the process of self-discovery involves five steps that allow us to know ourselves through giving expression to the drives within us. The first step in knowing yourself is to liberate yourself from the fear of others and the demands of convention—to "Be yourself!" The second step is to take responsibility for your own life—to build the bridge across the stream of your life that only you can take. The final three steps involve identifying the trajectory of your drives and discovering a horizon of values at which to aim your life.

> **[Step 3]** Let the young soul look back on its life with the question: What have you up to now truly loved, what attracted your soul, what dominated it while simultaneously making it happy? **[Step 4]** Place this series of revered objects before you, and perhaps their nature and their sequence will reveal to you a law, the fundamental law of your authentic self. **[Step 5]** Compare these objects, observe how one completes, expands, surpasses, transfigures the others, how they form a stepladder on which until now you have climbed up to yourself; for your true being does not lie deeply hidden within you, but rather immeasurably high above you, or at least above what you commonly take to be your ego. (*UO* III.1, 174)

The third step involves identifying all the things you have loved over your life. It is important to note that what you have loved is not only what gave you a thrill, but what has captured you in such a way that it mastered you and enhanced or elevated your life. When you are in the grips of something you love, you lose track of time; you are completely entranced by the object of your love. Notice that in this step, Nietzsche is directing you to tap into the Dionysian drive within that expresses your passions. He is asking you to ask yourself "What makes me happy?"—not what *should* make you happy, but what actually makes you happy and elevates your life. Living an authentic life requires that you be faithful to your own unique drives.

The fourth step asks you to examine the things you love and try to identify a pattern or order inherent within them. Here Nietzsche directs you to tap into your Apollonian drive that seeks to organize your passions and give them a lawful order. Imagine, for example, that you love music, justice, and friendship. These things really capture you and elevate your life. Ask yourself what the nature of each one is. What you will discover is that the nature of each of these things is a particular value. The nature of music is order; the nature of justice is equity; the nature of friendship is loyalty. In the final step, Nietzsche asks you to consider how these values that are inherent in what you love fit together and complement each other. Taken together these values represent the trajectory of your unique drives and form a horizon at which you can aim your life. This is why Nietzsche claims that who you are "does not lie deeply hidden within you, but rather immeasurably high above you" (*UO* III.1, 174). Once you know who you are, you can begin the process of self-education.

Self-Education

Nietzsche was a harsh critic of the educational system of his day. In his view, schools had become factories of social conformity; instead of awakening students to who they were and liberating them to live authentic lives, the education system had sedated them with "objective" knowledge and enslaved them to social norms. Nietzsche saw this problem as a symptom of the modern quest for certainty that Descartes had inaugurated, and he was determined to show that this quest was futile. The point of education is not to fill a student's head with "objective knowledge" like a museum filled with artifacts of the past; education is *for life*—it is a way of "coming to oneself out of the stupor in which we usually float as in a dark cloud" (*UO* III.1, 175). Education must emancipate us from convention and introduce us to ourselves, so that we can create ourselves like works of art. However, Nietzsche did not think that this kind of education was on offer in any of the modern schools or universities. Instead, he recommended that we take on the responsibility of self-education and make use of exemplary individuals as our true educators.

Nietzsche thought one should study models of genius and human greatness in order to inspire human greatness in oneself. For him, exemplary individuals like Julius Caesar, William Shakespeare, Johann Wolfgang von Goethe, Napoleon Bonaparte, Ludwig van Beethoven, and Arthur Schopenhauer, revealed human possibilities in their lives.

He thought that if one availed oneself of these models, one could liberate oneself and live a flourishing human life. Nevertheless, self-education is not a process of imitating great human beings; that would amount to walking someone else's bridge instead of building one's own. Self-education means taking responsibility for one's own liberation and using exemplary individuals as models for how to wake up to oneself and transform the mediocrity of one's life into something excellent. Nietzsche found his own model in the philosopher Arthur Schopenhauer.

Three exemplary qualities of an authentic life

Everyone who studies philosophy eventually stumbles on an author or a book that seems to speak directly to him or her. This experience has the effect of jolting one out of the stupor they have been living in and showing them a new way to think and live. A genuine philosopher will introduce you to yourself not them. This was Nietzsche's experience upon reading Arthur Schopenhauer for the first time when he was twenty-one years old:

> I am among those readers of Schopenhauer's who after having read the first page, know with certainty that they will read every page and pay attention to every word he has ever uttered. My faith in him appeared immediately, and today it is just as complete as it was nine years ago. To express it in a comprehensible, if yet immodest and foolish manner: I understood him as though he had written expressly for me. (*UO* III.2, 179)

Nietzsche discovered three exemplary qualities in Schopenhauer he wanted to cultivate in his own life. The first was *sincerity* or *honesty*. Schopenhauer never wanted to appear to be more than he was; in fact, Schopenhauer was not concerned at all with how he appeared to others—he was only concerned with living honestly and authentically. As Nietzsche puts it, Schopenhauer's fundamental maxim was "Never deceive anyone, not even yourself!" (*UO* III.2, 180). To live sincerely requires courage because it summons one to face up to one's strengths and weaknesses; a sincere person knows what they are capable of and what they are not, and they are unconcerned with how they are perceived by others. Schopenhauer did not care if people thought he was a great writer or philosopher; what mattered was what he thought of himself. He gave the measure of greatness to himself rather than deriving it from others. This is an important trait for the philosopher. To pursue the truth of reality, one must first pursue the truth about oneself.

The second quality that Nietzsche discovered in Schopenhauer was *cheerfulness*. Nietzsche distinguished between two kinds of cheerfulness. One is simply a shallow pleasantness that is in denial of the sufferings and dangers of life. This is the kind of cheerfulness depicted in the film *Pleasantville* (New Line Cinema, 1998), in which the characters become trapped in the town of a 1950s sitcom where everything is wholesome and nothing bad ever happens, so everyone smiles in an overly sentimental way. The other kind of cheerfulness, which Nietzsche admired in Schopenhauer, is a state of happiness that can only arise from overcoming great suffering and danger. Nietzsche viewed Schopenhauer like a "victorious god amid all the monsters that he has conquered" (*UO* III.2, 182). Schopenhauer had argued that the essence of a human being is the will that is constantly striving to acquire what it lacks, which means human existence is plagued by pain and suffering that results from not having enough of what it wants. We constantly want what we do not have, and when we get what we want, we discover it does not last, and then want more. Life, Schopenhauer wrote, "swings like a pendulum, back and forth, between pain and boredom."[7] The remedy for this pain and suffering is to extinguish the will—to realize we will never have enough of what we want, and it is precisely our will to have it that causes us to suffer. Once we stop expecting life to be other than it is—an existence full of pain and suffering—we suddenly experience a great contentment and inner tranquility, like a god who has triumphed over a monster, because, as Nietzsche understood, "there is cheerfulness only where there is victory" (*UO* III.2, 182).

The final quality that Nietzsche admired in Schopenhauer was *constancy*. Schopenhauer did not waver in his commitment to live

---

[7] Arthur Schopenhauer, *The World as Will and Representation I*, trans. Judith Norman, Alistair Welchman, and Christopher Janaway (New York: Cambridge University Press, 2014), §57.

consistently with his insights into the reality of human existence. As Nietzsche puts it, Schopenhauer was steadfast in his commitments because he "cannot be otherwise" (*UO* III.2, 183). Nietzsche describes Schopenhauer as a runner driven by gravity, by which he means to indicate that Schopenhauer lived according to his natural drives, and in so doing achieved a natural and uninhibited freedom (*UO* III.2, 183). Once Schopenhauer understood who and what he was, he could not be anyone or anything else—he acquired an inner integrity that he took as the measure of his life. However, living in this way has its dangers.

The dangers of an authentic life

Living an authentic life sets one immediately in opposition to social norms and in violation of the demand to conform. The truth of one's existence—the singularity of one's being—is frightening for most people to witness, Nietzsche argues, because it is disorderly, it breaks with the common social order. Living such a singular life can result in one's exclusion from the mainstream of social life; one can easily become marginalized as an outsider. Nietzsche calls this kind of life "unfashionable," and he sees it exhibited only rarely, in those who possess an "iron nature" like Beethoven, Goethe, and Schopenhauer, all of whom lived bold and honest lives that put them at odds with the standards of their day. However, living authentically requires an inner strength to endure the solitude of such a life. Those who fail to endure this solitude experience the first of three dangers: *loneliness* (*UO* III.3, 186). Philosophers can escape the conformity of the world into their own inner freedom, but this freedom requires strength to bear it. The lonely philosopher is free when he takes refuge in his solitude, but he is also cut off from the world, and when he reappears in the world, he seems to others to be a monstrous figure because the things he says and does are so at odds with common beliefs and practices. This can leave the philosopher with few friends; the task for the one who lives authentically is to find a group of companions with whom one can be oneself.

The second danger of living authentically is that one might *despair of the truth*. The more one knows, the more one realizes how much one doesn't know; and the more one realizes how much one doesn't know, the more one begins to see the impossibility of ever knowing the truth of reality, which can lead to what Nietzsche calls a "corrosive and disintegrating skepticism and relativism" (*UO* III.3, 188). Skepticism gives up on truth by denying the possibility of knowledge, while relativism gives up on truth by making knowledge dependent on the individual knower's perception, so that everything becomes true, and therefore nothing is true. Nietzsche claimed that Kant's philosophy leads inevitably to skepticism and relativism because it denies that we can know the essential nature of anything (skepticism) and restricts our knowledge to appearances (relativism). Schopenhauer's first book, *On the Fourfold Root of the Principle of Sufficient Reason*, tried to overcome this problem in Kant's theory of knowledge by arguing on the basis of the *principle of sufficient reason*—everything must have a reason that explains its existence—that the will of the knowing subject and the representation of an object in the world are two sides of the same coin. For Schopenhauer, the unknowable thing-in-itself does not produce sensations in the body of the knowing subject, as Kant had argued (skepticism), nor does the subject construct a representation of the unknowable thing-in-itself (relativism). Instead, the subject (will) and object (representation) are two aspects of a single reality. Nietzsche saw that Schopenhauer's philosophy was like a ship moving through a narrow passage between two cliffs (skepticism and relativism) and thereby avoided the second danger.

The final danger one must face when living an authentic life is the possibility of *being ruined by the desire for greatness or genius*. To understand this danger we must remember that greatness for Nietzsche results from the creative tension between the two drives within us—the Apollonian drive toward order and the Dionysian drive toward disorder. There is always a danger that one will give in to one or the other drive. Giving in to the Dionysian drive could result in one going completely mad. As Nietzsche writes, anyone who "gives free rein to his talent" might "perish as a human being and merely live a ghostly existence in the realm of 'pure knowledge'" (*UO* III.3, 192). But giving in to the Apollonian drive is equally as dangerous because it results in a "moral or intellectual hardening ... The uniqueness of his being has become an unpartable, unimpartable atom, a cold stone" (*UO* III.3, 192). Like a volcano that erupts with hot lava that then cools into hard rock, the one who seeks to live a great and unique life can succumb to *being* great instead of continuing to *become* great. Schopenhauer did not fall victim to any of these dangers, and for this reason he can serve, Nietzsche writes, as a model for how to live an authentic life. Notice that Nietzsche is not recommending that we *imitate* the *content* of Schopenhauer's life, but rather that we *appropriate* the *form* of his life. The person who chooses to live an authentic life like Schopenhauer must refuse to conform to the demands of society and instead affirm the truth of her own existence.

Summary

Nietzsche understood philosophy as a practical endeavor for living an authentic life that required self-knowledge, self-education, and self-creation. He claimed that we come to know ourselves by liberating ourselves from the fear of others and identifying our deepest drives and the values they entail. These values provide a horizon at which to aim our lives. However, Nietzsche thought we needed exemplary guides to help us along the path to self-knowledge. These are our true educators who liberate us for self-education and self-creation. Arthur Schopenhauer was Nietzsche's true educator, and he admired the sincerity, cheerfulness, and constancy that Schopenhauer acquired by overcoming the dangers of loneliness, skepticism, and being ruined by his own genius. Schopenhauer offered Nietzsche a model for living authentically.

Questions

1. Does Nietzsche think there is a stable and unchanging self?
2. How can we know if we are living an authentic life, according to Nietzsche?
3. What are the ethical implications of Nietzsche's philosophy of life?

10

Nietzsche: The Creative Life
(*Schopenhauer as Educator*, 4–6)

> **Key terms**
>
> Culture – the archive of human excellence and creativity
> Egoism – an ethical position that seeks to maximize one's self-interests
> Cultural Duty – the duty to perfect nature in ourselves and contribute to culture
> Creative Spirits – free individuals who create their own values

If there is one question that Nietzsche was preoccupied with in *Schopenhauer as Educator*, it is the question of the value of human existence: "How can your life, the life of the individual, obtain the highest value, the deepest significance? How is it least wasted?" (*UO* III.6, 216). How can we live so as not to waste our life? This is an important question, and to ask it is to ask what makes life worth living—what is the purpose of a human life? Nietzsche thought he had discovered the answer in the life of Schopenhauer, who lived "for the benefit of the rarest and most valuable specimens" (*UO* III.6, 216). The purpose of self-knowledge, self-education, and self-creation is to become an exemplary individual and contribute to a culture that can produce other exemplary individuals. For Nietzsche, culture and identity are not mutually exclusive; they are interdependent. The whole point of living more authentically is to make a creative contribution to the world around us, that in turn makes it possible for us to become who we are.

It might seem that Nietzsche's emphasis on non-conformity and his advocacy for an uncompromising individualism is deeply anti-social.

If, as Nietzsche has argued, living an authentic life requires liberation from social conformity through self-knowledge, self-education, and self-creation, this would seem to require a withdrawal from the world and society. After all, one of the dangers that one must face in living authentically is loneliness. This, however, was, not Nietzsche's intention. What he saw in Schopenhauer's exemplary life was the possibility of redeeming human nature from the social forces that would seek to domesticate it, and perfecting it through a creative act of the will to create a culture that fostered and supported human freedom and flourishing. The point was not to withdraw from society but to recreate it within a new kind of *culture*—a culture that could produce more exemplary individuals like Schopenhauer. For Nietzsche culture was both the product of exemplary human achievement and the source of exemplary individuals. We are conditioned by our culture, and in turn we condition the cultures we live in. Culture can be humanizing or dehumanizing; it can foster human freedom and flourishing or diminish them. Nietzsche saw modern culture as dehumanizing, and he discovered in the life of Schopenhauer a way to transform it into something higher. The agents of this kind of transformation have always been *creative spirits* like philosophers, artists, and saints—individuals who overcame the desire to conform and acted against the current of their times in order to fashion themselves into a new work of art that inspired others to do the same. But what is the process for developing such a creative spirit?

Modern culture is dehumanizing

The modern world of the nineteenth century appeared to many as the dawn of a new age of progress for humanity. Modern science had expanded our knowledge of the material universe and the evolution of the human species, and made it possible to traverse the earth in ships, trains, and eventually automobiles, and to discover new lands and people. The American and French revolutions had liberated human beings from political tyranny, granted them inalienable rights, and ushered in an age of freedom and equality. Additionally, technological innovations like the steam engine and the factory system fostered an industrial revolution that accelerated capitalist economies across Europe, creating immense wealth and prosperity. However, for Nietzsche, modernity was not an age of progress; it was an age of decline. Instead of producing better human beings, it was producing human beings who were fearful, lazy, submissive, and complacent. Modern science had stripped humanity of its illusions about an orderly and meaningful universe and confronted it with a meaningless and contingent universe. In "The Parable of a Madman," Nietzsche describes this experience as a kind of disorientation that results from the horizon of transcendent ideas and values like God, goodness, beauty, and truth being wiped away by reason and science.[1] Without a unifying ideal to impose order on the chaos of a contingent universe, modern human beings were confronted with a terrifying and meaningless existence. This existential fear led most to seek comfort in consumption and safety in conformity. The widespread materialism that modern wealth made possible had turned human beings into ravenous consumers habitually engaged in trying to escape their fears through the satisfaction of an array of desires that the tempting products of commercial markets produced in them. Additionally, the modern state sought to provide stability and safety through law and education, creating human beings who were obedient and conventional. The result of the modern age was a human being driven by fear and greed to maximize his own self-interests. Instead of liberating human beings, modernity had created a new breed of dehumanized slaves who sought comfort and conformity rather than excellence. For Nietzsche, the remedy for this modern sickness was a new kind of culture that aimed at human greatness, and only exemplary individuals like Schopenhauer could produce it.

When you hear the word *culture*, you might immediately think of things like traditions, foods, language, or religion—the things that locate someone in a particular group. However, Nietzsche meant something different. Culture, from the Latin word *colere*, which means "to tend, guard, or cultivate," is the result of a process of overcoming one's animalistic nature through self-cultivation in order to realize one's freedom and produce work that is excellent and valuable—culture is the result of a transformation of the animal, which is driven by "blind instinct" and necessity, into a human being who is free to create (*UO* III.6, 216). But how does this transformation happen?

---

[1] Friedrich Nietzsche, *The Gay Science: With a Prelude in Rhymes and an Appendix of Songs*, trans. Walter Kaufmann (New York: Random House, 1974), III.125, 181–2.

How to become a child

Nietzsche described this process of transformation in what was arguably his most important work, *Thus Spoke Zarathustra*. In the first book of that work, he described the psychological evolution of an authentic human being through the metaphorical transformations of a camel into a lion and a lion into a child. The camel, a load-bearing animal, represents the beginning of our life when we are loaded down with the burdens of traditions, values, lessons, and practices that others place on us. During this phase of our life, we are all students, learning the ropes, and gaining strength and endurance under the loads placed on us. However, everyone eventually reaches a stage in their life when the burdens become too much to bear, and they refuse to live by the rules and values of others. This is the transformation of the camel into the lion. During this stage we rebel against everything in order to become the masters of our own lives; we seize our freedom from the hands of the masters who have burdened us with their values. As Nietzsche puts it, the lion declares "I will" and defies every "Thou shalt!"[2] However, no one can live as a rebel forever; the repudiation of every value leaves a person without any sense of what is important and valuable. But if we cannot rely on the traditions of the past for our values, where shall we find them? Nietzsche argued that we must create our own values to live by, and this requires a further transformation from a lion into a child. Children represent pure creativity; they possess unrestricted imaginations that open them to new possibilities. The child, Nietzsche wrote, "is a forgetting, a beginning anew, a play, a self-propelling wheel, a first movement, a sacred Yea-saying" (*TZ*, I.1, 24). The child is free from the burden of tradition and the tyranny of moral values; the child is free to create its own values and affirm its own life. This is the goal of the process of self-knowledge and self-education: to become a creative spirit. How does one become a creative spirit? Nietzsche tells us that "The marvelous, creative human being is supposed to answer the question: 'Do *you* affirm your existence from the bottom of your heart? Are you willing to be its advocate, its savior? For all it takes is one single truthful "Yes!" from your mouth—and life,

---

[2] Friedrich Nietzsche, *Thus Spoke Zarathustra: A Book for Everyone and Nobody* (*TZ*), trans. Graham Parkes (New York: Oxford University Press, 2005), I.1, 23–4.

now facing such grave accusations, will be set free'" (*UO* III.3, 195). To affirm one's existence is to reclaim ownership of one's life from an age of "atomized chaos" that shapes us into egoistic consumers, to face one's mortality honestly and courageously, and to cease living in a passive way that allows external forces and influences to determine one's life—the creative spirit is a "self-propelled wheel" (*UO* III.4, 199). These are the conditions of human freedom, according to Nietzsche.

Modern culture is egoistic and tyrannical

It may seem strange that the philosopher who declared the death of God would lament the decline of Christianity in the Middle Ages, but Nietzsche understood that during that period the Catholic Church had synthesized the Apollonian and Dionysian drives of human life into a harmonious theological order, providing a divine ideal for human beings to organize their lives around. Its stories, rituals, doctrines, and values organized the chaos of human passions into an image of divine order within which human beings could understand themselves. However, according to Nietzsche, when the Protestant Reformation emancipated itself from the authority of the Catholic Church, it shattered this order, and the opposing cultural manifestations of the Apollonian and Dionysian forces were unleashed (*UO* III.4, 199). With the rise of modern science, the religious image of man began to lose its hold on the minds of human beings, leaving the modern human being "determined by the crudest and most evil forces": *egoism* and *despotism* (*UO* III.4, 200).

To become a free, creative spirit, we have to "educate ourselves against our age," as Schopenhauer did, and this requires that we resist the attempts of the modern market and the modern state to impose their image of humanity upon us. The image of the market is the egoistic consumer, and the image of the state is the obedient citizen. To understand how commercial markets shape us into egoistic consumers, consider the contemporary example of online shopping. When you search for an item in a search engine, an algorithm stores that search as an individual consumer interest, which is then sold to businesses who begin targeting you with advertising tailored to your specific interests. Advertisers know that a consumer has to encounter a product frequently and consistently before they decide to purchase it, and so they serve up pop-up ads, discount codes, direct mailers, product placements, and commercials to influence consumers to purchase their products. The algorithms are so quick and comprehensive that whenever you log on to the Internet, your identity as a consumer has already been formulated, and the more you engage with these digital networks, the more you come to understand yourself through this online identity. Nietzsche saw the dangers of the egoistic drives of the modern market economy. The speed of the market destroys the tranquility of the human spirit and replaces it with a kind of frenzied madness—the human being becomes a slave to its desires instead of their master. But there is another danger: the state. For Nietzsche the modern nation-state had taken the place of the medieval Church: "the state wants people to worship in it the very same idols they previously worshipped in the church" (*UO* III.4, 200). The state seeks to organize the chaotic passion of humanity into an obedient and docile citizenry. Against these images of the egoistic consumer and the obedient citizen, modern creative spirits offered three alternatives in an attempt to "spur mortals on to a transfiguration of their own lives" (*UO* III.4, 201).

Three images of creative spirits

One modern image of humanity was the *contemplative image* exemplified in the life of the poet and philosopher, Johann Wolfgang von Goethe. The Goethean human being is like the camel of Zarathustra's "Three Metamorphoses"; he moves through life gathering the wisdom of the ages and seeks in it a unifying ideal by which to organize the chaos within him. The Goethean human being seeks order through contemplation and therefore is an expression of the Apollonian drive. The second alternative was the *revolutionary image* of the philosopher Jean-Jacques Rousseau, who sought inspire human beings to emancipate themselves from tyranny through violent revolution. The Rousseauian human being is like the lion of the "Three Metamorphoses"; he challenges the existing order and seeks freedom by any means necessary. The Rousseauian human being seeks freedom through disruptive action and therefore represents the Dionysian drive. The final modern image of humanity was the *redemptive image* of Arthur Schopenhauer. Nietzsche wrote that "The Schopenhauerian human being voluntarily takes upon himself the suffering inherent in truthfulness, and this suffering serves to extinguish his individual will and to prepare the way for that complete revolution and reversal in his being whose achievement is the true meaning of life" (*UO* III.4, 203). The Schopenhauerian human being is a creative synthesis of the Goethean and Rousseauian images, and therefore represents the child of the "Three Metamorphoses." The Schopenhauerian human being seeks a principle of order by which to organize his life like the Goethean human being, and acts against the conventional forces of his age like the Rousseauian human being, but he also moves beyond both in a joyful tranquility to create a new world and new values. It is precisely this image of humanity that Nietzsche recommends as the model for living an authentic life in the modern world. The Schopenhauerian image is an ideal that is capable of educating us, Nietzsche writes. It is not that we should imitate Schopenhauer by learning German, growing sideburns, dressing like him, and adopting a pessimistic worldview; rather, we should learn from his way of life—make use of him as ideal for living a freer, more creative, and more truthful life. So, what would that kind of life look like? What would be its meaning or purpose?

The meaning of life is to contribute to culture

Schopenhauer represents a human ideal that can serve as a model for living authentically, but his life also reveals "a new set of duties" that can give our lives purpose and meaning (*UO* III.5, 207):

> One thing, above all, is certain: those new duties are not the duties of a solitary individual; on the contrary, through them one is integrated into a powerful community, one that to be sure is not held together by external forms and laws, but by a fundamental idea. This is the fundamental idea of *culture*, insofar as it is capable of charging each of us with one single task: to foster the production of philosophers, artists, and saints within us and around us, and thereby to work toward the perfection of nature. (*UO* III.5, 213)

It is the duty of creative spirits "to work toward the perfection of nature" in themselves and in the works they produce. Indeed, Nietzsche would say that every individual is obligated by nature and by future generations to realize humanity's highest potential in works of genius. What is most important to note in this passage is the interdependence of the individual and the community. In order for any individual to become what they are through self-knowledge and self-education, they must make use of culture. For example, it was through Schopenhauer's writings that Nietzsche discovered his model for an authentic human life—Nietzsche never met or studied with Schopenhauer—and these writings were cultural products. Culture is the archive of humanity's highest achievements in art, philosophy, and religion. Consequently, it generates artists, philosophers, and saints. Culture, you might say, is the soil of human greatness. Individuals are shaped by culture, and through their work they create culture that then shapes others.

The American novelist and essayist, James Baldwin, exemplifies the duty of creative spirits that Nietzsche describes. In his essay "The Creative Process" he described the duty of the artist as twofold: to conquer himself and to illuminate the world.

> But the conquest of the physical world is not man's only duty. He is also enjoined to conquer the great wilderness of himself. The precise role of the artist, then, is to illuminate that darkness, blaze roads through that vast forest, so that we will not, in all our doing, lose sight of its purpose, which is, after all, to make the world a more human dwelling place.[3]

For Baldwin, like Nietzsche, the artist must perfect his nature by overcoming his animality that is driven by instinct and governed by external forces ("the great wilderness of himself"), but he must do so in order to become free to contribute to the perfection of nature in culture ("to make the world a more human dwelling place"). In making his contributions to culture, the artist, like the philosopher and the saint, tells the truth about reality and how we have failed to live in accordance with it. As Baldwin put it, the artist tries to "correct the delusions to which we fall prey in our attempts to avoid this knowledge."[4] The exemplary works of the artist tell the truth about human potential—

---

[3] James Baldwin, "The Creative Process," in *The Price of the Ticket: Collected Nonfiction: 1948–1985* (New York: St. Martin's Press, 1985), 315.
[4] Ibid., 316

they show us what we can become, which is always more than we think we are. It is only in creating exemplary works, Nietzsche tells us, that our lives can have value (UO III.6, 216). For Nietzsche, a human life can only have value if it is lived for exemplary ends, namely the realization of the human potential in culture. The most exemplary models for this kind of life are artists, philosophers, and saints (UO III.5, 213). But wait a minute! Nietzsche is beginning to sound very elitist. Artists, philosophers, and saints are quite rare. Is he arguing that only a hand full of lives can have value? What about the rest of us?

The two sacraments of culture

One way of reading Nietzsche is as an *aristocrat* who thinks human beings are not created equal—some people are born to be great, but most people are common and average. Another way of reading him is as an *egalitarian* who thinks everyone is equally great. Both readings miss an important nuance in Nietzsche's thinking: he thinks that everyone is capable of greatness, but few have the strength to realize this potential. As he stated at the beginning of the essay, most people are lazy—they take the path of least resistance and conform to the demands and values of others (UO III.1, 171). In order to fully realize one's potential, Nietzsche argues, one must receive two *sacraments of culture*: faith in culture and the creation of culture. The *first sacrament* is internal and requires a self-knowledge sufficient to recognize one's deficiencies, "being ashamed of oneself without distress, hatred of one's shriveled narrowness," which provokes one to overcome these deficiencies in order to realize something "loftier and more human" than one is. When we encounter a great work of art—a piece of music or a painting—we recognize the great skill, insight, or power that it took to create it, and likely, our own lack of such skill, insight, or power. Works of genius reveal how we have not realized our full potential. Faith in culture delivers us from mediocrity and opens up a horizon of greatness and genius at which we can aim our life, for who we are is immeasurably high above us (UO III.1, 174). The second sacrament of culture is external; it is an inversion of the inward activities of self-knowledge and self-education into cultural production: creating exemplary cultural works. Our internal vision of humanity's highest potential must be realized in external works of art, music, literature, theater, and philosophy; the creative spirit must answer the call of nature that cries out, "Come! Help us! Complete us! Put together what belongs together! We have an immeasurable longing to become whole!" (*UO* III.6, 217). The creative spirit must "make the world a more human dwelling place," as Baldwin put it.

Beware of the four enemies of culture

The creative spirit will inevitably encounter impediments in their attempt to fulfill their cultural duties by overcoming their animality and realizing their human potential. Nietzsche describes these impediments as forms of escape from taking ownership of our own lives. As he puts it, "we hasten to sell our soul to the state, to moneymaking, to social life, or to scholarship just so we will no longer possess it" (*UO* III.5, 210). Living authentically is difficult because, even though everyone is capable of it, most lack the courage to resist the forces of conformity and convention. There are also powers that seek to exploit culture for their own selfish ends; these are the four enemies of culture—the *market*, the *state*, *society*, and *scholarship*—and they present a unique challenge that must be overcome. Each of these enemies promotes culture while undermining its ultimate goal: the production of exemplary and authentic individuals.

The first enemy is the modern *market* economy, which views culture as a commodity to be bought and sold, and consequently seeks to "dictate the goal and standards of culture" (*UO* III.6, 218). Consider how the pop music industry produces only the music that the public wants. The music that tops the charts does not necessarily represent exemplary musical talent but merely the music that has generated the highest sales. Pop music is simply an expression of mass desire. The market is driven by an egoistic desire to increase profits rather than realize human potential.

The second enemy of culture is the modern *state*, which views culture as a tool for extending its power and control. It puts exemplary individuals in the service of political power. Nietzsche uses Christianity as an example of how state power coopts cultural power.

> Christianity is certainly one of the purest manifestations of that drive for culture, and especially of that drive for the ever-renewed

production of the saint, but since it was used in a hundred ways to drive the mills of state power, it gradually became sick to the very marrow, hypocritical and dishonest, until it degenerated to the point of standing in contradiction to its original goal. (*UO* III.6, 220)

Nietzsche understood the power of Christianity to lie in its drive to overcome the animal nature in order to produce an exemplary human being—the saint. When this drive is redirected by state power to produce stable and obedient citizens, it loses its ability to produce saints.

The third enemy of culture is modern *society*, which views culture as a performance before an audience of one's peers. Instead of answering the call of one's conscience to "Be yourself!," one answers the call of society to "Impress us!" As Nietzsche writes, "culture is demanded by all those who are conscious of an ugly or boring content and who want to disguise it behind what is called 'beautiful form'" (*UO* III.6, 220). Instead of cultivating the content of our character, we adopt a form that will impress others. Society demands that we never be boring or ugly—that we always conform to the current standards of beauty and interest. Consider the way that fashion and cosmetic surgery function to conceal our flaws behind masks of cotton and collagen, or how we represent our boring lives as endlessly exciting on social media platforms. In society, we no longer seek to be great, only to appear great.

The final enemy of culture is modern *scholarship*, which views culture as an object of intellectual analysis, and converts seekers of wisdom into seekers of truth. The scholar is driven "to discover *certain* 'truths,' motivated by his servility to certain ruling people, classes, opinions, churches, or governments, since he senses that he will profit from placing 'truth' on their side" (*UO* III.6, 225). Scholarship drains the life out of culture and the scholars who analyze it—they become mummies instead of human beings, according to Nietzsche. Whereas Schopenhauer sought wisdom *in* his suffering, scholars seek truth *without* suffering (*UO* III.6, 225). The "certain truths" of scholarship are nothing more than solutions to problems. For Nietzsche, there is no love or passion in the scholars; they are merely servants of truth who hate philosophy—the passionate pursuit of wisdom (*UO* III.6, 225).

The one who chooses to live authentically must cultivate their own genius without allowing these enemies of culture to destroy it.

Schopenhauer's life provides a model for how to resist the antagonistic forces of the market, the state, society, and scholarship, but as Nietzsche reminds us, "Schopenhauer as educator must actually *educate*" (*UO* III.6, 234). We must allow the ideal of Schopenhauer to liberate us so that we can realize our own potential. This leads us to an important point: the study of philosophy can put us in contact with exemplary individuals who can show us why and how to live more authentically. If the theoretical aim of philosophy is to liberate us from our delusions, then the practical aim of philosophy is to emancipate us from inauthenticity, so that we can become who we truly are.

Summary

Nietzsche was chiefly concerned with the question of how our lives can obtain the highest value. The answer he discovers through his encounter with Schopenhauer is that our lives have value when they are devoted to a form of culture that seeks to produce exemplary individuals. Modern society, which is driven by egoism and despotism, dehumanizes us through the market, the state, and society, but Nietzsche argues that we can resist these dehumanizing forces by becoming creative spirits who fashion themselves into exemplary individuals like works of art and live according to their own values. In fact, we have a duty to realize our highest potential and translate that potential into exemplary contributions to culture. Schopenhauer serves as a model for this kind of life.

Questions

1. If our lives are largely the product of the cultures we inhabit, how can we transform ourselves or culture?
2. Is Nietzsche an elitist thinker?
3. Nietzsche sees a conflict between culture and politics. Is he right?

11

Arendt: Think What We are Doing!
("Labor, Work, Action")

Key terms

Communicative Action – the public disclosure of who we are to others through words and deeds
vita activa – the active (political) life
vita contemplativa – the contemplative (philosophical) life
World – the shared network of objects and orientations between human beings
Worldlessness – the modern loss of trust in the shared world

One point should be clear by now: philosophy is not simply a way of thinking; it is a way of living in accordance with what we know to be real. This means our metaphysical conceptions of reality and our epistemological orientations to reality inform our ethical judgments about how we might live our lives. As we have seen, Nietzsche understood reality in terms of becoming, and his ethical imperative was to realize one's potential through creative acts of the will. For Nietzsche, philosophy fosters a *creative* way of life. It helps us understand that, in order to live in accordance with reality, we have to know ourselves and emancipate ourselves from the influences of society, politics, scholarship, and markets in order to create our lives as works of art and devote our lives to culture. This is the path to an authentic life, according to Nietzsche.

Hannah Arendt did not consider herself a philosopher, although she had studied with some of the most significant continental philosophers of the twentieth century: Edmund Husserl, Martin Heidegger, and Karl Jaspers, to name just a few. Instead, she described herself as a *political theorist*. This is an important appellation because it suggests that she understood thinking and action to be interrelated. For Arendt, being a political theorist did not entail the abandonment of thinking in favor of action, or the abandonment of action in favor of thinking, but rather the practice of *political thinking* that aimed at understanding human action, or as she put it in *The Human Condition*, "to think what we are doing."[1] This is what Arendt attempts to do in her lecture, "Labor, Work, Action"; she wants to think about what we do when we act—she wants to theorize our political life in order to restore the dignity it had lost in the modern age. As we will see, the modern turn inward, with its emphasis on individual liberty and private interests, produced human beings who were atomized, alienated, and lonely. This resulted in the loss of a shared public world, which in Arendt's estimation had contributed to the emergence of totalitarian regimes and genocide in the twentieth century. For this reason, she recommended the political way of life as an authentically human way of life. But to understand why Arendt focused on the political life of action, we need to understand what she viewed as the *prejudice of philosophy*.

The prejudice of philosophy and worldlessness

For Arendt, the traditional practice of philosophy as a contemplative way of life—a life devoted to thinking—was disconnected from the world of human activities and had diminished the dignity of the active life of politics and culture. For her, philosophy was an empire of thinking ruled by philosopher kings who sought to subject the political life to the tyranny of reason, robbing it of its dignity. Even her own teacher, Martin Heidegger, had succumbed to this philosophical prejudice, arguing that our everyday life with others in the world was a diminished mode of existence marked by conformity and inauthenticity.[2] Like Nietzsche, Heidegger understood the existential dangers of conforming to the demands and interests of others, and thought

---

[1] Hannah Arendt, *The Human Condition* (*HC*), second edition (Chicago: University of Chicago Press, 1998 rev.), 5.

[2] Martin Heidegger, *Being and Time*, trans. John Macquarrie and Edward Robinson (New York: Harper and Row, 1962), I.5, 220 (176).

that our only hope of an authentic existence was to retreat from our absorption with others in the world. However, as Arendt came to understand, Heidegger's retreat from the world of everyday life into the empire of thinking resulted in the loss of a common world, an experience she called "worldlessness." Arendt thought this experience was characteristic of the modern age, and that it had made human beings vulnerable to the monstrous forces of authoritarianism and totalitarianism in the twentieth century.

Beginning with Descartes' turn inward to the individual thinking substance, modern philosophy had separated thinking from being and self from the world. As we have seen, Hume and Kant both argued that reality as it is in itself (being) is out of reach for the human mind (thinking). Nietzsche was aware of how this separation of thinking and being had led to a world of atomized individuals who lived frenzied lives without a unifying principle to bring order to the chaos of their lives. Nietzsche thought the answer to this modern dilemma was culture and the creation of exemplary individuals, but for Arendt this solution still left human beings alienated from one another and the world. For her, the experience of worldlessness began with philosophy's retreat from the public world of action into the private world of thinking. Like Nietzsche, Heidegger had tried to overcome the separation of thinking and being, but in his turn to thinking he separated thinking (theory) from action (*praxis*). Arendt sought to join them together again. In understanding herself as a political theorist instead of a philosopher, Arendt was seeking to recover the public world and the life of action. The political life—the life of action—cannot be divorced from the life of thinking, according to Arendt; they inform and illuminate one another; they are interrelated.

The recovery of the public world

Instead of loving wisdom, as the philosophers did, Arendt sought to *love the world*—a public network of orientations and objects constituted through human speech and action and held in common by a plurality of unique individuals. Instead of trying to escape Plato's cave into an intelligible realm of ideas that could be imposed on the world, as Plato, Descartes, and Heidegger had done, Arendt proposed a return to the cave of political life, where human beings search for reality together through independent thinking and communicative action. For Arendt, reality was not outside the world, it was immanent in the world human beings build together through their words and deeds that communicate who they are to each other and establish a web of relations that provides a horizon for human action. She thought we could only live authentically human lives when we speak and act with others in a common world. This means that, in contrast Plato's claim in the *Sophist*, being and appearance are one—to be is to appear with others through our speech and action. Whenever we lose our common world, we lose what Arendt called the "web of human relationships"—the immaterial threads of references, orientations, and meanings that emerge from the words of deeds of human beings over time, and that bind us together in a shared world—and so live lives that are inauthentic and inhuman (HC V.25, 183). In *The Human Condition*, Arendt used the metaphor of a table to illustrate how the common world functioned. Like a table that joins and separates individuals the world joins us together as human beings while allowing us to express our unique differences. In the common world of political life, as Arendt envisioned it, our shared humanity (universal) and our individual differences (particular) are preserved and can be recognized through communicative action. When this world is lost, however, we lose the space in which to appear, to speak, and act with others.

Arendt disagreed with Heidegger's claim that the political life is inauthentic; she argued that we live authentically human lives when we communicate who we are through speech and action. This is because whenever we speak and act, we always do so in the company of others, and the words and actions we use are initiated by our thinking and express our unique perspectives (HC V.24, 176). This way of life involves attending to what is given in our immanent experiences with others in the world, withdrawing from these experiences to think about them independently, and then returning to the world to share with others what we have judged to be good, beautiful, or true, and listening to their responses. Arendt developed this approach from Kant's three rules for common understanding, outlined in his *Critique of Judgment*, and applied them to our political life together: We begin by withdrawing from the world we share with others in order to think for ourselves, then use our imaginations to "let our minds go visiting" in order to think from the perspective of others, and then think consistently between our perspective and the perspective of others.[3] This allows us to bring the world into our thinking and our thinking into the world. In this way, the political life is characterized by communicative action, where each person shares their thoughts with others in a back-and-forth exchange, and it is through this speaking and acting with others that we create the common world. Arendt's focus on the political life of action in her lecture "Labor, Work, Action" is an attempt to recover this common world.

The two ways of life

Arendt begins her lecture with what she says is an "odd question": "What do we do when we are active?" (291).[4] It is an odd question because it seems to include its answer and suggests that *doing* and *acting* are the same thing. However, Arendt thought there were important distinctions to be made between the various acts that we do, distinctions that philosophers had overlooked as a result of their prejudice against the political life. For example, there are qualitative differences between taking a shower, making breakfast, writing a poem, and protesting an injustice. Arendt wanted to think about what we do when we are active—to examine the active life that philosophy has left unexamined.

It is important to note that Arendt is assuming a traditional philosophical distinction between the contemplative way of life (*vita contemplativa*) and the active way of life (*vita activa*), which she says existed until the modern age (291). The contemplative way of life was the life of thinking, the way of life pursued by the few, rare individuals who had the leisure to engage in it. This is the life of philosophers and religious mystics, who withdraw from the world of action into the pure and tranquil realm of the mind or spirit. The active way of life was the

---

[3] Immanuel Kant, *Critique of Judgment*, trans. Werner S. Pluhar (Indianapolis: Hackett Publishing, 1987), Ak. V: 294–5.
[4] All quotations and references to Arendt's lecture, "Labor, Work, and Action" in these final two chapters are from Hannah Arendt, "Labor, Work, Action," in *Thinking Without a Bannister: Essays in Understanding, 1953–1975* (New York: Schocken Books, 2018), 291–307. The lecture was given on November 10, 1964 as part of the "Christianity and Economic Man: Moral Decisions in an Affluent Society" conference held at the Divinity School of the University of Chicago.

life of action pursued by the rest of humanity, who had to keep themselves alive, raise families, build a common world, and organize their lives together in a way that made it possible for everyone to flourish and live in peace. This is the life of parents, workers, artists, activists, and politicians. Each of these ways of life, Arendt says, is derived from a collection of human capacities that make up what she called the *human condition*—the collection of capacities for thought and action that allow human beings to condition the world, which, in turn, conditions them. Arendt avoided using the term *human nature* because it suggested that humans have a knowable essence that determines what they are or who they can become. Like Nietzsche, Arendt understood human existence to be characterized by openness, movement, and freedom, and this is reflected in the way she understood the relationship between the two ways of life. Let's take a closer look at Arendt's historical understanding of the active life.

The pre-philosophical view of the active life

When Arendt examined how the active life had been understood historically, she approached the past like a wreckage that we can no longer put back together but from which we can recover parts. So, when she discusses the "pre-philosophic" view of the active life in ancient Greece, prior to the rise of philosophy in general and Plato's philosophy in particular, her aim is not to return to a pre-philosophic life—this is impossible—but to recollect the essential features and meaning of the active life. What Arendt discovered as she surveyed the wreckage were three distinctive activities in the active life that had been overlooked by philosophers: labor, work, and action. She also discovered that these activities had been organized in different hierarchies, and that this organization makes a significant difference in how the active life has been understood. In the pre-philosophic view, the activity of labor occupied the lowest level of the hierarchy, work occupied the next level, and action, which corresponded to the political life, occupied the highest level (293). In her book *The Human Condition*, on which Arendt's lecture is based, she argued that each of these activities arises from a fundamental condition of human life and has a particular aim. Labor is the external expression of *life* itself—it is the biological process that seeks to metabolize nature in order to preserve and maintain the living organism. Work is the external expression of *worldliness*—the impulse to create an artificial and durable world as a shelter from natural forces. Action is the external expression of each individual's unique identity through what they say and do in the world with others. It is a manifestation of the essential characteristic of humanity, plurality—the fact that we are all equally human and distinctly different, giving rise to different perspectives, ideas, and values—and it aims to begin something new (*HC* I.1, 7–8; V.24, 175). These conditions of life, worldliness, and plurality are the sources of our existence between our birth and eventual death, and the active life is what takes place between these two momentous events. Unfortunately, as Arendt points out, the active life was largely neglected in the philosophical tradition. To understand how and why this happened, we need to explore how the active life was understood in ancient and modern history.

The philosophical view: political action as work

Historically, philosophers understood the activities of the active life to be the necessary conditions for the contemplative way of life—contemplation was understood as the end or purpose of action. Though the active life was characterized by "un-quiet" (292), it made the contemplative life possible because in order to achieve the quiet and tranquil atmosphere necessary for thinking, one must labor to stay alive, work to build a shelter from nature, and act to establish a peaceful community. As Arendt points out, we spend the majority of our lives acting, and even if we are able to engage in philosophical thinking or religious contemplation, we can do so only for short periods of time, because everyone has to eat, sleep, do the laundry, work, pay taxes, and vote, etc. As she writes, "no man can remain in the contemplative state throughout his whole life. Active life, in other words, is not only what most men engaged in but even what no man can escape all together" (291). In spite of the importance of the active life, and the contemplative life's dependence on it, philosophers had viewed it with disdain. For them, it was an ignoble means to a noble end—the way of life practiced by the unenlightened herd of humanity.

For ancient philosophers, politics was simply the handmaiden of philosophy—it was tasked with fashioning a stable political community, so that a privileged few who could outsource their labor and work to others could retreat into solitude to think (291). Consequently, the active life derived its meaning from the contemplative life instead of the other way around. Arendt understood that the life of thinking was the primary way of life for philosophers in the ancient world, and hence the active way of life—the ethical and political life of the citizen—was always described by philosophers "from the viewpoint of contemplation" (231). If we think of Plato's conception of the philosopher as a contemplator of the forms, we can see what Arendt means. The philosopher looks at the active life of ethics and politics *from above*—through the lens of the forms—or, using the cave analogy, the philosopher views the shadows on the cave wall from outside the cave. This perspective led philosophers to understand political action as *work*—the activity of making a stable and tranquil world for contemplation.

When Arendt distinguishes between work and action, she is drawing on a distinction made by Aristotle between *poiesis* (making) and *praxis* (action). Aristotle had claimed that each of these activities had distinctive purposes. The purpose of making was to produce a product. For example, when a carpenter makes a table, he aims to produce a table. However, the purpose of action is quite different, according to Aristotle. When we act, the purpose of the action is the action itself—action is an end in itself—and this action reveals who we are. For example, when someone acts courageously, they reveal themselves to be virtuous.[5] With the introduction of contemplation as the highest goal of human life, action ceased being an end in itself and became a means to making a world fit for contemplation. This was the triumph of *homo faber*—man the maker.

As Arendt points out, "Labor, to be sure, remained at the bottom, but political activity as something necessary for the life of contemplation was now recognized only to the extent that it could be pursued in the same way as the activity of the craftsman" (293). Once political action was seen as work—fabrication or making—it could be trusted to produce lasting results: a stable environment for contemplation (293). Plato had argued in his *Republic* that the only way to achieve a peaceful political order was for philosophers to rule. They would act

---

[5] Aristotle, *Nicomachean Ethics*, in *The Complete Works of Aristotle*, trans. J. O. Urmson (New York: Oxford University Press, 1984), VI.2, 1139b.1–4.

as craftsmen, looking at the transcendent forms like blueprints, and making political communities in the image of the forms.[6] Labor was outsourced to others, so that politicians could devote themselves to *making* laws, civic institutions, and educational systems to create a harmonious and peaceful society. The problem Arendt saw with this approach to political life was that the logic of work and action are entirely different. Work is a productive activity that aims at making a stable and peaceful community in the image of the forms. However, action is an endless and unpredictable activity—it is an ongoing process of initiating new beginnings (305–6). By understanding action as work, philosophers sought to bring order and stability to the political life of humanity—to put an end to the constant change and chaos of cave life. But, in doing so, philosophers put an end to the new beginnings that emerge when human beings come together to share points of view and opinions and to act in concert with one another. This philosophical subordination of the active life did not change with the rise of Christianity either. Despite its practical emphasis on loving one's neighbor, Christianity still posited an afterlife where the soul could achieve union with God. Instead of affirming the dignity and relevance of the active life of service to one's neighbor, Arendt argues, Christianity reaffirmed the superiority of the contemplative life—loving one's neighbor as a *means* of loving God (292). So, the active life for both philosophy and religion, until the modern age, was treated as a mere means to a contemplative end.

The problem Arendt saw with the philosophical and religious views of the relationship between the active and contemplative ways of life was that in posing contemplation as the highest aim of human life and action as the means of achieving that aim, the active life was reduced to insignificance. There is an important principle at work in Arendt's diagnosis here: in every relationship organized in terms of a means (the path to the goal) to an end (the goal), the end is always superior to the means. For example, if you form a friendship with someone because they work at company where you would like to be employed, and you hope to use that friendship as a means to obtain a position at that company, the friendship is emptied of its significance and meaning, and

---

[6] Plato, *Republic*, 501a–e.

the friend is reduced to a mere object to be used as tool for achieving your ends. For Arendt, philosophy had treated politics and public life in a similar way: in using politics as a means to a philosophical end, it had robbed politics of its value and dignity. One might think that when contemplation was no longer the highest aim of human life, the dignity of the active life would be restored, but, as Arendt points out, this was not the case.

The modern view: political action as labor

In the modern age, two intellectual reversals took place that severed the ties between the philosophical and political traditions of the past and those of the modern age: one was made by Friedrich Nietzsche and the other by Karl Marx. Nietzsche declared that all of the transcendent ideas of the philosophers—being, God, truth, goodness, beauty—were empty abstractions.[7] Philosophers, he claimed, had turned away from the immanent reality of the world to other-worldly and transcendent ideas. Nietzsche sought to reverse this orientation, returning to the immanent world of bodies, passions, wills, and the creative activities of human beings. Marx sought to make a similar reversal by declaring that philosophers were too theoretical and sought only to interpret the world through transcendent ideas, when the actual goal was to change the world through revolutionary action.[8] These reversals might suggest that the philosophical hierarchy that privileged the contemplative life over the active life would be reversed, but as Arendt points out, the only thing that changed was the elimination of the contemplative aim. Nietzsche eliminated contemplation and reinterpreted action as the *work* of the artist, and Marx eliminated contemplation and reinterpreted action as *labor*, something no Greek or Roman philosopher had ever done because they thought the labor of our bodies was an inescapable and contemptable activity (294). Political *action* remained overlooked by modern philosophy.

---

[7] Friedrich Nietzsche, *The Twilight of the Idols: or How to Philosophize with a Hammer*, trans. Duncan Large (New York: Oxford University Press), III.4, 17.

[8] Karl Marx, "Concerning Feuerbach," in *Karl Marx: Early Writings*, trans. Rodney Livingstone and Gregor Benton (New York: Penguin Books, 1992), XI, 423.

Marx, like Arendt, rejected the idea that human beings have an essential nature that determines them. Instead, he argued that human beings possess a "species-being" that provides them with the freedom to *make* themselves through purposive activities like productive labor.[9] Marx sought to organize human labor power to restore human freedom. From his perspective, human beings were being alienated and exploited by a capitalist mode of production that forced them to sell their labor power as a commodity to those who owned the means to produce other commodities for the market. Instead of finding meaning in their work and making a living wage, workers found themselves exhausted and alienated from the products they made, their fellow workers, and themselves. Instead of becoming free through their labor, they had become slaves to the system of exploitation. Marx thought that if the workers organized themselves and took over the means of production from the owners, they could emancipate themselves from exploitative labor and engage in voluntary creative work. Arendt was not convinced.

As she points out, labor and work are distinctly different activities. Labor is the cyclical process of the human effort to transform natural resources into resources to sustain its life: "by laboring, men produce the vital necessities that must be fed into the life process of the human body" (295). Work, on the other hand, is a linear process of producing consumer goods—it has a beginning, and it has an end (295). What Arendt understood was that labor is governed by necessity not freedom, because human beings *must* produce the necessary goods to sustain their lives. When Marx attempted to liberate humanity through productive labor, Arendt argued, he failed to see that labor is governed by necessity and can never liberate humanity; only political action can liberate human beings because only action is capable of creating new beginnings. The only effective revolution would be through free and collective political action; Marx's revolution, in Arendt's view, was doomed to failure.

---

[9] Marx, "Economic and Philosophical Manuscripts (1844)," in *Karl Marx: Early Writings*, trans. Rodney Livingstone and Gregor Benton (New York: Penguin Books, 1992), 327.

Summary

Hannah Arendt argued that the political life of communicative action in the public world was the most authentically human form of life. She sought to recover the public world of human action that had been robbed of its dignity by the philosophical prejudice against politics. In this recovery, Arendt discovered three distinct activities within active life: 1) *labor*, the necessary activity that sustains the human organism; 2) *work*, the productive activity that makes the world; and 3) *action*, the highest activity that reveals who we are to others and creates new beginnings. Against the philosophical view that understood political action as work, and the modern view that understood political action as labor, Arendt argued that only political action could liberate human beings to build a new and common world, and that we should "think what we are doing."

Questions

1. What does it mean to "think what we are doing"?
2. What are some examples of the modern experience of worldlessness that Arendt describes?
3. Is it possible to change the world through labor or work, or can this only occur through political action?

12

Arendt: The Political Life
("Labor, Work, Action")

> **Key terms**
>
> Natality – human birth that initiates a new expression of humanity
> Plurality – the paradoxical condition of equality and distinction that makes action possible
> Labor – the cyclical and necessary activity for maintaining biological life
> Work – the productive activity of making an artificial and durable world
> Action – the unpredictable and irreversible activity of beginning something new

Arendt claimed we live authentic human lives when we appear with others in a shared world and engage in communicative action with them—the political life is the most authentically human way of life. Although she claims that action is the highest activity, each of the three activities of labor, work, and action has its own unique dignity and contributes to a fully human life. As we will see, each of the three activities are interrelated like the folds of a Möbius strip, with each activity informing the other. To understand this interrelationship, we will need to analyze the sources, conditions, purposes, and logics of each activity. Living an authentically human life will turn out to include all three. Let's begin our analysis with the activity of labor.

Labor is natural and necessary

The activity of labor is a natural and necessary activity that every living organism must engage in to sustain its life (295). The source for labor is the earth, which provides the natural and material resources for nourishing and sustaining life, and the condition for this activity is life itself—life requires labor to continue living. The activity of labor connects human beings to all the other animals on the earth who have to sustain their lives by gathering, producing, preparing, and consuming water, food, and oxygen to sustain their lives. Labor is, therefore, natural and necessary.

For Arendt, as for Marx, labor was the human power that transformed the natural resources of the earth into products that could be consumed to sustain the human body. This can be seen in the agricultural labor that plants seeds and harvests crops for the production of food that can be eaten to sustain the life of the human species. Arendt noted that the internal logic of labor was cyclical and necessary, and was composed of two stages: production and consumption (see Figure 12.1).

"Labor," Arendt claimed, "stands under the sign of necessity" (295). This means that we are never free to stop laboring. We can outsource our labor by paying or forcing someone else to do it or by creating machines that will do it for us, as Marx proposed, but the labor will still have to be done. Labor is eternally necessary to sustain human

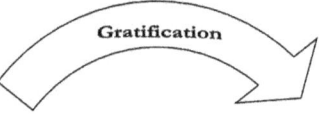

Consumption   Production

Figure 12.1

life. However, even though the activity of labor is endless, its products are temporary—they are produced quickly and consumed or decay just as quickly. Consider, for example, the labor required to produce a loaf of bread. The farmer plants, nurtures, and harvests wheat, which can then be ground and processed into a flour that can be made into dough that can then be baked into a loaf of bread. The bread must be eaten before it decays with mold. Once the bread has been eaten or becomes moldy, more bread must be made. Labor is endless, but it produces nothing durable.

Nevertheless, Arendt points out that in the process of spending our energies in producing consumable goods, and in the enjoyment we find in consuming them, there is a "blessing of labor" (297). Think about the joy and satisfaction you find in preparing and eating a meal. Sure, you have to drive to the grocery store, purchase the food, bring it home, prepare it, eat it, and then clean up the kitchen, but the joy of eating a well-prepared meal is deeply satisfying. However, not all labor is marked by happiness, and some forms of labor leave us miserable or simply bored (297). We do not feel joy, for example, when we work long hours doing back-breaking work for low pay, get up each morning to do it all over again, only to barely make ends meet at the end of each month; we feel exhausted and depressed. Similarly, when we work a repetitive and meaningless job, even if the pay is good, we do not feel joy; we feel bored. The blessing of labor is found in *meaningful labor*—labor that is satisfying because the effort we put into it produces a gratifying product that nourishes and sustains our lives. This kind of labor gives us a sense of dignity and mastery of our own lives. There is, however, a danger in conflating labor with work.

Labor is not work

Arendt was a critical, yet attentive, reader of Karl Marx, whose labor theory shaped the modern age. One of her chief criticisms of Marx was that he failed to distinguish labor from work, and this error stemmed from a glaring contradiction in his work. He had sought to replace the Aristotelian conception of the human being as a rational animal—*animal rationale*—with a conception of the human being as a laboring animal—*animal laborans*. However, Marx had argued in the *Grundrisse* that in a post-capitalist society wealth would be measured by the amount of free time one had outside of necessary productive labor. In fact, the stated goal of the communist revolution was to abolish labor altogether, through the development of technologies of automation, which would liberate human beings from the labor process and allow them to engage in creative work instead.[1] This struck Arendt as inherently contradictory: if the essence of the human being is her labor power, and the goal is to liberate human beings from this essential quality, then "we are left with the rather distressing alternative between productive slavery and unproductive freedom" (HC III.14, 105).

Marx understood that all animals labor, but human beings were distinguished from animals by their ability to transform nature through their productive labor power into a means for their own subsistence.[2] This labor power could be sold as a commodity to anyone (i.e. capitalists) who owned the means to produce other commodities that could, in turn, be sold for a profit on the market because every commodity has a twofold value: the value of its usefulness (use-value) and the value others are willing to pay for this usefulness (exchange-value).[3] The problem, as Marx pointed out, is that once human labor power becomes a commodity, the human being becomes a commodity as well, because labor is its essential nature; and because every commodity can be bought and sold based on its use or exchange value, human beings are inevitably exploited for their labor power. Capitalists buy labor power at the lowest wage in order to increase productivity and profits, and consequently laborers are treated as things rather than persons. To remedy this problem, Marx sought to liberate human beings from the labor process by reconceiving labor in terms of work, and taking the means of production out of the hands of the capitalist and placing them in the hands of workers. If labor is the essence of the human being, Marx reasoned, and human beings make and sustain themselves through their productive labor (work), then human beings can only be free through their labor—in other words, Marx thought

---

[1] Karl Marx, *Grundrisse: Foundations of the Critique of Political Economy*, trans. Martin Nicolaus (New York: Penguin Book, 1993), VII, 702–6.

[2] Karl Marx, *The German Ideology*, in *The Collected Works of Karl Marx and Frederick Engels*, trans. Clemens Dutt (New York: International Publishers, 2004), I.I.2, 31.

[3] Karl Marx, *Capital, Volume 1*, trans. Ben Fowkes (New York: Penguin Books, 1990), I.1.1–3, 125–77.

labor could be an expression of human dignity and freedom. The problem with Marx's strategy, from Arendt's perspective, was that it failed to understand that the activity of labor cannot be engaged in as if it were work, because it is governed by necessity and only produces goods that must be consumed to sustain the human organism.

To appreciate why Arendt thought this distinction was important, we have to understand how she understood concepts to originate. Concepts are mental models of reality that we create and express in language; they allow us to organize reality in an intelligible representation. To understand a concept, we must trace its intellectual development and expressions in language throughout history. Arendt does this with the concept of *labor* when she notes how it differs from the concept of *work* in Latin, Greek, French, and German, each of which is a source of the English language. As she explains, in each of these languages, the word for labor connotes a "bodily experience, of toil and trouble, and in most cases they are significantly also used for the pangs of birth" (294–5). When she examined Marx's use of the concept of *productive* labor, she found a similar connotation of bodily experience, and concluded that Marx had overlooked the distinction between labor and work. Consequently, his political theory led humanity into slavery rather than freedom.

Work makes the world

If labor is the activity that reveals our biological needs and produces consumer goods to keep us alive, work is the activity that reveals human creativity and produces *use-goods* to stabilize our lives in an objective and durable world (297–8). Work is the activity that distinguishes the human being from the animal because it seeks to build an artificial world as a shelter from the natural world. While its source for this artificial world is nature, its condition is worldliness—the artificiality of human production. Work builds an artificial border between nature and the human being—it creates an objective and durable shelter to house the human being and protect it from the violent forces of nature. Consider, for example, a high-rise apartment building in midtown Manhattan. Nothing could be more unnatural than this dwelling made of stone, steel, and glass harvested from natural resources deep within the earth and transformed into raw materials through a highly industrialized production process. The apartments within these buildings are protected from the natural world by double-glazed windows and insulated walls, so that the climate inside each unit can be controlled by electric air-conditioning systems. Nature is completely mastered by these artificial dwellings. Work, then, is the activity of producing material things like houses, tables, chairs, bicycles, iPhones, novels, poems, films, and constitutions, with and within which human beings can live meaningful lives. These are the objects that constitute our shared world, and once created they are independent of us and begin to condition us. The products of work endure longer than the consumer goods produced by labor. We have to eat the bread we make quickly, but the table at which we eat it will last for years.

Work produces an objective and durable world, independent of us and built to last. However, as Arendt points out, "alone with his image of the future product, *homo faber* [the human maker] is free to produce and facing alone the work of his hands, he is free to destroy" (300). Work is always violent insofar as it makes use of natural materials that must be forcibly removed from their natural environments and transformed (299). Consider a tree that must be chopped down, cut up, and planed to make a table. This process is governed by a means–end logic—the violence is the means and the table is the end. In the modern age, *homo faber* "becomes lord and master of nature herself insofar as he violates and partly destroys what was given to him" (299). This violent aspect of work, while necessary, can also prevent human beings from living fully human and dignified lives.

Consider, for example, how technology increases the speed of production and changes the relationship of the worker and the machine from one where the worker controls the machine to one where the machine controls the worker. A person can use a blender to make healthy green smoothies and remain largely in control of the machine, but consider the way smartphones have allowed human beings to outsource their memory to such an extent that they have become reliant on the operations of their phones—the person no longer controls the machine; the machine controls the person. Arendt reminds us of this destructive aspect of work because she understood that the chief characteristic of modern technology is speed and automation, and that human beings are expected to adjust to their machines for the sake of higher production, with the result that "everything and everybody is judged in terms of suitability and usefulness for the desired end product, and nothing else" (301). As she notes in *The Human Condition*, "The question therefore is not so much whether we are the masters or the slaves of our machines, but whether machines still serve the world and its things, or if, on the contrary, they and the automatic motion of their processes have begun to rule and even destroy world and things" (*HC* IV.20, 151). The modern worker is simply a replaceable cog in a machine. Nevertheless, there is another kind of work that creates a world that inspires human beings to live more authentically: art.

Art, Arendt tells us, is the only kind of work that escapes the productive velocity of means–end logic; consequently, art is entirely useless—it is not judged for its usefulness but for its *meaning*. The purpose of a work of art is "to attain permanence throughout the ages" (303). The artist does not simply fabricate in the way the craftsman makes a chair; the artist transfigures nature: "a veritable metamorphosis in which it is as though the course of nature which wills that all fire burn to ashes is reverted and even dust can burst into flames" (*HC* IV.23, 168). In transfiguring reality, poetry, literature, plays, paintings, sculptures, and films form and illuminate our shared world, allowing us to escape, for a time, our mortality and find meaning together.

Action reveals who we are

Each of the interrelated activities of the active life reveals something about the human condition. While labor and work reveal *what* a human being is through their physical and creative capacities—labor reveals human need and work reveals human artisanship—action reveals *who* a human being is, their unique and irreplaceable individuality and dignity. It is important to note that it is the labor of our bodies that makes the work of our hands possible, and it is the world made by work within which we act. So, the activities of labor, work, and action are not organized in terms of a regional hierarchy but in a relational process, akin to a Möbius strip that folds over itself (see Figure 12.2).[4]

Arendt describes action in terms of two births: our physical birth that inaugurates our biological life and makes action possible, and our

---

[4] See Patchen Markell, "Arendt's Work: On the Architecture of 'The Human Condition.'" *College Literature*, vol. 38, no. 1 (Winter 2011): 15–44.

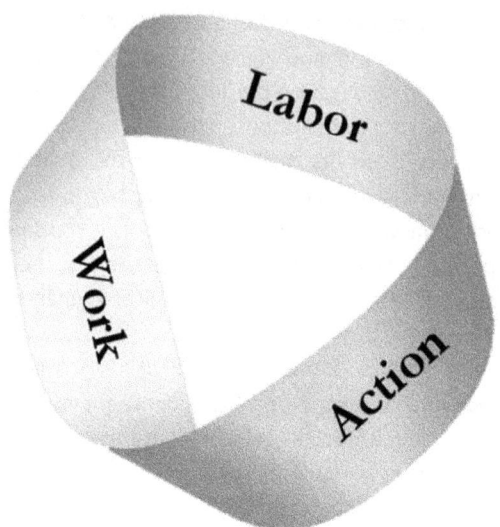

Figure 12.2

second, worldly birth through speech and action that communicates our distinctive individual life. For Arendt, human life stretches between our physical birth and our eventual death; our birth represents a new beginning for humanity because each newly born human being constitutes a new and unique expression of humanity, and our death represents the loss of this unique possibility. As Arendt noted, "action, with all its uncertainties, is like an ever-present reminder that men, though they must die, are not born in order to die but in order to begin something new" (307). Action, then, fulfills the purpose of human life—to begin something new. When a human being is born, he or she appears in the world as a newcomer on earth—like a new actor appearing on stage in a play, who must disclose who they are and make a contribution to the performance. Each human being is a unique and irreplaceable expression of humanity, and this uniqueness is expressed in the words and deeds each human being performs on earth (303). Action is, therefore, a *communicative* activity that discloses who we are through what we say and do.

If the source of action is our birth, its condition is human plurality—the fact that humans are all equally human but also distinguished from one another by their unique differences. As Arendt put it in *The*

Human Condition, "plurality is the condition of action because we are all the same, that is, human, in such a way that nobody is ever the same as anyone else who ever lived, lives, or will live" (*HC* V.24, 176). There is something paradoxical about the human condition that makes action possible: human beings have to be equal to understand each other, but they also have to be distinct for speech and action to be meaningful. We are born *human* like everyone else, but we are born a second-time as *persons*, when we distinguish ourselves through speech and action (303). Action, it turns out, is the most authentically human activity because—unlike labor, which can be outsourced to others, or work, of which we can be mere recipients rather than contributors—action must be done by each individual with others. Whenever we act, we never act alone, but always within a world and with others. Any life that ceases or fails to speak or act is no longer human, according to Arendt.

Human beings live in a common world they share with other human beings. When we are born, we enter a durable and objective world of things that existed before we were born, and will likely exist long after we are dead. Nevertheless, we are also born into an "already existing web of human relationships," and everything we do and say initiates a new and unpredictable process within this web (305). This relational web is comprised of unique individuals, each with their own interests, values, wills, and intentions. The realm of human action—the public realm—is always competitive; there is always a back-and-forth exchange between human beings, who express their unique perspectives in their words and deeds. For Arendt, we live authentically when we engage in communicative action with others. Wherever this public space for human action is denied—for example in totalitarian states—our human dignity is destroyed because we can no longer act in a distinctive human way.

The logic of human action is spontaneity, and this means that human action will always be unpredictable and irreversible (305, 306). Whenever we speak or act, we cannot know what the results of our words and deeds will be, and once we have spoken or acted, we cannot take our words back or undo our actions. This is very different from the activity of work, where the craftsman knows what he is doing. When we act "we can really never know what we are doing" (306). Given that each human being is unique, and their actions introduce a new beginning into the world, it is impossible to know how any human being will speak or act. Human beings can use their words and deeds to illuminate and enhance the world, or they can use them to destroy the world: democracy and totalitarianism are both products of human action.

The unpredictability and irreversibility of human action creates two serious problems for the web of human relationships. On the one hand, the unpredictability of human action makes the future uncertain; on the other hand, the irreversibility of human action makes the past a prison. Arendt suggests there are two remedies for these problems: promise-making and forgiveness (306–7). Whenever we make a promise, we illuminate the future with our intentions and commitments to act in a particular way—we provide stability for ourselves and others, and thereby constitute ourselves as persons, as individuals who are free and responsible for what they do and say. However, it may turn out that we fail to live up to our values and commitments—we may break our promises or act in ways that are harmful to others. In these situations, we cannot undo what we have done, and so we stand in need of forgiveness—of being "released from the consequences of what we have done" (307). Forgiveness, Arendt reminds us, is a necessary remedy for human action because without it we would "be confined to one single deed from which we could never recover; we would remain the victims of its consequences forever, not unlike the sorcerer's apprentice who lacked the magic formula to break the spell" (307). Forgiveness liberates us from the past so that we can have a future, and promise-making ensures that we will have one.

Behavior vs. action

There are of course ways of acting that do not reveal who we are or express our human dignity. These are ways of speaking and acting that are neither spontaneous nor communicative of our uniqueness but instead express our conformity with social rules and expectations. Arendt calls this way of acting *behavior* (*HC*, II.6, 40). For example, whenever we use clichés, jargon, or tired phrases to express ourselves, we don't say what *we* think; we say what *everyone else* thinks; we say what we are expected to say. This kind of speech is neither infused with thinking nor guided by reflection, and therefore it cannot reveal who we are to others. When we behave in conformity with prevailing social norms, values, or even laws without thinking about what we are doing, we do not reveal our dignity but forfeit it, and become, like Han van Meegeren, forgers of our lives instead of artists.

Arendt's description of the Nazi officer, Adolf Eichmann, in her final work, *The Life of the Mind*, exemplifies the distinction between action and behavior. She says she was struck by how shallow Eichmann was; he was a man without convictions or qualities: "There was no sign in him of firm ideological convictions or of specific evil motives, and the only notable characteristic one could detect in his past behavior as well as in his behavior during the trial and throughout the pre-trial police examination was something entirely negative: it was not stupidity but thoughtlessness."[5] Eichmann's "thoughtlessness" was his refusal to think for himself and to speak and act thoughtfully. Instead of facing the reality of himself and reflecting upon the situation in which he found himself, he hid behind "clichés, stock phrases, adherence to conventional codes of expression and conduct," so that, consequently, he never encountered the reality of himself, others, or the world. What is so terrifying about Eichmann is that his thoughtless behavior allowed him to mindlessly facilitate the murder of millions of human beings. His failure to live in accordance with reality led him to commit monstrous deeds, and when he was asked to give an account of why he had done what he did, he could only respond, "I was only following orders. What else could I have done?" In other words, he was only behaving, doing what was expected of him by his superiors in the Nazi regime. Arendt would have us realize that political thinking—thinking what we are doing—might help us avoid evil, and preserve both our own dignity and the dignity of the common world.

---

[5] Hannah Arendt, *The Life of the Mind*, one-volume edition (New York: Harcourt and Brace, 1977), 4.

Summary

Arendt claimed that we live an authentically human life when we engage in communicative action with others to build and sustain a common world. However, all three activities of the active life are interrelated and contribute to a fully human life. Labor is a natural and necessary activity that sustains the life of the human organism by transforming nature into consumable goods through a cyclical process of production and consumption. Labor makes possible the activity of work, which is a creative activity governed by a means–end logic that produces an objective and durable world of things. The durable world produced by work creates a space for human action, which is the highest activity that human beings engage in because it is governed by freedom and spontaneity and reveals who we are in our words and deeds.

Questions

1. Is Arendt's criticism of Karl Marx legitimate, or did she misunderstand Marx's conception of labor?
2. Arendt claimed that the work of our hands conditions us. What are some examples of human inventions positively or negatively impacting human life?
3. How can we know if we are speaking and acting authentically?

Conclusion: Philosophy for Life

We began this book with a conception of philosophy as a *practice* of distinguishing what is real from what is fake, and we ended with a consideration of philosophy as a *way of living* an authentically human life. This suggests that there is an intrinsic connection between *theory* and *praxis*—how we think and how we live. Similarly, the movement of our continental tour through the history of philosophy began in the transcendent realm of stable ideas and descended into the immanent activities of human life. These conceptual movements from transcendence to immanence, identity to difference, and thinking to acting were intended to convey that philosophy is *for life*—it is a theoretical practice in the service of living a flourishing human life. I hope this book has introduced you to key problems in philosophy, as well as the essential concepts and methods you need to engage in the persistent questioning of your experience, so that you can think for yourself, and speak and act authentically. The point of this book was not only to *introduce* you to the topic of philosophy, but also to *initiate* you into the practice of philosophy. If we return to the metaphor of an art gallery that I used in the Introduction to describe the history of philosophy, we can see that the point of becoming familiar with the various representations of reality on display is not to imitate them, but to be inspired to create your own representations of reality. To do this, you must take up the three questions anew and formulate your own answers.

One way to begin asking these questions anew is to critically examine the answers offered by the philosophers in this book in order to formulate new answers. As we saw, *critique* is central to philosophical practice and a precondition for the *creation* of new concepts. Each philosopher we examined questioned the insights and claims of their predecessors: Plato questioned Parmenides, Descartes questioned Aristotle, Hume questioned Descartes, Kant questioned Hume, and Nietzsche and Arendt questioned philosophy itself. This practice of critique can also help us realize how philosophical concepts and practice have marginalized or excluded women, people of color, the poor, or people of different sexual orientations. In short, critique allows us to become aware of how the various conceptions of reality, ways of knowing, and forms of life on offer in this book have been complicit in the oppression of others. To challenge this oppressive tendency, we can put the philosophers we have considered into dialogue with other philosophers and thinkers from different cultures or disciplines to raise new questions about reality, knowledge, and human life. New philosophical insights often emerge in the conflict of opposing ideas, where we become aware of what has been overlooked or forgotten.

The philosophers we have examined are from the Western European philosophical tradition, and with the exception of Hannah Arendt they have all been male. While this tradition has generated rich and valuable insights into reality, our knowledge of reality, and the various ways we might live in accordance with reality, it does not have an exclusive purchase on truth. Non-western philosophical traditions have equally significant contributions to make to our understanding of metaphysics, epistemology, and ethics. For example, we might contrast Plato's conception of reality as consisting of stable and unchanging *forms* with the Aztec (Nahua) conception of *teotl*, which conceives reality in monistic but dynamic terms as a singular, encompassing unity of ceaseless becoming.[1] By contrasting reality as being (Plato) with reality as becoming (Aztec), we might come to see difference as constitutive of reality instead of something to be excluded from reality. Additionally, feminist and queer approaches to epistemology might allow us to critically examine our concepts of gender and sexuality and how our embodied lives inform our understanding of the world and our relationships with others. As we begin to challenge our assumptions and

---

[1] For an introduction to Nahua philosophy, see James Maffie, *Aztec Philosophy: Understanding a World in Motion* (Boulder: University Press of Colorado, 2014).

conceptual frameworks by widening our conversations to include a multiplicity of perspectives, we can begin to create our own philosophical views. Philosophical insights are born from conflict and dialogue.

As I mentioned in the Introduction, philosophy is the ongoing inquiry into reality and the perpetual creation of concepts that enable us to come to terms with that reality in order to live more authentically. We are never finished philosophizing, but we can become better at it. It is my hope that this book has given you what you need to begin philosophizing for life.

Suggestions for Further Reading

Continental philosophy

Continental philosophy is best understood as a modern mode of philosophy, practiced primarily on the European continent, that is both critical and historical. It is critical in its resistance to the modern overreliance upon reason and science, and it is historical in its emphasis on human finitude and the contingency of human knowledge. Its primary representatives are Hegel, Marx, Kierkegaard, Nietzsche, Husserl, Saussure, Heidegger, Arendt, Sartre, Merleau-Ponty, Lacan, Beauvoir, Gadamer, Adorno, Levinas, Derrida, Foucault, Lyotard, Althusser, Deleuze, Irigaray, Kristeva, Badiou, Agamben, Nancy, Stiegler, and Žižek. While these thinkers draw on a common philosophical tradition including Parmenides, Heraclitus, Plato, Aristotle, Descartes, Leibniz, Spinoza, Locke, Hume, and Kant, their interpretations of this tradition are decidedly different. These differences arise from the various responses to Kant's distinction between "intuitions" and "concepts." Andrew Cutrofello's *Continental Philosophy: A Contemporary Introduction* offers an excellent overview of how continental philosophy developed from this distinction. Readers will also find David West's *Continental Philosophy: An Introduction* helpful for understanding the various and sometimes conflicting currents within continental thought. *The Continental Philosophy Reader*, edited by Richard Kearney and Mara Rainwater, contains some of the most important primary texts by continental philosophers and offers readers insight into the richness and diversity of continental thought.

Metaphysics

Plato

Plato's writings are immense and fundamental to the philosophical tradition. They are usually divided into the early, middle, and late dialogues. The *Sophist* is one of Plato's late dialogues; it purports to be a continuation of the conversation in the *Theaetetus* and gestures toward the conversation taken up in the *Statesman*. Readers of the *Sophist* would benefit from a knowledge of these dialogues, as well as the other dialogues devoted to Plato's metaphysics, such as the *Euthyphro*, *Meno*, *Parmenides*, *Phaedo*, *Phaedrus*, *Timaeus*, *Symposium*, and parts of the *Republic*.

The secondary literature on Plato's dialogues is a vast labyrinth of competing interpretations. Continental interpretations of Plato are often difficult to find; however, *Being and Logos: Reading the Platonic Dialogues* by John Sallis offers a superb introduction to Plato's thought in general, as well as a chapter specifically devoted to the *Sophist*. Adriaan Peperzak's *Platonic Transformations: With and After Hegel, Heidegger, and Levinas* also offers a distinctly continental interpretation of Plato. Drew Hyland's *Finitude and Transcendence in the Platonic Dialogues* is helpful for understanding how Plato's dialogues dramatize the practice of philosophy. For a more detailed study of Plato's *Sophist*, readers should consult Martin Heidegger's *Plato's Sophist* and Jacob Klein's *Plato's Trilogy: Theaetetus, the Sophist, and the Statesman*.

Descartes

Although Descartes' works are not as vast as Plato's, they are no less fundamental to the history of philosophy. Descartes wrote for both academic and non-academic audiences. His *Meditations on First Philosophy* was written for an academic audience, and he included objections he received from readers along with his responses. Readers will want to consider these objections and replies when reading the *Meditations*. The *Meditations* draw explicitly on insights developed by Descartes in his *Rules for the Direction of the Mind*, his *Discourse on Method*, and his *Geometry*. Descartes' *Principles of Philosophy* was written as a textbook and can be read as an interpretive companion with the *Meditations*. Descartes' final work, *The Passion of the Soul*, offers further insights into the relationship between the body and the mind developed in the *Meditations*.

The *Cambridge Companion to Descartes*, edited by John Cottingham, provides an excellent survey of the scholarship on Descartes' philosophy, including articles by leading continental philosophers. Readers will find Kurt Brandhorst's *Descartes' Meditations on First Philosophy* an indispensable guide to understanding Descartes' arguments in the *Meditations*. Jean-Luc Marion is the most prominent continental interpreter of Descartes, and his *Cartesian Questions: Method and Metaphysics* is a superb primer on Descartes' metaphysics. Readers interested in Descartes philosophy of mind and the role of the imagination will want to consult Dennis Sepper's *Descartes' Imagination: Proportions, Images, and the Activity of Thinking*.

Epistemology

Hume

While David Hume's writings are not vast, they have had an enormous impact on the history of philosophy. His most significant and most difficult work is the *Treatise of Human Nature*, which went largely unread, prompting Hume to write the more concise *An Enquiry Concerning Human Understanding*. A comparative reading of these two texts will reveal significant changes that Hume made in his philosophy of mind, theory of the subject, and moral theory. His *Dialogues Concerning Natural Religion* further develops his skeptical arguments in the *Enquiry* regarding religious claims, and his *An Enquiry Concerning the Principles of Morals* further develops the moral theory developed in the *Treatise*.

Continental interpretations of Hume are not as common as analytic interpretations. Peter Millican's edited volume of essays, *Reading Hume on Human Understanding*, is a good introduction to analytical interpretations of Hume, while the work of Gilles Deleuze on Hume is certainly one of the most important continental readings. Deleuze's essay "Hume" in *Pure Immanence: Essays on A Life* is a concise and accessible introduction to Hume's empiricism and the significance of his theory of associationism. Readers will also want to consult Deleuze's *Empiricism and Subjectivity: An Essay on Hume's Theory of Human Nature* for a more detailed interpretation of Hume's *Treatise of Human Nature*.

Readers who are interested in an illuminating overview of Deleuze's reading of Hume should consult Jeffrey Bell's *Deleuze's Hume*.

Kant

Kant's transcendental philosophy is presented systematically in three "Critiques": the *Critique of Pure Reason*, the *Critique of Practical Reason*, and the *Critique of Judgment*. In addition to his *Prolegomena to Any Future Metaphysics*, Kant's metaphysics and epistemology are developed early in his dissertation *On the Form and Principles of the Sensible and the Intelligible World* and in his lectures on *Logic*.

Kant's importance in philosophy cannot be underestimated. It is no exaggeration to say that Kant represents a watershed moment in the history of philosophy, and the philosophy that follows him is unintelligible without a knowledge of his philosophy. The secondary literature on Kant's philosophy is enormous, but little has been written specifically on the *Prolegomena*. Readers will find Beryl Logan's edited collection of essays, *Immanuel Kant's Prolegomena to Any Future Metaphysics: In Focus*, a helpful place to begin. Henry Allison's *Kant's Transcendental Idealism* is indispensable for understanding Kant's epistemology, and Gilles Deleuze's *Kant's Critical Philosophy* offers a brief and accessible discussion of Kant's critical philosophy in his three "Critiques."

Ethics

Nietzsche

Nietzsche wrote on a variety of topics like art, education, culture, science, politics, religion, and mortality, and his style ranged from pithy aphorisms to bombastic prose and poetic fiction. *The Birth of Tragedy* is an illuminating text to read alongside Nietzsche's four essays in *Unfashionable Observations*. Nietzsche's greatest work is *Thus Spoke Zarathustra*, but it is a difficult and complex text and should be read only after gaining an understanding of Nietzsche's more accessible works like those previously mentioned, as well as *The Gay Science*, *On the Genealogy of Morality*, *Beyond Good and Evil*, and *Twilight of the Idols*.

There is a massive body of secondary literature on Nietzsche, but there are three excellent introductions to his work that will help readers understand his thinking: Gianni Vattimo's *Nietzsche: An Introduction*, Ashley Woodward's *Understanding Nietzscheanism*, and Keith Ansell-Pearson's *How to Read Nietzsche*. Jeffrey Church's *Nietzsche's Unfashionable Observations* is especially helpful for understanding Nietzsche's four unfashionable essays.

Arendt

Arendt wrote widely on literature, religion, philosophy, politics, and morality. Her major works are *The Origins of Totalitarianism*, *The Human Condition*, *Between Past and Future*, *On Revolution*, *Eichmann in Jerusalem*, and *The Life of the Mind*. There are five collections of her essays that can serve as entry points into her thought: *Essays in Understanding: 1930–1954*, *Responsibility and Judgment*, *The Promise of Politics*, *The Jewish Writings*, and *Thinking Without a Banister: Essays in Understanding, 1953–1975*. A good place to begin reading Arendt is with *Between Past and Future*, and then *The Origins of Totalitarianism*, then *The Human Condition*, and then *The Life of the Mind*. This order will provide the reader with a sense of the trajectory and style of Arendt's thought, and will make the essay collections much more accessible.

The secondary literature on Arendt is broad and varied, but *The Cambridge Companion to Hannah Arendt*, edited by Dana Villa, is a good place to begin. Elizabeth Young-Bruehl's *Hannah Arendt: For the Love of the World* remains the standard biography of Arendt, but Julia Kristeva's *Hannah Arendt* is also an excellent introduction to Arendt's life and thought. Readers should also consult Margaret Canovan's *Hannah Arendt: A Reinterpretation of Her Political Thought* and Seyla Benhabib's *The Reluctant Modernism of Hannah Arendt*, as well as her edited volume, *Politics in Dark Times: Encounters with Hannah Arendt*.

Bibliography

Allison, Henry E. *Kant's Transcendental Idealism: An Interpretation and Defense.* New Haven: Yale University Press, 2004.

Ansell-Pearson, Keith. *How to Read Nietzsche.* New York: W. W. Norton and Company, 2005.

Arendt, Hannah. *Eichmann in Jerusalem: A Report on the Banality of Evil.* New York: Penguin Books, 1977.

Arendt, Hannah. *The Life of the Mind.* One-volume Edition. New York: Harcourt and Brace, 1977.

Arendt, Hannah. *Between Past and Future: Eight Exercises in Political Thought.* New York: Penguin Books, 1993.

Arendt, Hannah. *Essays in Understanding: 1930–1954: Formation, Exile, and Totalitarianism.* Ed. Jerome Kohn. New York: Schocken Books, 1994.

Arendt, Hannah. *The Origins of Totalitarianism.* New York: Harcourt and Brace, 1994.

Arendt, Hannah. *The Human Condition.* Second Edition. Chicago: University of Chicago Press, 1998.

Arendt, Hannah. *Responsibility and Judgment.* Ed. Jerome Kohn. New York: Schocken Books, 2003.

Arendt, Hannah. *The Promise of Politics.* Ed. Jerome Kohn. New York: Schocken Books, 2005.

Arendt, Hannah. *The Jewish Writings.* Ed. Jerome Kohn. New York: Schocken Books, 2007.

Arendt, Hannah. "Labor, Work, Action." In *Thinking Without a Banister: Essays in Understanding: 1953–1975*. Ed. Jerome Kohn, New York: Schocken Books, 2018, 291–307.

Aristotle. *Categories*. In *The Complete Works of Aristotle*, Volume 1. Trans. J. L. Akrill. New York: Oxford University Press, 1984, 3–24.

Aristotle. *On the Soul*. In *The Complete Works of Aristotle*, Volume 1. Trans. J.A. Smith. New York: Oxford University Press, 1984, 641-692.

Aristotle. *Nicomachean Ethics*. In *The Complete Works of Aristotle*, Volume 2. Trans. J. O. Urmson. New York: Oxford University Press, 1984, 1729–1867.

Aristotle. *Physics*. In *The Complete Works of Aristotle*, Volume 1. Trans. R.P. Hardie and R.K. Gaye. New York: Oxford University Press, 1984, 315–446.

Baldwin, James. "The Creative Process." In *The Price of the Ticket: Collected Nonfiction: 1948–1985*. New York: St. Martin's Press, 1985, 315–18.

Bell, Jeffrey A. *Deleuze's Hume: Philosophy, Culture, and the Scottish Enlightenment*. Edinburgh: Edinburgh University Press, 2009.

Benhabib, Seyla. *The Reluctant Modernism of Hannah Arendt*. Second edition. Lanham: Rowman and Littlefield, 2003.

Benhabib, Seyla (ed.). *Politics in Dark Times: Encounters with Hannah Arendt*. New York: Cambridge University Press, 2010.

Bostrom, Nick. "Are You Living in a Computer Simulation?" *Philosophical Quarterly*, vol. 53, no. 211 (2003): 243–55.

Brandhorst, Kurt. *Descartes' Meditations on First Philosophy*. Edinburgh: Edinburgh University Press, 2010.

Canovan, Margaret. *Hannah Arendt: A Reinterpretation of Her Political Thought*. New York: Cambridge University Press, 1992.

Church, Jeffrey. *Nietzsche's Unfashionable Observations: A Critical Introduction and Guide*. Edinburgh: Edinburgh University Press, 2019.

Cottingham, John (ed.). *The Cambridge Companion to Descartes*. New York: Cambridge University Press, 1999.

Cutrofello, Andrew. *Continental Philosophy: A Contemporary Introduction*. New York: Routledge, 2005.

Deleuze, Gilles. *Nietzsche and Philosophy*. Trans. Hugh Tomlinson. New York: Columbia University Press, 1983.

Deleuze, Gilles. *Empiricism and Subjectivity: An Essay on Hume's Theory of Human Nature*. Trans. Constantin V. Boundas. New York: Columbia University Press, 1991.

Deleuze, Gilles. *Kant's Critical Philosophy: The Doctrine of the Faculties*. Fourth edition. Trans. Hugh Tomlinson and Barbara Habberjam. Minneapolis: University of Minnesota Press, 1993.

Deleuze, Gilles. "Hume." In *Pure Immanence: Essays on a Life*. Trans. Anne Boyman. New York: Zone Books, 2001, 35–52.

Deleuze, Gilles. "Nietzsche." In *Pure Immanence: Essays on a Life*. Trans. Anne Boyman. New York: Zone Books, 2001, 53–101.

Descartes, René. *Discourse on Method*. In *The Philosophical Writings of Descartes*, Volume 1. Trans. John Cottingham, Robert Stoothoff, and Dugald Murdoch. New York: Cambridge University Press, 1993, 111–51.

Descartes, René. *Meditations on First Philosophy*. Third edition. Trans. Donald A. Cress. Indianapolis: Hackett Publishing, 1993.

Descartes, René. *Principles of Philosophy*. In *The Philosophical Writings of Descartes*, Volume 1. Trans. John Cottingham, Robert Stoothoff, and Dugald Murdoch. New York: Cambridge University Press, 1993, 179–291.

Descartes, René. *Rules for the Direction of the Mind*. In *The Philosophical Writings of Descartes*, Volume 1. Trans. John Cottingham, Robert Stoothoff, and Dugald Murdoch. New York: Cambridge University Press, 1993, 7–78.

Descartes, René. *The Passions of the Soul*. In *The Philosophical Writings of Descartes*, Volume 1. Trans. John Cottingham, Robert Stoothoff, and Dugald Murdoch. New York: Cambridge University Press, 1993, 326–404.

Descartes, René. *Geometry*. In *Discourse on Method, Optics, Geometry, and Meterology*. Revised Edition. Trans. Paul J. Olscamp. Indianapolis: Hackett Publishing, 2001, 177–262.

Dolnick, Edward. *The Forger's Spell: A True Story of Vermeer, Nazis, and the Greatest Art Hoax of the Twentieth Century*. San Francisco: Harper Collins Publishing, 2009.

Du Bois, W. E. B. *The Souls of Black Folk*. New Haven: Yale University Press, 2015.

Freud, Sigmund. "Repression." In *The Complete Psychological Works of Sigmund Freud*, Volume XIV. Trans. James Strachey. London: The Hogarth Press. Reprinted, 1981, 146–58.

Freud, Sigmund. *The Ego and the Id*. In *The Complete Psychological Works of Sigmund Freud*, Volume XIX. Trans. James Strachey. London: The Hogarth Press. Reprinted, 1986, 3–68.

Heidegger, Martin. *Being and Time*. Trans. John Macquarrie and Edward Robinson. New York: Harper and Row, 1962.
Heidegger, Martin. *Plato's Sophist*. Trans. Richard Rojcewicz and Andre Schuwer. Bloomington: Indiana University Press, 2003.
Hume, David. *An Enquiry Concerning Human Understanding*. Second edition. Ed. Eric Steinberg. Indianapolis: Hackett Publishing, 1993.
Hume, David. "Of National Characters." In *David Hume: Selected Essays*. Ed. Stephen Copley and Andrew Edgar. New York: Oxford University Press, 1993, 113–25.
Hume, David. *Dialogues Concerning Natural Religion*. In *Dialogues and Natural History of Religion*. Ed. J. C. A. Gaskin. New York: Oxford University Press, 1998, 29–133.
Hume, David. *An Enquiry Concerning the Principles of Morals*. In *David Hume: Moral Philosophy*. Ed. Geoffrey Sayre-McCord. Indianapolis: Hackett Publishing, 2006, 185–310.
Hume, David. *A Treatise of Human Nature: A Critical Edition*, Volume 1: Texts. Ed. David Fate Norton and Mary J. Norton. New York: Oxford University Press, 2007.
Hyland, Drew. *Finitude and Transcendence in the Platonic Dialogues*. Albany: SUNY Press, 1995.
Jaspers, Karl. *Philosophy of Existence*. Trans. Richard F. Grabau. Philadelphia: University of Pennsylvania Press, 1995.
Kant, Immanuel. *Critique of Judgment*. Trans. Werner S. Pluhar. Indianapolis: Hackett Publishing, 1987.
Kant, Immanuel. *On the Form and Principles of the Sensible and the Intelligible World*. In *The Cambridge Edition of the Works of Immanuel Kant: Theoretical Philosophy: 1755–1770*. Trans. David Walford. New York: Cambridge University Press, 1992, 373–416.
Kant, Immanuel. *The Cambridge Edition of the Works of Immanuel Kant: Lectures on Logic*. Trans. Paul Guyer and Allen Wood. New York: Cambridge University Press, 1992.
Kant, Immanuel. *Critique of Pure Reason*. Trans. Werner S. Pluhar. Indianapolis: Hackett Publishing, 1996.
Kant, Immanuel. *Prolegomena to Any Future Metaphysics*. Second edition. Trans. James. W. Ellington. Indianapolis: Hackett Publishing, 2001.
Kant, Immanuel. *Critique of Practical Reason*. Trans. Werner S. Pluhar. Indianapolis: Hackett Publishing, 2002.
Kearney, Richard, and Mara Rainwater (eds). *The Continental Philosophy Reader*. New York: Routledge, 1996.

Klein, Jacob. *Plato's Trilogy: Theaetetus, the Sophist, and the Statesman*. Chicago: University of Chicago Press, 1977.
Kristeva, Julia. *Hannah Arendt*. Trans. Ross Guberman. New York: Columbia University Press, 2001.
Lawlor, Leonard. *Early Twentieth-Century Continental Philosophy*. Bloomington: Indiana University Press, 2012.
Logan, Beryl (ed.). *Immanuel Kant's Prolegomena to Any Future Metaphysics: In Focus*. New York: Routledge, 1996.
Maffie, James. *Aztec Philosophy: Understanding a World in Motion*. Boulder: University Press of Colorado, 2014.
Marion, Jean-Luc. *Cartesian Questions: Method and Metaphysics*. Chicago: University of Chicago Press, 1999.
Markell, Patchen. "Arendt's Work: On the Architecture of 'The Human Condition.'" *College Literature*, vol. 38, no. 1 (Winter 2011): 15–44.
Marx, Karl. *Capital*, Volume 1. Trans. Ben Fowkes. New York: Penguin Books, 1990.
Marx, Karl. "Concerning Feuerbach." In *Karl Marx: Early Writings*. Trans. Rodney Livingstone and Gregor Benton. New York: Penguin Books, 1992, 421–3.
Marx, Karl. "Economic and Philosophical Manuscripts (1844)." In *Karl Marx: Early Writings*. Trans. Rodney Livingstone and Gregor Benton. New York: Penguin Books, 1992, 279–400.
Marx, Karl. Grundrisse: Foundations of the Critique of Political Economy, Translated by Martin Nicolaus. New York: Penguin Books, 1993.
Marx, Karl. *The German Ideology*. In *The Collected Works of Karl Marx and Frederick Engels*, Volume 5. Trans. Clemens Dutt. New York: International Publishers, 2004, 21–584.
Millican, Peter (ed.). *Reading Hume on Human Understanding: Essays on the First Enquiry*. New York: Oxford University Press, 2003.
Nietzsche, Friedrich. *The Gay Science: With a Prelude in Rhymes and an Appendix of Songs*. Trans. Walter Kaufmann. New York: Random House, 1974.
Nietzsche, Friedrich. *Schopenhauer as Educator*. In *The Complete Works of Friedrich Nietzsche, Volume 2: Unfashionable Observations*. Trans. Richard T. Gray. Stanford: Stanford University Press, 1995, 169–255.
Nietzsche, Friedrich. *Twilight of the Idols: or How to Philosophize with a Hammer*. Trans. Richard Polt. Indianapolis: Hackett Publishing, 1997.
Nietzsche, Friedrich. *The Birth of Tragedy: Out of the Spirit of Music*. Trans. Shaun Whiteside. New York: Oxford University Press, 2003.

Nietzsche, Friedrich. *Thus Spoke Zarathustra: A Book for Everyone and Nobody*. Trans. Graham Parkes. New York: Oxford University Press, 2005.

Nietzsche, Friedrich. *The Complete Works of Friedrich Nietzsche, Volume 8: Beyond Good and Evil/On the Genealogy of Morality*. Trans. Adrian del Caro. Stanford: Stanford University Press, 2014.

Parekh, Bikhu. "Hannah Arendt's Critique of Marx." In *Hannah Arendt: The Recovery of the Public World*. Ed. Melvyn A. Hill. New York: St. Martin's Press, 1979, 67–100.

Peperzak, Adriaan. *Platonic Transformations: With and After Hegel, Heidegger, and Levinas*. Lanham: Rowman and Littlefield, 1997.

Plato. *Sophist*. Trans. Nicholas P. White. Indianapolis: Hackett Publishing, 1993.

Plato. *Euthyphro*. In *Plato: Complete Works*. Ed. John M. Cooper and Trans. G. M. A. Grube. Indianapolis: Hackett Publishing, 1997, 1–16.

Plato. *Letter VII*. In *Plato: Complete Works*. Ed. John M. Cooper and Trans. C. D. C. Reeve. Indianapolis: Hackett Publishing, 1997, 1646–67.

Plato. *Meno*. In *Plato: Complete Works*. Ed. John M. Cooper and Trans. G. M. A. Grube. Indianapolis: Hackett Publishing, 1997, 870–97.

Plato. *Parmenides*. In *Plato: Complete Works*. Ed. John M. Cooper and Trans. Marie Louise Gill and Paul Ryan. Indianapolis: Hackett Publishing, 1997, 359–97.

Plato. *Phaedo*. In *Plato: Complete Works*. Ed. John M. Cooper and Trans. G. M. A. Grube. Indianapolis: Hackett Publishing, 1997, 49–100.

Plato. *Phaedrus*. In *Plato: Complete Works*. Ed. John M. Cooper and Trans. Alexander Nehamas and Paul Woodruff. Indianapolis: Hackett Publishing, 1997, 506–56.

Plato. *Republic*. In *Plato: Complete Works*. Ed. John M. Cooper and Trans. C. D. C. Reeve. Indianapolis: Hackett Publishing, 1997, 971–1223.

Plato. *Theaetetus*. In *Plato: Complete Works*. Ed. John M. Cooper and Trans. Myles Burnyeat. Indianapolis: Hackett Publishing, 1997, 157–234.

Plato. *Timaeus*. In *Plato: Complete Works*. Ed. John M. Cooper and Trans. Donald J. Zeyl. Indianapolis: Hackett Publishing, 1997, 1224–91.

Plato. *Statesman*. In *Plato: Complete Works*. Ed. John M. Cooper and Trans. C. J. Rowe. Indianapolis: Hackett Publishing, 1997, 294–358.

Plato. *Symposium*. In *Plato: Complete Works*. Ed. John M. Cooper and Trans. Alexander Nehamas and Paul Woodruff. Indianapolis: Hackett Publishing, 1997, 457–505.

Sallis, John. *Being and Logos: Reading the Platonic Dialogues*. Third edition. Bloomington: Indiana University Press, 1996.

Schopenhauer, Arthur. *The World as Will and Representation I*. Trans. Judith Norman, Alistair Welchman, and Christopher Janaway. New York: Cambridge University Press, 2014.

Sepper, Dennis. *Descartes's Imagination: Proportions, Images, and the Activity of Thinking*. Berkeley: University of California Press, 1996.

Vattimo, Gianni. *Nietzsche: An Introduction*. Trans. Nicholas Martin. Stanford: Stanford University Press, 2002.

Villa, Dana. *Arendt and Heidegger: The Fate of the Political*. Princeton: Princeton University Press, 1996.

Villa, Dana. *The Cambridge Companion to Hannah Arendt*. New York: Cambridge University Press, 2000.

West, David. *Continental Philosophy: An Introduction*. Second edition. Malden: Polity Press, 2010.

Woodward, Ashley. *Understanding Nietzscheanism*. New York: Routledge, 2011.

Young-Bruehl, Elizabeth. *Hannah Arendt: For the Love of the World*. New Haven: Yale University Press, 1982.

Index

a posteriori, x, 92, 97, 104, 109, 110
a priori, vii, x, xii, 80, 92, 96–9, 100, 101, 103–4, 105, 106, 107, 109–10, 116–17
abstraction, 124, 158
action, vii, viii, x, xi, xiii, 4, 18, 22, 44, 69, 70, 84–5, 88, 91, 101, 114, 121, 142, 149, 150–9, 160
active, vii, xii, 53, 55, 60, 92, 107, 108, 109, 149, 150, 153–9, 160, 167, 172
affect, 48, 69, 71, 73, 79, 93, 100, 101
African philosophy, 89–90
alienation, 125, 126, 150–1, 159
allegory of the cave, 13–14, 22–3, 53, 151, 156–7
Allison, Henry, 179, 181
Amo, Anton Wilhelm, 89–90
analytic, x, 92, 97–8, 104, 109–10
analytical philosophy, 108, 178
angler, 20–3
animal, 22, 40, 56, 88, 139, 140, 144, 146, 147, 162, 163, 164
animal laborans, 163
animal rationale, 163

Ansell-Pearson, Keith, 180, 181
antinomies of reason, x, 105, 111, 112–14
anti-philosophy, 120
Apollonian, x, 123, 127–8, 129, 130, 135, 141, 142
appearance, v, vii, x, 2, 6, 12, 13, 14, 15–17, 22, 24, 25, 27, 29, 32, 36, 37, 44, 45, 86, 99, 100, 105, 106–7, 109, 110, 112, 113, 114, 120, 121, 127, 128, 132, 135, 147, 152, 161, 168
Arendt, Hannah, vii, x, xi, xii, xiii, 4, 6, 14, 119, 120–1, 149–60, 161–72, 174, 178, 180, 181–2, 185, 186, 187
  "Labor, Work, Action", xiii, 149, 150, 153, 161
  The Human Condition, 14, 150, 152, 154, 167, 168–9, 180, 181, 185
  The Life of the Mind, 171, 180, 181
Aristotle, 3, 39–40, 42, 76, 77, 96, 101–2, 156, 174, 176, 182
  Categories, 40, 101, 182
  Nicomachean Ethics, 156, 182

INDEX

On the Soul, 40
Physics, 76
art, 1–2, 4, 56–7, 70, 80, 90, 124, 129, 138, 149, 167, 173, 183
artist, 1, 4, 6, 16, 19, 80, 102, 128, 129, 138, 143, 144–5, 154, 158, 167, 171
assemblage, vi, 67, 72, 77
associationism, vi, 71, 178
   cause and effect, vi, 71, 73, 75, 76–7, 78, 81, 82, 83, 86, 89, 90, 96, 115
   contiguity, 71, 73, 75
   resemblance, 71, 73, 75, 89
atomism, vi, 71
atomization, 141, 150, 151
attribute, 40, 41, 42, 51, 55, 82, 84, 86, 111
authentic, vii, xii, 1, 2, 3, 4, 6, 16, 18, 19, 25, 80, 119, 120, 121, 123, 124, 127, 128, 130, 131, 132–6, 137, 138, 140, 143, 144, 146, 147, 148, 149, 150, 151, 152, 160, 161, 167, 169, 172, 173, 175
automation, 164, 166
Aztec philosophy, 174, 185

bad conscience, 125
Baldwin, James, 144, 146, 182
Barma, Kocc, 90
beauty, 17, 22, 23, 139, 147, 158
becoming, x, 26, 35, 108, 127, 129, 148, 149, 159, 174
Beethoven, Ludwig, 131, 134
behavior, viii, 170–1

being, v, vi, x, 15–16, 22, 24, 26, 27–31, 33–6, 37, 56, 94, 106, 124, 127, 129, 151, 158, 174
being and appearance, v, x, 13, 14, 15–16, 24, 36, 106, 152
belief, vi, xi, 12, 24, 32–3, 43–6, 69, 71, 74–7, 79, 80–1, 83, 85–6, 87, 88, 89, 90, 91, 134
Bell, Jeffrey, ix, 179, 182
Benhabib, Seyla, 180, 182
Bergson, Henri, 4
Berkeley, George, 105, 106
Bernier, François, 88–9
billiards, 81–3, 95, 115
birth, xi, 22, 47, 125, 155, 161, 165, 167–8
body, x, 34, 38, 44, 45, 46, 48, 49, 53, 59, 61, 62, 70, 82, 85, 126, 135, 159, 162, 178
Bonaparte, Napoleon, 131
Bostrom, Nick, 61, 182
Brandhorst, Kurt, ix, 178, 182

Caesar, Julius, 131
Camera obscura, 17, 32
Canovan, Margaret, 180, 182
Canterbury, St. Anselm, 58
capitalism, 138, 159, 163–4
Caravaggio, Michelangelo Merisi, 1–2
Cartesian ego, vi, 47, 69, 72
categories, xi, 5, 13, 19, 20, 92, 96, 101–4, 111, 112, 115, 117, 125
Catholic Church, 141

cause, xi, 45, 48, 49, 50, 51, 59, 71, 76, 77, 79, 81–3, 84–5, 86, 94, 95, 98, 102, 103, 105, 112–14, 115
four causes (Aristotle), 76
causal adequacy principle, 50, 59
cause and effect, vi, 50, 51, 71, 73, 75, 76–7, 78, 81–3, 86, 89, 90, 96, 97, 98, 115
certainty, xi, 6, 45, 59, 74, 79, 81, 83, 87, 92, 94, 105, 106, 131, 132
change, 9, 12, 17, 26, 35, 36, 46, 47, 74, 157, 158, 160, 166
chaos, 127–8, 129, 139, 141, 142, 151, 157
cheerfulness, 133, 136,
Christianity, 5, 141, 146, 147, 153, 157
Church, Jeffrey, ix, 180, 182
claims, 8–9, 38, 74, 83, 84, 87, 90, 95, 97, 108, 112–15, 117, 174, 178
clear and distinct, x, 38, 47–8, 51, 54, 56, 57, 58, 59, 60, 62, 68, 69, 74
cogito, 111
cognition, 93, 104, 109–10, 111
commodity, 146, 159, 164
common world, 6, 120, 121, 151–3, 154, 160, 169, 171, 172
communicative action, x, 149, 152–3, 160, 161, 169, 172
compatibilism, x, 79, 84–5
concept, 4–6, 7, 8–9, 22, 27, 29, 35, 62, 66, 67–9, 72, 74, 88, 90, 93, 94, 96, 97–104, 106–11, 112, 113, 115–16, 117, 120, 123–4, 125, 126, 127, 128, 149, 156, 163, 165, 173, 174, 175, 176
empirical concept, 103, 109
pure concept, 104, 107, 109, 115, 116, 128
concepts of the understanding, 100–1, 103–4, 106, 107, 109, 110, 111, 112, 113, 115, 116, 117, 128
conformity, 120–1, 125, 127, 131, 134, 136, 137–8, 139, 145–7, 150, 170, 171
constancy, 133, 136
consumerism, 139, 141–2
consumption, 139, 162, 172
continental philosophy, vi, 4–6, 14, 108, 149, 173, 176–80, 182, 184, 187
contingent, 49, 53, 112, 139
contradiction, 36, 60, 62, 73, 86, 94, 112, 114, 117, 147, 163, 164
contrary, 44, 75, 84, 86, 94, 104, 113, 124, 143
Copernicus, Nicolaus, 5, 95
copy, xi, 15, 17, 23, 25, 32, 67
Cottingham, John, 40, 178, 182, 183,
creative spirits, vii, x, 137, 138, 142, 143, 144, 148
creativity, x, 120, 137, 140, 165
critique, 94, 95, 174
critical philosophy, vi, 4, 66, 95–6, 104, 105, 176, 179, 182

culture, vii, x, 6, 121, 124, 137, 138–48, 149, 150, 151, 174, 179, 182
cultural duty, x, 137, 143–6
Cutrofello, Andrew, ix, 176, 182

death, 51, 155, 168
deception, 16, 18, 19, 42, 46, 51, 54–5, 59, 60, 62, 85, 94, 132
decision, xi, 53, 56, 82, 84, 85
dehumanization, vii, 138–9, 148
Deleuze, Gilles, 4, 14, 176, 178–9, 182–3
delusion, 2, 14, 45, 68, 111, 144, 148
Democritus, 34
demonstration, 36, 57, 76, 80–1
denial, 55, 94, 133
Descartes, René, v, vi, x, xi, xii, xiii, 3, 5–6, 11, 12, 38–63, 66, 68–9, 72, 73, 74, 77, 79, 82, 90, 92, 94, 105, 105, 110, 111, 112, 124, 131, 151, 174, 176, 177–8, 182, 183, 187
  Meditations on First Philosophy, vi, xiii, 38–9, 41, 53, 124, 177–8, 182, 183
  Principles of Philosophy, 40, 47, 55, 177, 183
desire, 51, 54, 55, 84, 124, 125–6, 127, 128, 135, 138, 139, 142, 146, 167
despotism, 141, 148
dialectical illusions, vii, 110–16
  antinomies, 112–14
  ideals of pure reason, 115–16
  paralogisms, 111

dialogue, 12, 13–15, 16, 19, 20, 24, 31, 33, 35, 36, 39, 174, 175, 177, 178, 184, 186
difference, 5, 15–16, 18–19, 35, 36
dignity, 150, 157, 158, 160, 161, 163, 165, 167, 169, 170, 171
Dionysian, xi, 123, 128, 129, 130, 135, 141, 142
Dolnick, Edward, 1, 183
double consciousness, 126
doubt, vi, x, xi, 38, 42–6, 47, 48, 50, 51, 52, 54, 57, 59, 72, 79, 80
drive, x, xi, 123, 127–8, 129–31, 134, 135, 136, 139, 141, 142, 144, 146–7, 148
Du Bois, W.E.B, 126–7, 183
durability, xii, 155, 161, 163, 165, 166, 169, 172

education, 12, 13, 27, 39, 88, 89, 124, 129, 131–2, 136, 137–8, 139, 140, 144, 145, 147, 179
egalitarianism, 145
ego, vi, 69, 72, 128, 183,
egoism, xi, 137, 141–2, 148
Eichmann, Adolf, 171
emotion, 12, 68, 69
Empedocles, 34,
empiricism, xi, 66, 67, 89, 90, 95, 104, 107, 108, 178
Enlightenment, The, 66, 89, 90
epistemology, vi, 3, 12, 65, 66, 81, 93, 106, 107, 117, 123, 174, 178–9

equivocation, 111
error, 36, 42, 55–7, 62, 66, 70, 71, 95, 111, 112, 163
essence, 5, 31, 37, 40, 47, 51, 58, 62, 88, 89, 93, 100, 104, 105, 106, 111, 133, 154, 164
ethics, 3, 12, 90, 119, 120–1, 156, 174, 179–80
evidence, xi, 8, 17, 61, 79, 80–1, 83, 85–6, 89, 90
evil genius, 45, 46, 48
existence, 3, 5, 40, 41, 45, 46–7, 49, 50–1, 52, 53–5, 57, 58–60, 62, 83, 86, 100, 102, 105, 110, 112, 114, 116, 118, 129, 130, 133–6, 137, 139, 140, 141, 150, 151, 154, 155
existential, 139, 150
experience, x, xi, xii, 5, 6, 8, 9, 17, 27, 31, 38, 39, 42, 44, 47, 60, 61, 62, 66, 67, 68–9, 70, 71, 73, 74, 75, 76, 77, 78, 79, 80, 81, 82, 83, 84, 85, 86, 92, 93, 94, 95, 96–7, 98, 99, 100, 101, 102, 103, 104, 105, 106, 107, 108–9, 110, 111, 112, 113, 114, 115, 116, 117, 120, 123, 124, 125, 126, 127, 128, 132, 133, 134, 139, 151, 152, 160, 165, 173
Extension, 42, 51, 55, 57–8

fabrication, 48, 68, 156
fallibilism, xi, 92, 95
Fanon, Franz, 4
feeling, 27, 44, 46, 75, 83, 84
fiction, 75
forgery, v, 1–2, 16–18, 32, 37, 56–7, 80, 90, 111, 129, 171
forgiveness, 170
form(s), v, xi, 5, 13, 15–17, 19, 20, 21, 22–3, 25, 26, 27, 29, 34–5, 36–7, 38, 39–40, 56, 68, 71, 76, 92, 94, 106, 107, 109, 123, 136, 143, 146, 147, 148, 157, 160, 174
freedom, x, 54, 75, 79, 83–85, 113–14, 116–17, 120, 134, 138, 139, 140, 141, 142, 154, 159, 164–5, 172
Freud, Sigmund, 126
friendship, 131, 157

Galilei, Galileo, 5
genera, 20
genius, 131, 135, 136, 144, 145, 147
genocide, 150
geometry, 17, 39, 58
giving an account, v, 19–22, 28, 31, 37, 76, 171
God, vi, 12, 40, 41, 45–6, 47–51, 52, 53–4, 55–9, 60, 62, 68, 73, 81, 82–3, 84, 85–6, 87, 90, 93, 95, 110, 113, 114, 115–17, 118, 124, 139, 141, 157, 158
Goering, Hermann, 2
Goethe, Johann Wolfgang von, 131, 134, 142–3
Great Chain of Being, 56

habit, 8, 9, 73–6, 80, 83, 125, 139
happiness, 127, 130, 133, 163
Hegel, G.W.F., 4, 176, 177
Heidegger, Martin, 14, 120, 149, 150–1, 152, 176, 177
Heraclitus, 34
homo faber, 156, 166
honesty, 132
human condition, 154, 167, 169
Human Genome Project, 90
human nature, 69, 70, 75, 79, 91, 138, 154
Hume, David, vi, x, xi, xiii, 3, 6, 65, 66, 67–77, 79–91, 92–5, 96, 97, 98, 103, 104, 105, 109, 112, 151, 174, 176, 178–9, 184
   A Treatise of Human Nature, 72, 184
   An Enquiry Concerning Human Understanding, xiii, 67, 68, 69, 72, 79, 87, 178, 184
   "Of National Characters", 87–8, 184
humility, 117
Husserl, Edmund, 4, 120, 149, 176
Hyland, Drew, 177, 184

Id, 128
idea, vi, xi, 5, 8, 9, 22, 47, 48–51, 53, 54, 55, 56, 57, 58, 59, 60, 62, 66, 67, 69, 71, 72, 73, 74, 75, 77, 78, 79, 80, 81, 83, 86, 87, 89, 90, 94, 97, 98, 103, 105, 112, 116, 117, 120, 124, 139, 143, 151, 155, 158, 159, 173, 174
   complex ideas, 73
   innate ideas, vi, 48, 49, 51, 54, 58, 59, 60, 69, 72, 73–4, 75, 77, 94, 103
   simple ideas, 73, 75
ideal, 114, 115–16, 126, 139, 141, 142, 143, 148
idealism, 33, 35, 95, 104, 105, 107, 117, 179
   transcendental idealism, 105, 107, 181
ideals of reason, xi, 105, 111, 115–16
identity and difference, v, xi, 13, 18–19
illusion, vi, vii, 3, 6, 12, 60, 72, 81, 101, 110, 111, 112, 115, 116, 123, 139
images, vii, 4, 17, 22, 28–30, 32, 37, 44, 46, 48, 49, 56, 57, 73, 75, 103, 124, 141, 142–3, 157, 166, 178, 187
Imagination, xi, 39, 44–5, 46, 47, 48, 49, 53, 55, 57, 58, 59, 60, 69, 73, 74, 75, 103, 109, 140, 152, 178, 187
imitation, vi, 2, 16, 17, 32–3, 129, 132, 136, 143, 173
   appearance-making, 32
   likeness-making, 32
immanence, 5, 38, 42, 51, 70, 71, 96, 120, 123, 124, 152, 158, 173
immaterial, xi, 13, 15, 17, 22, 25, 26, 27, 28, 30, 31, 34, 38, 39, 40, 42, 47, 49, 53, 55, 57, 59, 68, 69, 72, 79, 86, 124, 152

implication, 8–9, 16, 18, 22, 33, 35, 43, 45, 47, 58, 66, 78, 85, 106, 107, 136
impression, xi, 67, 69, 71, 73–4, 75, 77, 81, 82, 83, 86, 89
inauthenticity, 18, 148, 150, 152
incompatibilism, 84
inference, 72, 76, 77, 79, 81, 83, 86, 94, 103, 110, 112, 116, 117
instinct, 124, 125, 126, 127, 139, 144
intellect, xi, 4, 5, 12, 53, 55–6, 57–8
intelligibility, 26, 28, 36, 66, 92, 93, 94, 96, 100–03, 105, 106, 107, 109, 151, 165
intrasubstantialism, 81
intuition, 99–100, 103–4, 106–8, 109–10, 111, 112, 116, 117, 128, 176
  empirical intuition, 103, 111
  pure intuition, 99–100, 104, 107, 111, 112, 117
irreversibility, 170

Jaspers, Karl, 1, 120, 149, 184
Jesus, 39, 49
judgment, vi, vii, x, xi, xii, 48, 53, 54–7, 59, 62, 63, 75, 85, 90, 92, 94, 96–8, 101, 102, 103, 104, 109–10, 115, 116, 125, 149
  analytic, x, 92, 97, 104, 109, 110
  of experience, 103
  of perception, 103
  synthetic, xii, 92, 97, 104, 110
  synthetic a priori, vii, 97, 98, 100, 104, 110, 116–17

Kant, Immanuel, vi-vii, x, xi, xii, xiii, 3, 4, 6, 65, 66, 92–104, 105–18, 128, 135, 151, 152, 153, 174, 176, 179, 184
  Critique of Judgment, 152, 153, 179, 184
  Critique of Pure Reason, 93, 95, 99, 107, 108, 111, 112, 114, 179, 184
  Prolegomena to Any Future Metaphysics, 92, 93, 98, 105, 110, 179, 184, 185
Kearney, Richard, 176, 184
Kepler, Johannes, 5, 95
kinds, vi, 18, 19, 35–6, 40, 71, 73, 96, 97, 104, 109, 133
Klein, Jacob, 177, 185
knowledge, vi, x, xii, 6, 12, 15, 22, 26, 28–31, 32–3, 35, 36, 37, 38, 40, 42, 43, 44, 45, 46, 47, 51, 53–4, 57, 58, 62, 63, 66, 69, 70, 71, 74–76, 77, 79, 84, 86, 87, 92–5, 96–8, 99–100, 104, 105–8, 110, 114, 116, 117, 118, 123, 129–31, 135, 136, 137–8, 140, 144, 145, 174, 176, 177, 179
Kristeva, Julia, 176, 180, 185

labor, vii, xi, xiii, 149, 150, 153, 154, 155, 156–7, 158–9, 160, 161, 162–5, 166, 167, 169, 172, 182
labor power, 159, 164
language, v, xi, 5, 6, 7, 9, 13, 14–16, 17, 19, 24, 25, 26, 27–32, 36, 37, 76, 89, 97, 108, 139, 165

law, 12, 85–6, 95, 100, 126, 128, 130, 139, 143, 157, 171
Lawlor, Leonard, 4
Leclerc, George-Louis, 89
Levinas, Emmanuel, 4, 14, 176, 177
liberation, xii, 14, 68, 71, 90, 107, 120, 123, 124–5, 127, 130, 131–2, 136, 138, 139, 148, 159, 160, 164, 170
liberty, 84, 150
Libet, Benjamin, 82
life, vii, viii, xi, xii, 6, 9, 39, 54, 56, 60, 69, 81, 85, 87, 97, 120, 121, 123–4, 127, 128, 129, 130, 131, 132–6, 137, 138, 140, 141, 142, 143–5, 146, 147, 148, 149, 150, 151, 152, 153–5, 156, 157, 158, 159, 160, 161, 162, 163, 167, 168, 169, 172, 173–5
Linneaus, Carolus, 89
Literature, 108, 145, 167, 180
Logan, Beryl, 179, 185
logic, 5, 8, 12, 14, 36, 39, 73, 74, 94, 96, 98, 102, 104, 106, 108, 109, 110, 111, 112, 115, 116, 157, 161, 162, 166, 167, 169, 172, 184
logos, 13, 19, 20, 27, 28
loneliness, 134, 136, 138
love, 17, 19, 34, 39, 72, 130–1, 147, 151
Loyola, Ignatius of, 39
lying, 54, 80

Marion, Jean-Luc, 178, 185
market economy, 139, 141–2, 146, 148, 149, 159, 164
Marx, Karl, 158–9, 162, 163–5, 172, 176, 185, 186
 Capital I, 164, 185
 "Concerning Feuerbach", 158, 185
 Economic and Philosophical Manuscripts (1844), 159, 185
 Grundrisse, 163–4, 185
 The German Ideology, 164, 185
master, 2, 140, 142, 166, 167
mastery, 130, 163, 166
Matrix, The (film), 45
matter, 34, 40, 113
materialism, 33, 34, 139
mathematics, 12, 39, 58, 94–5, 97, 98–100, 104, 106, 110, 117
matters of fact, 73–4, 77, 80, 94, 96, 97
meaning, vii, 8, 28, 31, 42, 70, 97, 100, 139, 143–5, 152, 154, 156, 157, 159, 163, 166, 167, 169
mediocrity, 124, 132, 145
meditation, vi, 39, 42, 44, 46, 47, 48, 49, 51, 53, 54, 57, 58, 59, 61, 62, 72
 as spiritual exercise, vi, 39
Merleau-Ponty, Maurice, 4, 176
metaphysics, v, 3, 11, 12, 66, 93, 97, 98, 107, 110, 117, 174, 177–8, 179
method of division, xi, 13, 20, 23, 24
Miedl, Alois, 2
Millican, Peter, 185

mind, vi, xi, 5, 6, 7, 18, 22, 26, 27, 29, 32, 35, 38, 40, 42, 46–51, 52, 54–62, 66, 67, 68, 69–70, 71, 72, 73–4, 75–6, 77, 79, 81, 82, 83, 85, 87, 92, 93–6, 98, 99, 100–4, 105, 106–10, 111, 112, 113, 114, 116, 117, 141, 151, 152, 153, 178
miracle, vi, 85–6, 87, 90
Möbius strip, 161, 167–8
modality, 102, 112–13, 115
mode, 42, 51, 56, 71, 116, 150, 159, 176
model, xi, 2, 7, 13, 15, 16, 17, 22, 25, 26, 58, 79, 87, 124, 131–2, 136, 143, 144, 145, 148, 165
modern, vii, vii, 3, 5, 39, 126, 131, 138–9, 141–3, 146–8, 149, 150, 151, 153, 155, 157, 18–9, 160, 163, 166, 167, 176
modern science, 138, 139, 141
monism, 33
monogenesis, 89
morality, 78, 87, 90, 91, 135, 140, 178, 180
music, 19, 39, 124, 128, 130, 131, 145, 146
  pop music, 70, 146
Musk, Elon, 61–2

names, 18–19, 20, 21, 22, 27, 28–33, 35, 37, 50
natality, xi, 161
nation-state, 142
nature, x, 6, 14, 15, 19–20, 22, 23, 25, 27–31, 35, 36, 40, 46, 51, 57, 58, 59, 66, 69, 71, 84, 85, 86, 88, 93, 95, 100, 103, 104, 112, 113, 114, 116, 123, 127, 129, 130, 131, 134, 135, 139, 143–5, 147, 154, 155, 159, 164, 165–7, 172
Nazism, 1–2, 120, 171
necessary, vii, xi, 22, 28, 29, 31, 41, 49, 51, 83, 84–5, 92, 95–6, 99–100, 102–04, 107, 110, 112, 113, 114, 116, 139, 142, 155, 156, 159, 160, 161, 162–3, 164, 165, 166, 170, 172
  necessary connection, xi, 76–7, 79, 81–3, 85, 86
Newton, Isaac, 95, 98
Nietzsche, Friedrich, vii, x, xi, xii, xiii, 4, 6, 119, 120–1, 123–36, 137–48, 149, 150, 151, 154, 158, 174, 176, 179–80, 181, 182, 183, 185–6, 187
  "Schopenhauer as Educator", xiii, 123–36, 137–48, 185
  The Birth of Tragedy, 124, 127, 179, 185
  The Gay Science, 139, 179, 185
  "The Parable of the Madman", 139
  Thus Spoke Zarathustra, 140–1, 179, 185
  Twilight of the Idols, 123, 124, 158, 179, 185
  Unfashionable Observations, 124, 125, 179–80, 182, 185
non-being, xi, 26, 32–33, 35, 36, 56, 124

noumena, 105
nuerosis, 127

object, xi, xii, 15, 20, 28, 29, 31–2, 34, 40, 42, 48, 49, 50, 53, 55, 57, 59–62, 66, 71, 86, 93, 94, 96, 98–104, 106–10, 111, 112, 113, 116, 117, 130, 135, 147, 149, 151, 158, 166
objectivity, 5, 49–50, 66, 94, 95, 97, 102, 103–4, 106, 117, 131, 165, 166, 169, 172
occasionalism, 81, 83
ontological argument, 58
opinion, 22, 30, 37, 42, 43, 45, 103, 109, 125, 147, 157

Parmenides, 15, 32–3, 174, 176
particular, 20, 26, 28, 35, 40, 42, 72, 88, 99, 102, 116, 124, 131, 139, 152
passive, xi, 53, 55, 60, 62, 93, 96, 128, 129, 141
Peperzak, Adriaan, 177, 186
perception, x, xi, 31, 38, 45, 47–8, 55, 58, 60, 67, 68, 72, 73, 89, 103, 105, 106, 135
perfect, x, xi, 1, 13, 22, 41, 50, 51, 54, 59, 62, 83, 137, 138, 143–4
phenomena, 4, 7–8, 35, 99, 105
philosopher, 3, 4, 6, 7, 8, 9, 12, 13–19, 23, 24–5, 27, 28, 32, 33, 34, 36, 37, 42, 47, 51, 58, 61, 66, 67–8, 75, 76, 84, 86, 88, 92, 94, 95, 108, 111, 114, 120, 124, 125, 127, 132, 133, 134, 138, 141, 142, 143, 144, 145, 149, 150, 151, 153, 154, 155–8, 173, 174, 176, 178
philosophy, iii, v, vi, vii, xii, 2, 3, 4–7, 8–9, 12, 13–15, 22, 25, 26, 27, 31, 32, 34, 38–9, 40, 42, 51, 53, 66, 67, 69–71, 76, 77, 81, 86, 87, 89–90, 93, 95–6, 107, 108, 120, 121, 123, 124, 127, 132, 135, 136, 144, 146, 147, 148, 149, 150–1, 153, 154, 155–8, 160, 173–5, 176, 177, 178, 179, 180
  abstruse, 70
  as creative activity, 4, 8–9, 68, 175
  as practice, 7, 12, 13, 25, 33, 39, 51, 177
  as therapy, 87
  as way of life, viii, xii, 7, 9, 53–4, 121, 123, 136, 148, 149, 173–5
  easy, 70
Plato, v, vi, x, xi, xiii, 3, 5, 6, 11, 12, 13–25, 26–37, 38, 39–40, 42, 44, 53, 66, 68, 69, 71, 76, 92, 94, 105, 106, 124, 127, 151–2, 154, 156, 156, 157, 174, 176, 177, 184, 185, 186
  Letter VII, 28, 31, 186
  Republic, 13, 22, 157, 177, 186
  Sophist, xiii, 13, 14, 15, 16, 19, 20, 23, 38, 45, 152, 177, 184, 185, 186
  Statesman, 15, 177, 185, 186
  Theaetetus, 15, 38, 177, 185, 186

Pleasantville (film), 133
pluralism, 33, 34
plurality, xi, 5, 6, 33, 102, 121, 151, 155, 161, 168, 169
poet, 76–7, 167, 179
poetry, 167, 179
poiesis, 156
political theorist, 120, 150, 151
politics, 12, 108, 148, 149, 150, 155, 156, 158, 160, 179, 180
Pollock, Jackson, 15
polygenesis, 89
potential, 77, 144, 145, 146, 148, 149
power, 47, 49, 50, 54, 56, 59, 74, 81, 82, 83, 84, 86, 88, 113, 120, 124, 127, 143, 145, 146–7, 159, 162, 164
will to power, 120
practical, 53, 69, 70, 77, 83, 116, 123, 136, 148, 157, 179, 184
praxis, 151, 156, 173
predicate, x, xii, 30–1, 92, 97, 98, 109, 115
private, 2, 36, 150, 151
probability, vi, xi, 61, 77, 79, 80–1, 84, 85, 90, 91
production, 56, 143, 145, 146, 147, 159, 162, 164, 165–7, 172
progress, 87, 93, 138, 139
promise making, 170
proof, 45, 49, 80, 81
Protestant Reformation, 141
psychoanalysis, 4, 126
psychology, 70
public, vii, ix, x, 121, 146, 149, 150, 151–3, 158, 160, 169
pure, 55, 57, 93, 96, 98, 99–100, 102, 104, 107, 109, 111, 115, 116, 117, 128, 135, 146, 153

quality, x, 2, 8, 38, 101–2, 112, 113, 115, 133, 164
quantity, 74, 101–2, 112, 113, 115, 116
question, v, ix, 3–4, 5, 6, 7–8, 9, 12, 14, 15, 18, 19, 23, 28, 31, 34, 35, 38–9, 45, 51, 61, 66, 67, 70, 71, 79, 89, 93, 95–6, 98, 110, 120, 121, 127, 130, 137, 140, 148, 153, 167, 173–4

race, vi, 5, 87–90, 126,
racial elimitivism, 90
racial naturalism, 88
racism, 87, 89, 90
rational animal, 40, 163,
rationalism, vi, xi, 66, 67, 68–9, 79, 94, 95, 104, 107–8
relation, 69, 71, 74, 76, 101–2, 112–113, 115, 116, 152, 167, 169
relations of ideas, 73–4, 80, 94, 97
reality, vi, vii, xi, 1–6, 12–17, 20, 25, 27–31, 33–7, 38, 39, 42–52, 53–4, 56, 58–63, 66, 67–78, 79–81, 87, 90, 92–5, 99, 102–4, 105–6, 108, 109–11, 115–18, 121, 123–4, 127, 129, 133–5, 144, 149, 151–2, 158, 165, 167, 171, 173–5
formal reality, 49–50
objective reality, 49–50

referent, 28, 31, 36
relativism, 135
religion, 12, 139, 144,157, 179, 180
Rembrandt Society, 2, 57
representation, xi, 1, 4, 15, 28, 30, 48–9, 53, 57, 75, 100, 105, 107, 109, 111, 135, 165, 173
repression, 125–6
rest, 35–6
revolution, vi, 5, 67–8, 92, 95, 138, 142–3, 158, 159, 164
Rijksmuseum, 2, 90
Rousseau, Jean-Jacques, 142–3

sacraments of culture, vii, 145–6
saint, 39, 138, 143–5, 147
Sallis, John, 177, 187
sameness, xi, 5, 13, 35–6
Sartre, Jean-Paul, 4, 176
schema, 103, 109
scholarship, 146–8, 178
Schopenhauer, Arthur, xiii, 123, 125, 126, 131–6, 137–9, 141–4, 147–8
  On the Fourfold Root of the Principle of Sufficient Reason, 135
  The World as Will and Representation, 133, 187
science, vii, 45, 62, 69, 86, 88–90, 94–5, 97–8, 100–4, 106, 108, 110, 117, 125, 138, 139, 141, 147, 176, 179
self, vi, vii, xi, xii, 46–7, 69, 72, 73, 77, 78, 79, 111, 112, 117, 123, 124–34, 136, 137–8, 139, 140, 141, 144, 145, 147, 151
self-creation, 136, 137–8
self-cultivation, 139
self-education, 129, 131–2, 136, 137–8, 140, 144, 145
self-knowledge, 124–31, 136, 137–8, 140, 144, 145
sensation, 44, 48–9, 55, 59, 60, 62, 68, 69, 90, 96, 126, 135
Sepper, Dennis, 178, 187
Shakespeare, William, 131
sign, 27, 28, 98, 162, 171
signified, 28
signifier, 28
significance, 2, 3, 12, 14, 69, 137, 149, 154, 157, 165, 174, 178
simulation argument, 45–6, 61–2, 63, 182
sincerity, 132, 136
skepticism, vi, xi, 43, 66, 77, 79, 87, 90, 93, 94, 95, 104, 107, 117, 135, 136
  academic skepticism, 87
slavery, 88–9, 126–7, 131, 139, 142, 159, 164, 165, 167
social, 12, 90, 120, 126, 127, 128, 131, 134, 137–8, 146, 147, 170–1
society, 70, 125–8, 136, 138, 146–8, 149, 157, 163
Socrates, 12, 14–15, 18–19, 24–5, 28, 30–1, 36, 101, 115–16
solitude, 134, 156
sophist, 15, 18, 19, 20, 23–5, 26, 27, 28, 29, 31, 32, 33, 35, 36, 37, 44

soul, 24, 27, 53, 72, 93, 95, 116, 117, 126, 130, 146, 157
space, x, 38, 42, 57, 71, 99–100, 102, 104, 106, 107, 109, 110, 112–14, 117, 120, 121, 152, 169, 172
species, 20, 49, 89, 138, 162
species-being, 159
speech, 19, 36, 121, 151, 152, 168, 169, 171
speed, 142, 166
Star Trek, 49
state, 35, 101, 108, 133, 155
Steadman, Philip, 17
subject, x, xii, 17, 30, 46, 57, 72, 92, 96, 97, 98, 109–10, 111, 115, 116, 126, 135, 150, 178
subjectivism, 39, 103, 106, 109, 118
subjectivity, 47, 57, 59, 60
substance, vi, x, xi, 6, 38, 39–42, 49, 50, 51, 62, 68, 71, 72, 81, 83, 99, 101–02, 105, 111, 113, 116, 124
  extended substance, x, 38, 41
  finite, 40–1, 49, 53, 55
  infinite, 40–1, 53, 54, 55, 82
  thinking substance, xi, 38, 41, 46–9, 55, 57, 59, 72, 77, 111, 151
suffering, 133
sufficient, 1, 19, 21, 29, 54, 82, 83, 85, 91, 95, 145
sufficient reason principle, 135
superego, 128,
syllogism, 115–16
symptom, 88, 127, 131
synthetic, xii, 92, 97, 99, 103, 110

synthetic *a priori,* vii, 97–104, 110, 116–17

technology, 166
teotl, 174
Theodorus, 14, 15
theoretical, 4, 53, 67, 68, 69, 70, 71, 77, 83, 123, 148, 158, 173
thinking, ix, 3–5, 6, 7, 9, 12, 15, 25, 27, 39, 46, 47, 48, 49, 51, 55, 57, 59, 67, 69, 70–1, 72, 77, 87, 90, 94, 95, 103, 111, 120, 145, 149–51, 152, 153, 155–6, 171, 173, 180
Thirty Years' War, 12
threefold synthesis, vii, 108–110
time, 3, 5, 61, 71, 72, 99–100, 101, 102, 104, 106, 107, 109, 110, 111, 112–13, 114, 117, 130, 152, 155, 164
transcendent, xii, 5, 38, 105, 106, 107, 112, 114, 116, 123, 124, 139, 157, 158, 173
transcendental, xii, 105, 106, 107, 112, 114, 117, 179
true educator, xii, 123, 124–5, 131, 136
truth, vi, xi, 8, 16–17, 43, 45, 53, 54–7, 58, 59, 66, 79, 81, 87, 108, 133, 134–5, 136, 139, 140, 142, 143, 144, 147, 158, 174
tyranny, 18, 107, 138, 140, 142, 150

uncertainty, 68, 87
understanding, xi, 9, 49, 50, 53, 55–6, 58, 68, 69, 73, 76, 83,

86, 87, 90, 92, 96, 100–4, 106, 107, 108, 109, 110, 111, 112, 113, 115, 116, 117, 125, 126, 128, 150, 151, 152, 154, 157, 174, 176, 177, 178, 179, 180
unfashionable, xii, 123, 124, 125, 134, 180
universal, 25, 26, 31, 35, 40, 42, 92, 95, 96, 100, 102–03, 104, 107, 110, 115, 116, 117, 152
unpredictability, 170

validity, 58, 97, 103, 104
value, x, 6, 16, 39, 130–1, 136, 137, 139, 140, 141, 143, 145, 148, 155, 158, 164, 169, 170, 171
Van Meegeren, Han, 1–2, 16–18, 32, 49, 50, 56, 80, 90, 111, 125, 129, 171
 Christ at Emmaus, 2, 49, 50, 56
 Christ with the Woman Taken in Adultery, 2
Vattimo, Gianni, 180, 187
Vermeer, Johannes, v, 1–2, 16–18, 32, 56, 80, 129, 183
 The Music Lesson, 17
Villa, Dana, 180, 187
violence, 126, 166
virtual, vii, 61, 104, 105, 109, 111
Visitor from Elea, 14–16, 18–21, 23–4, 26–9, 31–6
vita active, xii, 149, 153

vita contemplative, xii, 149, 153
volition, 48, 55, 81, 82
voluntarism, 81, 82

West, David, 176, 187
wilderness, 144
will, xii, 31, 53, 54–7, 58, 59, 60, 62, 82, 83–4, 120, 124, 125, 126, 127, 133, 135, 138, 140, 143, 149, 158, 167, 169
wisdom, 3, 19, 22, 30, 32, 34, 68, 142, 147, 151
Woodward, Ashley, 180, 187
world, vi, vii, xii, 5, 6, 9, 22, 26, 27, 34–5, 38, 40, 42, 43, 44, 46, 47, 49–50, 53, 54, 57, 58, 59–62, 66, 68, 69–70, 71, 73, 75, 77, 79, 81, 87, 93, 95–6, 100, 105, 108, 109, 112, 113–14, 116, 117, 120, 121, 123, 126, 134, 135, 137, 138, 143, 144, 146, 149, 150–3, 154, 155, 156, 158, 160, 161, 165–7, 168, 169, 170, 171, 172, 174
worldlessness, vii, xii, 149, 150–1, 160
worldliness, 155, 165, 168
work, vii, xii, 129, 131, 139, 143, 144, 154–8, 159, 160, 161, 163–7, 169, 171, 172

Yaquob, Zera, 90
Young-Bruehl, Elizabeth, 180, 187

EU representative:
Easy Access System Europe
Mustamäe tee 50, 10621 Tallinn, Estonia
Gpsr.requests@easproject.com

www.ingramcontent.com/pod-product-compliance
Lightning Source LLC
Chambersburg PA
CBHW071115160426
43196CB00013B/2574